THE GENIUS OF HOME

*A family's path of homeschooling from
kindergarten through high school grade eleven*

THE GENIUS OF HOME

TEACHING YOUR CHILDREN AT HOME WITH THE WALDORF CURRICULUM

CATHERINE READ, PHD

Bell Pond Books | 2021

To Richard, Claire, and Sara, without whom…

And to all the Waldorf teachers and families, at home and in schools, who helped me. You know who you are.

2021
Bell Pond Books
an imprint of SteinerBooks | Anthroposophic Press, Inc.
PO Box 58, Hudson, NY 12534
www.steinerbooks.org

Copyright © 2021 by Catherine Read. All rights reserved. No part of this book may be reproduced, stored in a retrieval system, or transmitted in any form or by any means, electronic, mechanical, photocopying, recording, or otherwise, without the written permission of SteinerBooks.

ISBN: 978-1-952166-09-9 (paperback)

Contents

	Acknowledgements	8
	Preface	9
1.	Introduction: When You Are Your Child's Teacher	11
2.	What Is School at Home with the Waldorf Curriculum?	18
3.	Connecting with the Curriculum	43
4.	Making the Lessons Your Own	70
5.	Individualizing the Lessons and the School	93
6.	Rhythms of Teaching and Learning	121
7.	From Kindergarten to Grade Twelve: Growing New Faculties	160
	Epilogue: Waldorf after High School	188
	Bibliography and Resources	192

Appendices 197

1.	Anthroposophic Homeschooling: Fostering the Life of the Soul	198
2.	Colored Shadows and Afterimages	208
3.	Seeing the Twelve Grades through the Lens of the Twelve Senses	227
	About the Author	237

Acknowledgments

This book has been long in the making, and I truly stand on others' shoulders. I thank all the teachers I had in Waldorf teacher training at the Waldorf Institute of Teacher Training in Los Angeles; in Gradalis Teacher Training in Boulder, Colorado; in courses at Sunbridge College in Spring Valley, New York; and at Rudolf Steiner College in Sacramento. Gloria Kemp graciously provided me with curriculum ideas and explanations for grades five through eight as we taught them at the same time, she in a Waldorf school and I at home. Those who provided training specifically for Waldorf teaching at home, primarily Barbara Dewey of Waldorf Without Walls, were very important in my development. I especially thank the other Waldorf homeschool teachers and families I collaborated with over the years—fellow travelers on the path of teaching the curriculum in new circumstances—for the warm community you gave my family. My husband, Richard Carter, did everything—from being the janitor, the information technology expert, the research assistant, and the main funding source, to being the after-school parent while I prepared the next day's lessons. I literally couldn't have done it without him. I received help beyond the call of duty from Irene Cherchuck, manager of the Sunbridge College Bookstore, and from the two librarians at the Rudolf Steiner Library in Ghent, NY: Judith Kiely and Judith Swensigen. I thank Mado Spiegler, who read the book in draft form and gave me invaluable advice, and I thank Gabe Malarsky for copy editing. The editors at SteinerBooks are the main reason this book exists. Gene Gollogly had faith in me, Marsha Post kept me on track, and John-Scott Legg and Mary Giddens took up the baton. I owe you all. And, of course, I owe our daughters, Claire and Freya Sara, for initiating this journey in the first place.

Preface

To educate means to draw forth (Latin, *educare*: to lead, to bring up); the teacher must draw forth, but, also, must meet the new individual at her or his own level. But what does the teacher draw forth from the child? Is the teacher like the sun that draws forth the plants? Children do grow up, but at the same time, they come down. What if one is teaching one's own children? There are probably as many reasons to have school at home as there are families who do so. This book is for those who have decided to teach their own children at home, or are already engaged in that all-engrossing activity. I have written about the experience of one family, teaching at home with the Waldorf curriculum from kindergarten through high school grade eleven, in the hopes that this material can help others who are teaching their own children. I wish you strength and good fortune in the endeavor.

CHAPTER ONE

INTRODUCTION: WHEN YOU ARE YOUR CHILD'S TEACHER

School at home with the Waldorf curriculum: to some this is a contradiction. The Waldorf curriculum was originated by Rudolf Steiner in answer to the question of how school could be provided for all students, at that time specifically for children of workers in Emil Molt's Waldorf-Astoria Cigarette Factory. The school begun for that purpose was in Stuttgart, Germany and continues today. In these times, especially in the United States, many families realize that for various reasons their children will thrive better through an education at home than in an institution. Some see the strength of the Waldorf curriculum in its deep understanding of the human being and of child development in the context of body, life, soul, and spirit. When a parent is his or her own child's teacher, one individual fulfills two roles in a child's life—it can be done!

When I look back over fifteen years of teaching our children at home with the Waldorf curriculum, I am reminded of the book *We Didn't Mean to Go to Sea* by Arthur Ransome. This children's book tells the story of four siblings who are left tending a sailboat anchored at the mouth of a river on the edge of the English Channel. The captain leaves to get supplies, and for some unexplained reason, does not return. The tide rises, and through a series of events and decisions, the children, who are experienced sailors, find themselves crossing the North Sea at night in a storm. (They *do* reach the Netherlands safely.)

When our children were born, we had no thought of homeschooling; we didn't even consider the possibility. When our first daughter was born, a friend, who had attended the Edinburgh Steiner School, gave me the book *Education Towards Freedom*. I knew immediately that such an education would be right. A Waldorf education for our child became a given for me. When we moved to Connecticut, where there was no Waldorf school, I worked with a group of parents who had a playgroup and were interested in starting a school. When we moved again, this time to Southern California, now with two daughters, we were headed for a crisis.

The drive to the nearest Waldorf school was forty-five minutes on a crowded freeway. My daughter was a child who needed afternoon naps and long nights of sleep. She was also an introvert who needed plenty of quiet time to herself, yet she also liked people, especially other children. My strong intention that she should have a Waldorf education, and my equally strong intention to protect her from the life-draining aspects of modern living, led me to a crisis that I could only resolve by deciding to teach her myself at home using the Waldorf curriculum. We began in kindergarten the year she was five turning six, and we knew that we would decide about her schooling one year at a time. We taught her and her younger sister at home through grade eleven with the Waldorf curriculum. At that point they each went into a high school (a Waldorf high school for the younger sister) and graduated from there. It seems we did make it to the other shore.

Growing Up Meets Coming Down: The Curriculum as Guide

Just as flowing water alters the form of the earth and shapes even the hardest mineral, the currents of change as a child's physical and life bodies grow up while their soul and self come down are quite powerful in shaping their constitution and even the events and people around them. When currents flowing in opposite directions meet, a vortex results, out of which many forms and possibilities may arise. The indications Rudolf Steiner gave teachers about what to teach and how to teach grew both from his insights into the developing human being, as well as from the deeply held questions brought to him by the teachers with whom he was connected. This curriculum, as it has been developed and elaborated for 100 years, is still answering deeply held questions.

A curriculum is a course of classes or study (Latin *curricula*: a little running, a little course) and a course is a path for movement, not just a list of topics. Although a curriculum may originate in the context of an institution, as the Waldorf or Steiner Curriculum did, can it function outside the institution? Can the course be taught at home? This book is an extended answer of "yes" to these questions.

Rhythms: Day, Week, Season, Year, Life

How can home life provide the context for schooling? For us, the key has been a certain level of structure—structure for both the space and the time that is school. We have always had a room that is the schoolroom (even if it is sometimes also something else when school is out), with a large, freestanding, three-panel blackboard, artwork, a nature table, and, after kindergarten, the children's desks. I always ring my copper bell and greet the children at the door of the room with a handshake to begin the school day. Once in the classroom, we always begin with singing and the morning verse, and we always end the day with an ending verse. We all know when we are in school and when school is out.

Placing or finding ourselves in relation to time has been much more of a challenge than organizing our space, but certain rhythms have emerged. Once we decided not to structure our lives around the schedule of an institution, well then . . . what? I struck out into new territory and decided to honor my children's sleep. (When the subject of sleep comes up, I sometimes feel like Joan of Arc charging into the Battle of Orleans.) I decided that I would not wake anyone up, and that the children would wake on their own. So, coming out of sleep begins our day. On school days we begin work as soon as breakfast is completed and everyone is dressed. We have recess and lunch, and end the day when the schoolwork for that day is done—usually about six hours after we started.

Here is the weekly rhythm we developed that lasted fairly unchanged until eighth grade. Monday was a transition day after the weekend activities. On Mondays we had "exploring day," when we spent three or four hours in a quiet place in nature, away from people or buildings. The children were free to go where they wanted and I sat nearby or followed, saying nothing, like a mother bear going about her business but keeping an eye on the cubs. Tuesday, Wednesday, and Thursday were structured school days with the consistent pattern of greeting, circle, main lesson, breaks, specialty class, and closing. Tuesday's specialty class was painting, Wednesday's was handwork or modeling, and Thursday's was music. The three days together allowed for a rhythm of main lesson work that proceeded as follows: introduction of material—sleep—review and work on the lesson—sleep—review, elaborate, and finish the work. Friday was the day for practice with math and music, and for lessons with other teachers.

So far so good, but not all weeks are the same, and this is where the seasonal festivals took me by the hand and gently, little by little, led me into another world. Rudolf Steiner gave many indications on the renewal of festivals and the relation of festivals to the seasons. We were already part of a family festival group when we started homeschooling. The four major festivals, which fall a few days after alignments with the sun, except Easter, which aligns exactly with sun and moon, provide the structure of the year. Transitions between these festivals may also be felt and celebrated. Every day is a festival day; one must just work to be conscious of the festive quality present at the time. In relation to the curriculum, the festivals *are* the curriculum in kindergarten, but in the grades where topics are taught in main lesson blocks, the festivals are like the fixed stars in front of which the movable main lesson blocks take place. Each lesson takes on slightly different coloring depending on the season. Teaching about ancient Egypt, for example, with its emphasis on the physical body in relation to the spiritual world, becomes quite intense if it happens to fall around Easter. Teaching botany in the fall when plants are dying is very different from teaching botany in the spring when plants are sprouting. Chemistry, with its focus on fire and transformation, is intensified in the fall when nature is, in a way, "burning up."

The seasons provide a spiraling progression, but each school year, and each year in a human life, has an entirety, a completion. Our school year culminates in a class play in the spring and a final assembly the last day of school each year. As with the festivals we celebrate, class plays take place in the context of community. Every family is part of several communities. One of our communities is other homeschooling families. Every school year, including kindergarten, we work with other families to produce and perform plays for each grade that is represented in the group of children. The stories of the plays progress through the steps of the awakening that takes place as children come down to earth. These plays range from fairy tales to stories of the saints, from *The Paradise Play* to the *Kalevala*, from the Greek myths to Joan of Arc, from Goethe's *Magic Flute* to Shaw's *Pygmalion*. The plays always involve music, singing or playing instruments, blackboard art for the

Introduction: When You Are Your Child's Teacher

backdrop, and handwork on costumes. We all pull together until that magic moment when the audience is seated and quiet, the introduction is over, and the first line must be spoken. Each year's play is like a play-within-a-play, as the whole school year unfolds in miniature. The end of the year is complete with the final assembly, in which the children's music, movement, and recitation skills can be proudly presented.

Finally, there are rhythms in the course of a life that go beyond one year. Steiner has given extensive insights into the seven-year rhythms in life, but there are others. Simultaneously teaching grades that are three years apart (the age difference of my two children) has made me aware of a three-year pulse that beats through the curriculum. Although I didn't plan the coincidence of topics ahead of time, I sometimes found myself teaching the same topic in both grades, and through this I saw how the meaning is intensified and elaborated at three-year intervals.

For instance, I found myself teaching about Thor and his hammer—which he can fling to the ends of the world and which always returns—at the same time as I taught about the circulatory system, where the blood pulses to the farthest extremities of the body and returns to the heart. Likewise, I was teaching about magma and volcanoes, which included painting a very active watercolor, at the same time I taught, in the Thermodynamics block, about graphing the results of a physics experiment on phase changes. The topic of business math in grade six coincided with the history of revolutions in grade nine, both of which relate to the concept of the threefold social organism. One can experience, through this kind of teaching, how material is deepened and elaborated and made more conscious in three-year pulses.

Every Waldorf teacher experiences moments that clearly reveal the power of the curriculum to meet children at their level of consciousness. One such moment came for me in the eighth grade when my daughter—after having studied Plato's descriptions of God using the regular solid forms to create the elements—finished the long process of transforming clay from one solid form into the next, and finally into a dodecahedron. Then, remembering Plato's description of the dodecahedron (which he said God used "in the delineation of the universe"), she declared about the dodecahedron: "It is the human being." At such a time, one wants to jubilate for the forces that shape the growing child and for the gift that is the Waldorf curriculum!

Children are gradually stepping out into the world as they move into high school, and, we hope, taking up their destinies. In high school our daughters were engaged with more teachers: a shepherd and farmer for farm practicum, a horseback riding instructor and intramural basketball coach for sports, a German tutor for foreign language, a woodcarver for crafts. I taught art and music, as well as sewing. We also continued our work with other parents and children in festivals, plays, and specialty classes such as music. In high school we could no longer maintain the Monday exploring day in nature; we had German on Mondays, main lesson blocks Tuesday through Thursday, and outside lessons on Fridays. The rhythm of the school day remained much as before. We had movement, verses, and singing at the beginning of the lesson, then main lesson blocks, then a break followed by lunch and free time, and then practice classes in the afternoon. Homework was assigned, and, of course, each main lesson began with recalling what we had done in the previous lesson to provide continuity across time and sleep. In our case, when I presented two main lessons, I always worked with the younger daughter first; the older one had a separate space where she could work individually on her lesson before her work with me.

When young people wake up to their own individuality, we, as teachers, are called upon to meet them at that level. This type of meeting is beautifully described by Laurens van der Post in his book *A Mantis Carol*, where he imagines a medal for the "First Class in the Order of Being":

> For valor in the field of life, distinguished conduct in the battle of being and steadfastness in defending its quality and texture against aberration and distortion by the prevailing hatred, malice and envy of our collective time, ensuring thereby an example of how devotion to being for sheer being's sake and pursuing it to its own end, is the true glory of life on earth and the unique source of its renewal and increase of meaning and light in the darkness ahead.

One could well aspire to teach young people, especially adolescents, out of such an image—an image so close to the bone.

Introduction: *When You Are Your Child's Teacher*

Recipe for a Blackboard

Materials:

- 32 in. x 80 in. Masonite Primed Smooth Flush Hardboard Hollow Core Interior Door Slab (30 in. and 36 in. widths are also available depending upon your needs and space)

- 1.5 in. x 72 in. Brass Continuous (Piano) Hinge (alternate materials such as stainless steel are available; hinges might also be found in 2 in. width)

- Blackboard Paint: we used Blackboard Slating, Product Number BB-391, W.M. Barr & Co., Memphis, TN

- Handheld Power Paint Sprayer: we used a Wagner 305 (sprayers of this type are referred to as Cup Guns); you may be able to find other inexpensive quality models, but they need to be made to handle paint, not just stain, so look for 1,800 to 2,400 psi. We found that a sprayer produced superior results to a brush.

Construction:

Attach one piano hinge to the first two doors while they are standing face-to-face on their side edges. Then, lay the first door flat on its back face with the other door side upright; attach the second hinge. Finally, stand the two attached doors side upright and attach the third door to the open face of the second hinge.

In an outdoor covered space, stand the set of three panels upright angling the outside two so that the whole piece stands stably. Apply one coat of blackboard paint, let dry, sand with very fine steel wool, and repeat three times. The surface should have some texture as a slick surface does not take chalk as well. (See Figures 4 & 5, in chapter 2.)

Move to the classroom and season with white chalk rubbed off with erasers (wool erasers work best). When needed, clean with a wet cloth. Enjoy your new blackboard!

Chapter Two

What Is School at Home with the Waldorf Curriculum?

Kindergarten

Once there was a mother and father who had two daughters. The older was dark-haired, fiery, and active, and the younger golden-haired, airy, and flitting—a little like Rose Red and Snow White. When the older daughter, Claire, was five years old and ready for kindergarten, the mother made a classroom in a corner of the living room, a room with large windows and full of light. The kindergarten room was set off by wooden play stands draped with soft colored cloths so there was an enclosed spot to sit and listen to stories. We called this the Rainbow House. In front of this was an open space where the children could move and sing and follow the teacher in rhymes and games. In the adjoining kitchen was the table for snacks and painting.

At the entrance to the living room the teacher had a small copper bell that she rang to call the children to school. The mother held the younger child, who was two and a half years old and followed along or watched while her older sister had school. Every school day in the morning Claire came running in her school dress, face shining like the sun. The teacher greeted her saying, "Good morning, Claire," and saw the eager anticipation on her face. What would happen today in the little Rainbow House? Every school day after the greeting, the teacher let the girls go before her into the classroom. First, they stood together for a morning song, greeting the sun and the day:

> Very early every morning,
> All the birds awake and sing,
> Praising God that now the sunrise,
> Warmth and light to earth will bring

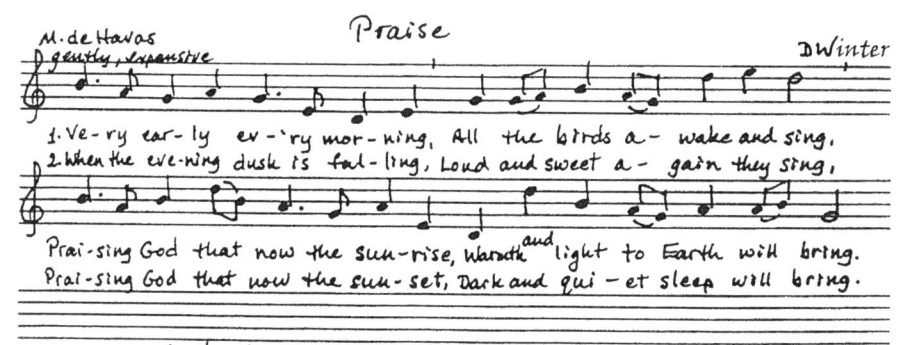

Figure 1. "Very early every morning"—song

Then they said a verse of thanks for the warmth and light:

> Morning has come
> Night is away
> Rise with the sun
> And welcome the day!

Morning has come

Figure 2. "Morning has come"—song

With singing, walking, skipping, and tossing beanbags all in a circle, the teacher brought the two girls into joyful movement and beautiful pictures of the world around them. Although this activity was fun, the children also had to concentrate and try hard at it, so they were glad just to go outside and play afterwards. The girls played outside by themselves (although mother could see them through the window) and they loved the bright sunshine, the warm air, and the wild grasses to run through and the small trees to climb. Once, when they were swinging and climbing on their play set, Claire, the big sister, saw something trotting down a small path beyond the yard. She looked closer and realized it was a coyote! Quickly she called to her little sister, "Come on! And don't run!" They both turned and hurried to the back steps, running up them to our back door. As they moved, the coyote, taken by surprise, stopped and turned to look back. Seeing no danger, he continued on his way down the path through the dry, brown grass of the green belt area behind our house. The teacher, watching them out of the window, saw the coyote before they did and knew that they were safe. She said the coyote wouldn't hurt them, but it was well they came inside.

After they all cut up food in the kitchen, they sat for grace and snack, and then it was time to paint, model little figurines in beeswax, or to knit—depending on the day of the week. On one of those kindergarten days, the girls were painting with transparent watercolors and one of the colors got the better of them, especially the younger daughter, Sara, who was usually so kind and helpful. It was a Tuesday, as usual—and they were sitting side by side at the table, a little too close together. Sara's active and excited movements disturbed Claire, who kept saying "Get away!" The teacher missed the hint and just kept encouraging their painting. Finally, Sara dipped her brush into red paint and flung the paint from the brush into the air. It went everywhere—including into Claire's hair and onto her clothes, and worst of all, onto her painting! Sara was gleeful, Claire was furious, and the teacher had to be quick to rescue Claire's painting. Red paint on a Tuesday (Mars day)—always a dangerous combination. After that, the teacher left more space between the painters at the table, and they painted happily from then on. (Three years after this, when Sara was in kindergarten for the second year, she was painting with blue and yellow, breathing back and forth between the two on the page, and she said, "Blue doesn't want to tell its secrets … yellow has no secrets." And, thus, blue and yellow live together still.)

Finally, they all went to the Rainbow House for the story that would end the kindergarten school day. In the Rainbow House the play stands made low shelves where table puppets could appear, and there was room for a child's chair. They would settle into the Rainbow House,

Claire sitting on her chair and the teacher sitting on the floor holding Sara. After the teacher lit a candle and said a verse about the fire, she would then always begin the story with "Once upon a time..." And then a whole rich and colorful world would unfold. She always told the story from memory. The first time she would just tell the story—maybe changing her voice a little when characters spoke directly or when there was a little verse, but just evenly and steadily.

For a whole week the teacher told the same story at the end of the school day. It was so good it was as if it were a special food, to be enjoyed over and over again. The second week she told the same story, but in a different way. This time when the children came into the Rainbow House, they saw that one of the shelves was covered with many layers of differently colored silk cloths. Now, at "Once upon a time," one of the floating layers of silk was lifted in a gentle wave, revealing small table puppet figures dressed to fit the characters of the story. The teacher moved the figures as she told the story, and when it was time for a new character, the next layer of silk was lifted, revealing a new person! This went on steadily until the whole story was finished. Then everyone was quiet for a minute drinking it in. Finally, the teacher said the closing verse before extinguishing the candle:

> In every seed that will be a tree
> There lives an image of all it will be.
> When I find the image of all I can be,
> Then I will be free.

That was the end of the school day. Mother would then sit on the couch reading a story, one girl on either side, while Claire did her finger knitting. And everyone felt tired in a good way, as if after hard and interesting work.

In the third week, the teacher and the children would act out the story. When it was time for the story, the teacher would say, "Remember we have the story of (for example) "Rapunzel." We have a girl, a prince, a witch. So, we need a crown, a cape, long braids, and what else? Now go find them!" The children would take off on a treasure hunt to find the costumes and props in the schoolroom—or anywhere in the house. When everything was gathered and roles decided, each helped the others dress, and then it was time for the story. As the teacher narrated the events, everyone carried them out and the story came alive. For the story of "Rapunzel," it was simple for the teacher to be the father, elder daughter Claire the mother, and little sister Sara the baby. Of course, the teacher also had to be the challenging figure of the witch, who raises the baby into young womanhood and keeps her in a tower where she feels, as all awakening young people do, alone and separate from the world. The elder daughter then becomes the prince, who searches for the young woman against all odds and rescues her from her loneliness. And all ends well after these trials have been sustained.

The fairy tales always end with a timeless moment, just as they begin. Sometimes it is, "The mouse has run, my tale is done," or, "And they live there still," or, "They lived happily together for a long time."

Creating the Space

We separated school from daily life in both time and space. In time we accomplished this differentiation by using a predictable rhythm for the day, the week, and the school year. This is described below. In space we created the school room in several ways that expanded as we progressed through the years of the curriculum.

Because kindergarten basically consists of a healthy rhythmic home life, we were only required to change our living space minimally. I, as the teacher, used a copper bell to call the children to school and I needed a doorway where I could meet them, shake their hands, and greet them individually before allowing them into the schoolroom. I needed open space for circle singing and movement activities, a table for art work, and a secluded, enclosed space for telling the story at the end of the school day.

We had already begun to have a nature table in our home before we started school, and that became a central part of the classroom. On a low table we kept a small, weathered, cedar tree stump with some short roots and colored silk cloths that mirrored the colors in nature at the time. We also had seasonal objects from nature, stones and plants, and wooden or wax figures of people and animals. Thus, a scene from nature always accompanied our work in the classroom.

To create a schoolroom, I hung a rainbow cloth in an entrance to the room. I moved furniture back for the circle activities. There was room for three or four people to sit comfortably and listen to the story. This enclosed space was important for gaining quiet and minimizing distractions. This space was always available during free play and when we were "out of school," and the girls played many hours in their make-believe games there. Claire made it a restaurant where she took orders, cooked on her wooden stove, served, and presented the bill! Sara had a farm set up on a felt landscape that she tended for years.

In the first grade, a major change in the space was required—the addition of the blackboard. First grade is an initiation into school life, a transition from the rhythmic home life of kindergarten into the time of more conscious and directed work that is specifically *school*. We spent a couple of weeks at the end of the summer before first grade constructing a blackboard. I used the design, described in detail on page 17, that a friend of mine used in her homeschool: three hollow core doors attached vertically with two piano hinges to make a freestanding triptych. It is stable and heavy, but can be moved. We painted the three inner panels with several coats of blackboard paint (warning: a smooth surface is not easy to achieve!) and set it up in one corner of the schoolroom. I did my work on the board at night, so there would be something new when the children came to school in the morning. This space was my working surface in school for the next fourteen years. That board has seen a lot of chalk...

The blackboard played a second important role: that of backdrop for our plays. Starting with first grade for Claire we produced, directed, and acted in one or two plays a year with other homeschool families, depending on which two grades I was teaching. In first grade for Claire we cooperated with another family to present

Figure 3. The blackboard in the classroom: kindergarten and Grade 2

the "Snow White" fairy tale in verse and song. The blackboard stood in the background covered with a chalk drawing of a castle and a forest. The audience saw the picture on the board through the action and story of the play as it was enacted before them. They also saw the story in the context of the background.

Figure 4. Photo: Blackboard with backdrop to Grade 7 play, Joan of Arc

The second significant change in the space for first grade was the addition of Claire's own desk (see Fig. 3 above). Now she would have her own space to sit for main lesson as well as to work in her math lesson books—a very big step. We bought a desk with adjustable height so it could grow with her. We only planned school one year at a time, but, as it turned out, she used that desk from grade one through grade eleven.

The one final characteristic of the classroom, if it is to be used for plays, pertains to entrances: if the room has more than one entrance, players can come "on stage" more easily. "Backstage" is just a space that is out of view of the audience. The Rainbow House can be redecorated to become structures as needed in plays.

The Mood of the Fifth

One important aspect of the surroundings for young children is the teacher! The mood and style of the teacher carries over into her actions, tone of voice, style of movement, and dress. All of these aspects of the teacher surround and enfold the children and can fit with the child's level of development—or not. From kindergarten through second grade, I tended to wear simple, natural fiber cloths in soft colors that could flow with and follow my movements when I was teaching. These garments also provided warmth when I was holding the child. Infants and young children, even up to age nine or ten, are drawn to imitate those around them. I tried not to be rushed or hurried. I had goals for each day, and I kept to the order of events, but not in a mechanical way or beholden to the mechanical clock. In all these areas we can be conscious of what we are giving the children to imitate—not just in actions, but in moods, feelings, and words that grow out of *goodness*. Goodness is the quality most important for young children's early development.

The idea of the "mood of the fifth" encompasses everything that nourishes young children in their surroundings and relates the evolution of human consciousness to the qualities of a progression of musical intervals or distances between tones. Steiner made the statement that children up to the ninth year live in the mood of the fifth and this understanding should guide our approach to young children (*Inner Nature of Music*, Lecture V). But what is the mood of the fifth? And how can we approach it through music or otherwise? When one quietly and contemplatively listens to fifths, for example, the tone A above middle C up to E or A down to D, one senses an openness, perhaps a gentle contact with a permeable boundary between "here" and "there." (See Nancy Foster, "The Mood of Early Childhood" and Sheila Johns, "Music, Mobility, and the Mood of the Fifth.")

The mood of the fifth challenges adults to somehow enter a consciousness that they once had, but is no longer theirs. Open and quiet attention to young children helps us enter this mood. We realize that young children are sponges that soak up, indiscriminately, what is around them in sound, color, gesture, mood—and that quiet voices, graceful movements, and flowing garments are healthful and stabilizing for them. So not only is the physical space important for kindergarten (which is based on home life, in any case), but the physical "space" of the teacher is also very important. As long as the children lived in the mood of the fifth, that is, through second grade, during school time I wore one-piece, long jumpers or soft color dresses of natural fiber fabric. (The three-year age difference between my children meant that this dress carried over somewhat into the older ages slightly for the older daughter and ended a little early for the younger daughter.) A flowing dress or skirt continues the movement of one's limbs and makes the movement visible, and the fabric provides warmth and breathable softness when the child is held. The colors, especially natural pigments, contribute to the child's gradual development of healthy visual perception and also affect mood, and I varied the colors to resonate with those of the season. There are also correspondences of planets with the days of the week: Monday (Moon day), Tuesday (French, *mardi*—Mars), Wednesday (French, *mercredi*—Mercury), Thursday (Thor—Jupiter), Friday (Freya—Venus), Saturday (Saturn day), and Sunday (Sun day). And the planets have traditionally been seen as corresponding to colors, although the particular pairings vary with time period and culture. One can work to experience the correspondences, as well as study up on the ones used in the past. The correspondence I used, and took into account in my dress on school days, is as follows: Monday, Moon, violet; Tuesday, Mars, red; Wednesday, Mercury, yellow; Thursday, Jupiter, orange; Friday, Venus, green. (Saturday, Saturn, corresponds to blue and Sunday, Sun, to incarnadine, or peach blossom.)

In the Grimm's fairy tale "Rumpelstiltskin," the king considers a miller's daughter for his wife under the pretense, perpetrated by her father, that the girl can spin straw into gold. When the king puts her to the test at risk of her life, a "manikin" appears and offers to spin the straw into gold if she will give him her firstborn child when she becomes queen. After she marries the king and has her child, the manikin reappears to claim the infant. But instead, he takes pity on the weeping mother and gives her three days to find out his name. She sends a messenger out far and wide to collect new names. By the third day the messenger returns, telling of a scene he had witnessed "at the end of the forest, where the fox and hare bid each other goodnight," where he learned the required name: "Rumpelstiltskin." This saved the day. The place where the fox and hare say "goodnight" to each other is a place "in-between," where daytime relations are suspended and a kind of twilight dreamy consciousness pervades. This is the mood of the fifth, where young children live. In a way the fairy tales all embody this mood—they all take place in some other, removed time and place, a place of "Once upon a time," outside of time and space. And this is why the fairy tales, especially when they can be told rather than read, provide such soul food for young children, and why they are so important for teaching in kindergarten and first grade.

In nature one can experience this mood in the few moments of twilight, when the whole dome of the sky is a transparent, even turquoise, and there are no directions. Interestingly, no such moment occurs before dawn. George MacDonald's poem from *At the Back of the North Wind* expresses this mood beautifully:

> Where did you come from, baby dear?
> Out of the everywhere into here.
> Where did you get your eyes so blue?
> Out of the sky as I came through.
> What makes the light in them sparkle and spin?
> Some of the starry spikes left in.
> Where did you get that little tear?
> I found it waiting when I got here.
> What makes your forehead so smooth and high?
> A soft hand stroked it as I went by.
> What makes your cheek like a warm white rose?
> I saw something better than anyone knows.
> Whence that three-cornered smile of bliss?
> Three angels gave me at once a kiss.
> Where did you get this pearly ear?
> God spoke, and it came out to hear.
> Where did you get those arms and hands?
> Love made itself into hooks and bands.
> Feet, whence did you come, you darling things?
> From the same box as the cherubs wings.
> How did they all just come to be you?
> God thought about me, and so I grew.
> But how did you come to us, you dear?
> God thought about you, and so I am here.

Setting the Rhythms—Day, Week, Season, Year

Given the physical space and the objects one needs for school, how does one use the time or even set the time? How does the teacher guide the students through the school day? Here the question of rhythm becomes all-important.

Rhythm means repetition, but not a mechanical, precise, by-the-clock repetition. Instead, living rhythm means regularity in variation. The word "rhythm" is related to "Rhea," the name of the Greek goddess of rivers. Flowing water is a wonderful representation of living rhythm. I will give some examples of spans of rhythm I worked to maintain in the school day, the week, the season, and the school year, beginning with the rhythm of the day in kindergarten.

The rhythm of the day and week in kindergarten. We had three school days a week in kindergarten: Tuesday, Wednesday, and Thursday. Mondays we explored in nature, and Fridays we had activities with other people, including lessons, such as music or physical activity. Mother would mention the night before that tomorrow would be a school day. Every day the children were allowed to wake up on their own so that the "breathing" between sleep and waking had a gradual and natural rhythm. That way, waking wasn't a "gasp," a quickly drawn in-breath, almost a shock. Young children, when they are not exposed to too much electronic and mechanical stimulation, are always in a sort of dreamy consciousness anyway. My younger daughter, Sara, when she was four years old, said one afternoon on our walk in the neighborhood, "I never sleep. I'm awake all night." Certainly I know that she slept at night, and was awake during the day, but I think what she said was meaningful. For her, the difference between waking and sleeping was not great—sleeping was light, and waking was dreamy. Every day can be in the expanded mood-of-the-fifth consciousness for the young child.

After waking, eating breakfast, and dressing, the teacher would stand at the entrance to the schoolroom and ring a copper bell to call Claire to kindergarten. After a greeting, the teacher would stand aside for the children to enter the schoolroom and then call them into the circle and sing the morning song. This activity brings lively singing and action after the still moment of gathering in the circle. One can lead the children in walking clockwise in a circle while singing and gesturing the words of the song. For instance, when the song "Autumn Winds" says "blows open the gate," I used my long dress or skirt to show this by swishing the fabric to one side. When the active song was finished everyone found their place to stand, breathe in, and concentrate on the morning verse.

> Here stand we
> Firm and free.
> From afar
> Shines our star.
> We enfold
> Sun's gold.

I used simple gestures related to the vowels i (ee), a (ah), and o (oh), including a moment of stillness at the end after returning to quiet standing. Then we moved into an active morning song such as "Wake up! Wake up!"— with gestures to follow the words.

Wake up!

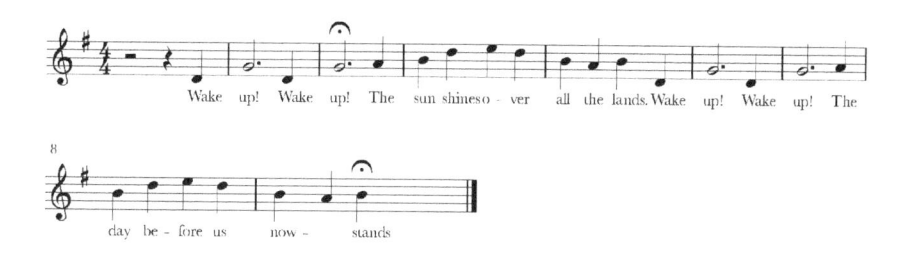

Figure 5. "Wake up!"—song

Each song and verse was repeated twice, to give it time to sink in.

At this point everyone was ready to concentrate on movement activities that required careful attention—beanbag games or body geography. (Beanbags are simple to make, stitched in square or round shapes, about two to three inches across, and filled with small dried beans.) I had beanbags ready in a basket that I carried to each child so she could select one for herself. (Sara joined in the circle in the winter after she turned three years old.) Then, standing in the circle, each of us holding a beanbag in the left hand, I recited the verse:

> Give and take (give own left hand to own right hand)
> Take and give (give own right hand to other's left hand)
> Each to the other (repeat first movement)
> As long as we live. (repeat second movement)

Each movement is careful and unhurried, so as to be a true embodiment of giving and taking in relation to both self and other. The whole sequence is repeated three or four times.

Then we moved into alliterative, rhythmic children's verses such as "Pease Porridge Hot" or a seasonal verse with actions that follow the words and rhythms of the speech. Here is a seasonal verse I used in the autumn:

> Four little pumpkins sitting on a gate
> First one said, "It's getting late!"
> Second one said, "We don't care!"
> Third one said, "There's witches in the air!"
> Fourth one said, "Let's get out of here!"
> Whoosh went the wind, out went the light
> And the four little pumpkins, rolled out of sight!

The motions that accompanied the verses were always the same, and I always sang the songs on the same pitches each time we had circle. Verses and songs were always repeated.

Finally, we came to our closing song and verse, which both stayed the same for the whole school year. Our closing song was "Sundrum," which includes the possibility of "drumming" on one's own body, which furthers children's musical experience.

Soltrumman
(Sundrum)

Come and let us dance now come a-long! Yes, I'm com-ing!

Come and let us drum now! We are drum-ming!

See the sun is shi-ni-ng bright-ly

Lis-ten to the Sun-Drum sound al-migh-ty

Look the sun is dan-cing a-rou-nd

Thous-and twin-kling stars in his crown

Alla Pauser Kan Markeras Med Lappn., Stampun. O.S.V. 1967

Figure 6. "Sundrum"—song

Then I spoke the closing verse while we stood quietly in the circle:

> Guarded from harm, cared for by angels,
> Here stand we, loving and strong, truthful and good.

In order to provide rhythm, stability, and also variation and interest for kindergarten-age children, the circle should remain the same yet also change over the course of the year. The beginning and end remain the same and provide a continuous frame. The inner sections can change with the season. To stay in the open, dreamy mood of the fifth, movements such as stepping and skipping are always forward, never backward. Backward stepping requires a very wakeful consciousness, and that begins later when the child is further along in the process of building up a healthy body. For the same reason, there is very little crossing the bodily midline with either hands or feet. (A large round rug, if you have it, helps show the physical boundaries of the circle.)

After the centered activity of the circle, the children breathe out into free play while the teacher prepares the space for snack. Free play outdoors in any weather is ideal because the light and air renew the children's life forces. Inside again, it is time for candle and grace, which we sang before snack. The days of the week correspond to plants and minerals as well as colors, and we had barley on Tuesday, millet on Wednesday, and rye on Thursday as part of the snack.

After snack we moved to an artistic activity, a different one each school day: wet-on-wet watercolor painting, modeling with beeswax or clay with beeswax, and handwork (stitching and finger knitting). Watercolor painting allows experience with transparent, flowing color (one at a time at first) that is only a few steps more material than atmospheric or prismatic color in light itself, especially if the pigments are plant derived. The girls played indoors while the teacher prepared for painting—first soaking the watercolor paper in a large tray, then laying out the painting boards, the large painting brushes, and one or two colors which were already diluted in small jars of water. When the paper was on the boards, the teacher called the children and they stood at the table and sang a painting song such as:

Painting Song

text: Robert Lewers
music: Catherine Read

1. Help me dear Angels of the light with tender care to paint a-right the colors that in me a-rise Bringing to Earth from out the skies

2. Help me to see in Earth's dark ways the golden sword of Mi-cha-el raised From out my heart I too would bring the colors of the rainbow ring

Figure 7. Painting song

Then the teacher painted on her paper quietly, maybe using a few words about the qualities or actions of the colors. (This wet-on-wet method with transparent colors gives the children a living experience of color in the material world. This matches and meets their consciousness, which consists of flowing, changing imaginations.) Then the children could paint on their own paper—how special! When they were finished, the paintings were left to dry.

If it was a day for modeling, they used small blocks of colored beeswax, one color at a time, to model simple figures related to the season or the story. Starting from the "outside in" and working with the whole piece, the teacher first used the palms of her hands to make a sphere and then elongated part of it making an egg shape. From there the form was revealed by pulling or pressing, always working with one whole piece of wax. Then the children made their own forms.

Likewise, the handwork of stitching or finger knitting was demonstrated by the teacher first, and natural fiber materials were used. We made objects for school and as gifts for others, or simply to experience the season.

After the artistic activity, they all moved quietly to the Rainbow House for the final event of the school day—the story. In kindergarten (as well as first grade), the story is always a fairy tale. But before the story could begin, the teacher lit a candle and said the verse: "Fire fairies burning bright, thank you for your golden light." In this quiet, enclosed space, surrounded by colored light, the teacher told fairy tales over the course of the year. She used clear speech and an even tone. When the story was finished, they sat quietly just to take it all in and let it work. Sometimes the most amazing moments happened in that quiet. Once, after a fairy tale that ended with the prince and princess together happily, Sara said wistfully to Teacher, "I want to marry you, really. But I know I can't, because you are already married...."

After the story and the priceless quiet they ended with the verse:

> In every seed that will be a tree
> There lives an image of all it will be.
> When I find the image of all I can be
> My heart and soul will then be free.

They then snuffed out the candle and repeated: "Fire fairies burning bright, thank you for your golden light." And school was over for the day! Hurray!

At the end of the school day there was always a feeling of accomplishment and of being nourished. The children, on a good day, have rosy cheeks at the end of school, and they are looking forward to the rest of the day. After having started around 9:30 AM, we usually ended school around 11:30 AM or noon.

The rest of the day had a rhythm too. The girls had free play, indoors or out, while Mother prepared lunch. After lunch they sat on the living room couch and Mother read them a picture book while they worked on handwork. When Father got home from work, he took over with the children through taking them to bed including more reading. Mother made dinner, they ate together, and then she studied for the next school day, taking a break to join Father and the children for the prayer before sleep. Thus went the school days in kindergarten which laid the foundation for all the years of school to come, although they didn't know then how many years that would be.

Moving into the grades. On the first day of first grade for our older daughter, Claire, she took her younger sister and disappeared into their bedroom right after breakfast. She knew this was the first day of her first "grade" (not just kindergarten) and the new blackboard was waiting, somehow mysteriously, in the classroom. And I had added a hanging rainbow cloth in front of the door to the classroom, making a distinct threshold between home life and school life. A little later, when I rang the bell and called "Time for school," they came excitedly down the hallway and presented themselves in the doorway dressed in their best dresses from last Easter. When I shook Claire's hand and said "Good morning, Claire," she replied solemnly, "Good morning, Teacher." Our career in school began at that moment.

In first grade the rhythm of day and week that we had established in kindergarten continued, except that right after the morning circle we had main lesson, a three-to-four-week block of lessons on one topic:

1. Form drawing—the straight line and the curve
2. Numbers and operations
3. The alphabet

The younger daughter had her own drawings or modeling materials to play with while the older daughter had her main lesson. At this early stage, main lessons were short. I alternated the morning circle activities' emphasis on language or numbers with the content of the day's main lesson. Thus, when the main lesson was language, the circle concentrated on numbers and number operations—and vice versa.

One of the most significant changes from kindergarten to first grade, in addition to the main lesson, is the school verse that the children say with the teacher to start the school day immediately after the greeting at the door. This gave me a chance to meet eye to eye and hand to hand with the children—to "take the pulse" of their mood and attention. We entered the classroom for the circle and said the following verse (translated from the German in *Wahrspruchworte*) while we faced a window looking out into our yard:

> The sun with loving light
> Makes bright for me each day.
> The soul with spirit power
> Gives strength unto my limbs.
> In sunlight shining clear
> I revere, Oh God,
> The strength of humankind,
> Which Thou so graciously
> Has planted in my soul
> That I with all my might
> May love to work and learn.
> From Thee stream light and strength
> To Thee rise love and thanks.

In first grade the teacher maintains the mood of the fifth that was established in kindergarten. The mood pervades the circle activities and continues in the story content, which is now drawn from the fairy tales as well as from nature stories.

As in the previous year, we had Nature Day on Monday, school on Tuesday, Wednesday, and Thursday, and on Friday I led a playgroup at a Waldorf school, which my younger daughter, Sara, attended. On Friday, Claire spent the day at the home of a friend who was a native speaker of German, so she would be immersed in another language in home life.

> ### Sample Circle activities in First Grade
>
> Morning song with gestures—"Two eyes to see"
> Morning verse, standing still—"The sun with loving light..."
> Walking in circle, body as drum—"Sundrum" song
> "Winter Goodbye" song
> Finger play—"Riders of the rain"
> Riddle—I went to town, but who went with me? I went up, I went down, but nobody could see me. (Answer: the wind.)
> Beanbags—mouse
> Body geography
> "Spring is coming" song
> "I came from the heavens" (closing song)
> Closing verse—"Guarded from harm..."

Mondays were a transition from weekend home life to school on Tuesday. On Monday we dressed for the outdoors, had breakfast, and then walked out our back door to the arroyo in the greenbelt area behind our house, or drove to a mountain canyon for a hike—or went to the beach. On these days, Nature was our teacher. We carried a snack with us so we could stay out as long as we wanted. I did not talk much to the girls; I answered their questions, but otherwise left it quiet. They chose where to go and what to do—I went along and stayed at a distance and made sure everything was safe. If there had been any rain, there might be mud in the arroyo, which always afforded a lot of inventive play. Once, Claire decided to use large burrs as curlers in her little sister's hair. (That took some careful work to undo!) I always said that if we came home dirty from exploring day, it had been a successful day. We saw an egret catch and eat a frog, we saw salamanders in the mud of a creek, and seagulls tried to steal the yarn out of our knitting bag at the beach. We did not see mountain lions or rattlesnakes, thank God!

We often went to the same place for weeks at a time; then we could experience the subtle change of seasons. We saw the late summer sky darkening from blue into the deeper indigo tinge of winter. And once again it lightened, right around Easter. Once, in a nature preserve in a canyon in the mountains, we returned to a spot we often visited, where large live oak trees grew near a creek. We found that a very big tree that had seemed a column holding up the sky had fallen—what a shock! Slow and sudden changes punctuated the rhythm of our explorations in nature.

School days, built on the rhythm established in kindergarten, but now with the main lesson added, were longer. The basic sequence was greeting at the door, circle, main lesson, recess, lunch, free time, artistic and craft activity, story, and closing verse. This rhythm maintains the same breathing between activity and quiet, between relaxing and concentrating, and between physical and mental activity that characterized the kindergarten day. The main lesson has a rhythm of its own, just as the circle does, but it is a rhythm of mental work, per se. The first step is to recall what happened in the previous lesson. This the teacher and student do together in order to build up the foundation for the new material. Then the teacher introduces the new material and is active while the student is quiet and receptive. Then it is the student's turn to be active and to work on the material, usually by working in the main lesson book that they are writing in or illustrating. Although the content of the lessons change, and the type of work the child can do advances, these basic rhythms hold at least through grade eight.

The sequence of topics in all the areas of a class day in the grades is detailed in several publications on the Waldorf curriculum, including *Rudolf Steiner's Curriculum for Waldorf Schools* by Karl Stockmeyer and *The Educational Tasks and Content of the Steiner Waldorf Curriculum,* edited by Martin Rawson and Tobias Richter. Steiner gave hundreds of lectures to Waldorf teachers and most of these are published and available. (Some of these include *The Kingdom of Childhood, Practical Advice to Teachers, Foundations of Human Experience,* and *Education for Adolescents*). His earliest writing on the subject is *The Education of the Child in the Light of Anthroposophy.* There are also various curriculum materials specifically for homeschool, such as Christopherus and Living Education.

I cannot leave the topic of the rhythm of the day without talking about time for the teacher—time for her mental, emotional, and intellectual study and preparation for school. I also cannot omit the question of the teacher's study space, a place of her own to keep and use study materials. I sometimes thought that in studying teaching and the curriculum it was I, not my children, who was receiving the education in this process. Each parent-teacher has their own "circadian" rhythm of the day, times of optimal alertness, and times when rest is needed. Self-knowledge in this area goes a long way toward achieving healthy study time. For example, I am a morning person, and begin to sleep lightly at 3:00 AM. Thus, when I was too tired to complete my study in the evening, I went to bed, got up at 3:00 AM and worked for an hour, then went back to sleep and awoke at the usual time for the school day. That is the flexibility of home!

Yearly rhythms. One finds an excellent resource for study and contemplation of the seasons in Rudolf Steiner's *Calendar of the Soul*, which he wrote for the year 1912–1913. He composed fifty-two verses, one for each of the weeks between Easter, 1912, and Easter, 1913. Already one can notice several riddles. Easter is determined by the relations of the sun, the moon, and the earth, and falls on the first Sunday after the first full moon following the spring equinox. The "year" from one Easter to the next has a variable number of weeks in it, as opposed to the (adjusted) solar year which has fifty-two weeks. If one follows the *Calendar of the Soul* each calendar year from Easter to Easter, certain adjustments are required, but it does help to be conscious of the relation of these three key heavenly bodies. Directly opposite Easter in the year is the fall celebration of Michaelmas, so this is the festival mood with which the school year begins.

Michaelmas was a traditional celebration in Europe starting in the Middle Ages and celebrated on September 29. Although festivals are associated with certain dates, they have an "aura" that extends around them in time, so that at any given time some festival is building, peaking, or waning. School for us started right after Labor Day—the first week in September. In the northern hemisphere, or at least far north of the equator where we lived, autumn is "in the air" in early September. The light is changing, annual and deciduous plants are "dying back," and the days are getting shorter and darker. Animals are preparing for winter and human beings are becoming more awake, more centered in an inner consciousness. These qualities are brought into school in the content of circle, in artistic and craft activities, and in the mood of the colors in the classroom. Luckily for the teacher, every day is a festival day and the time structure of the yearly seasons is a wonderful guide for material to use in school. Steiner's lectures on the seasons are of great value—for example, *The Cycle of the Seasons, The Four Seasons and the Archangels,* and *The Festivals and their Meaning.*

Michaelmas moves into an even darker and more inner time of winter, with festivals at the beginning of November (All Hallows' Eve, All Saints' Day, All Souls' Day) to remember those who are now in the spiritual world, among the dead. This darkness gives way to the depth of winter and the celebration of the birth of Jesus and Christ, which falls just after the winter solstice. After the first week in January, there are a few moments in the cycle of returning to Easter that one can be aware of. February 2 (Brigit's Day) is across the circle of the year from August 2; the former is the turning into spring, and the latter the turning into autumn and is roughly forty days after Christmas. Easter appears again in March or April, and then we begin the last leg of the school year. We marked May 1 which is the turning to summer, and I tried to end school in early June. Just as the school day works best when there is healthy breathing of activity and quiet, the school year works best when there is full breathing out into three months of summer, where there is no school or intellectual work required. Summer is the opposite of winter in human consciousness. In summer we are the most "expanded" and dreamy. This complete rest from school is the best preparation for the next year, the best time to "digest" all the new material and work of the previous school year.

Birthdays and the school year. One other celebration takes place yearly, and that is the celebration of the birth of the child. We had a celebration for birthdays that started before school age, and we continued this into the school years. I also actually brought part of it into school itself. Beginning when our older daughter was four years old, we said the birthday verse to her as the last thing before sleep the night before her birthday. Here is the birthday verse:

> When I have said my evening prayer
> And my clothes are folded on the chair
> When Mother switches out the light
> I'll still be __ years old tonight.
> But from the very break of day
> Before the children rise and play
> Before the rooftops turn to gold
> Tomorrow I'll be __ years old!

> __ kisses when I wake,
> __ candles on my cake.

When she woke in the morning, she received five kisses and later there were five candles on her cake. This ritual continued until she left home for college at age eighteen!

When Claire was in kindergarten at home, I added to the family ritual the step of writing a verse for her that captured something of the school year. I wrote it on a card in color, with illustration, and gave it to her as a birthday present along with her other presents. This tradition continued all the years she had school at home. Beginning in first grade, we brought the verse into the circle in school. Here is her verse given to her when she turned seven:

> I have started on my journey
> Traveling near and far
> Always on my path
> Guided by my star.
> What all shall I see?
> Sun and moon and stars
> Plants and animals
> And all people dear to me,
> The letters and numbers
> And rhymes and songs
> To help me grow
> Tall and strong.

I used this verse in the circle on the first school day of the week, on Tuesdays. After the morning verse and the morning song, I had her stand across from me and repeat the lines after me until she had it memorized. When she had it memorized, she would walk to me counting her steps, and then say the verse to me. Each year this developed, and the challenges of that year were captured in the birthday verse as well as in the accompanying movement task. These variations are given in chapter three, along with more detail on the material for each school year.

One final aspect of the school year was rhythmic: the beginning and the end of the school year itself. I tried to engender a festival mood and celebration for both the beginning and the end of the year. When the first day of school was near, we got new school dresses and shoes (even if they were from the consignment store, they were new to us). As a surprise, I bought a new set of school materials or tools that would be new for that year, something related to the more advanced work to be done. On the first day, after the greeting at the door but before the morning verse, I welcomed each child to her new grade, and rang the bell once for each year she had already completed plus one for the new one. I then presented her with her new materials, unveiled for her on her desk. This almost felt like a birthday celebration!

The last day of school was equally festive. We always had a year-end ceremony in which Teacher and Father called the child forward to receive a bouquet of flowers and our congratulations on completing the grade and being ready for the next one. In eighth grade there was a special graduation ceremony from the lower school to the high school, and when each had finished eleventh grade, there was a ceremony to mark graduation from our homeschool (before each went for her final year into an institutional school). These will be described in more detail in the section on the high school grades.

Of course, I am describing a school with our particular family configuration. Other families will have a different composition and different life circumstances. But the basic ideas and practices that I have shared apply, however they are manifested in particular family constellations.

Why the Waldorf Curriculum?

Even with my brief characterization of the Waldorf curriculum given so far, one can see that this method is distinct. It exists at the middle point between two poles, two opposite approaches to education. On the one hand, we have the traditional ideas that the teacher gives, pours, or somehow inculcates knowledge into the students and then tests this knowledge by demanding that it be demonstrated at given points in time decided by the teacher. At the other extreme is the completely child-centered approach known as unschooling in which children are allowed to engage in whatever activity holds their interest and the parent-teacher supports this interest and activity. In contrast, the Waldorf curriculum calls for the teacher to be educated in the development of the fourfold human being, as well as in methods of observing, studying, and teaching in an artistic manner based on an awareness of the evolution of human consciousness.

The Waldorf method and content, thus, is based on the child's developing consciousness and makes use of the materials we have from the past of humanity in myths, legends, and history, including works in science and mathematics. This curriculum is not quick and easy. So why use it? Everyone has their own answer to this question. In some ways I had decided that this was the right way to teach children even before I had a child or knew I would have a child. And I hadn't experienced anything in my own education other than state schools in America. The answer to this question for me was that I recognized something in a colleague I met at university, a professor of Geology, something that made his thinking distinctive. For example, he made a distinction between soul and spirit that wasn't familiar to me. When I asked why his views were so different, he replied that he had gone to a Waldorf school in Edinburgh, Scotland. I asked, "What is a Waldorf school?" and he gave me a book entitled *Education Towards Freedom*. After reading that book, there was no going back for me. I found later that the book was a great resource for teaching.

Chapter Three

Connecting with the Curriculum

Why Teach the Waldorf Curriculum at Home?

Everyone has their own reasons for deciding to school at home. There are many books on the subject, and that decision is not a focus here. But teaching with the Waldorf curriculum at home is innovative now—in its early days. Waldorf schools are institutions, and if one decides that one's child will be best educated outside of institutions, for whatever reason, then one is left with the challenge of finding a life in the curriculum that resonates to life at home. Before Steiner gave indications for an institutional school, he tutored one family's children at home, in all subjects, including one child with special needs. The first Waldorf school was begun when Emil Molt asked Steiner for indications of a curriculum and school for the children of the workers at his cigarette factory in Stuttgart, Germany. Yet as far as I know, no one ever asked Steiner for indications on how to school at home. We don't know what his answers might have been; we have to find the answers now ourselves. Steiner was clear, though, that starting a school as an institution within the state would require compromises (*Foundations of Human Experience*, August 20, 1919). School at home does not require those same compromises.

I often got the question, "How can the children be socialized if they go to school at home?" That question has many assumptions behind it. One assumption is that an institution in which children spend hours every weekday in a room with twenty or thirty other children the same age is the only way to provide them with group experience that will teach them how to interact in a socially acceptable way. This assumption is not true, even in Waldorf schools where teachers take into account the balance of temperaments in the group. Another assumption is that children who have school at home are not in social groups. This assumption is not true either. For instance, we were part of a group of families that celebrated festivals together and sometimes joined to teach our children in small groups. And we also hired specialty teachers for small groups throughout the fifteen years that we had school at home. Flexibility and adaptability are hallmarks of the Waldorf curriculum, and these qualities make the curriculum not only ideal but crucial as a foundation for teaching at home.

The Teacher's Own Relation to the Curriculum

If we go back to the word "curriculum" again, we can go deeper with its meaning. The word is from the Latin *curri*, a stem of the verb *currere*, "to run," and combines with *culum*, from *cule*, which is a diminutive suffix. Thus, a curriculum is "a little running" or "a little course." This is the type of course that stars follow, that rivers flow, and that runners run. But what does this "course" have to do with a predetermined set of lessons, which is what we now think of as a curriculum? If the course is a path, then schooling is a path, and the teacher and student are on that path together. There is movement and progress and change and adaptation.

As I stated earlier, my first contact with the Waldorf curriculum came before I had children, when a friend who had attended the Edinburgh Steiner School gave me *Education Towards Freedom* by Franz Carlgren. This book describes the curriculum and nature of the Waldorf schools of 1972 in England and Germany. When I first read it, a few things immediately struck me about the education: its beauty, depth, integrity, and wholeness. These qualities I was strongly drawn to, even though my own education and professional work were nothing like the schooling described. I was also drawn to the paintings and drawings, the classrooms themselves, and the expressions of interest and well-being on the children's faces, not to mention the breadth of topics and the detail of the thinking behind the topics—and also the sense that all the lessons were related to a larger whole. I felt that I would have children and that this Waldorf method would be the right education for them.

Once we had a daughter and had moved to New England, I gradually got "back on my feet," and when she was two and a half I started to be able hold my head above the "water" of daily life in order to think ahead about her schooling. I assumed there would be a Waldorf school nearby. But there wasn't. The closest one was one and a half hours away. I did find a Waldorf-inspired playgroup in a parent's house, and we started attending that weekly. Many things there were new for me, including forming a circle for songs and rhythmic movement, having a nature table, saying grace before snack, and having a quiet focus on the work at hand. Meanwhile, I began participating in a study group on one of Steiner's basic books, *An Outline of Esoteric Science*, with other mothers of young children.

I didn't directly encounter the curriculum again until we had our second daughter and moved again, this time to Southern California. As I stated earlier, the nearest Waldorf school was now forty-five minutes of freeway driving away—but they had a playgroup, and I began taking the children there once a week. This time the playgroup was held in a kindergarten room at the school, and led by a former Waldorf teacher along with some parents at the school. Again, I was struck by the beauty and peace of the kindergarten room and by the liveliness and enlivening rhythm of the playgroup activities.

I began to attend kindergarten in-service classes at the Waldorf school on the twelve senses (yes, there are twelve!)[1] and on child development. And though I continued to study the basic books in a group, I also started reading some of Steiner's lectures on education on my own. Several moments in this reading stand out for me. In a lecture of August 19, 1922, in Oxford, England (*Spiritual Ground of Education*, p. 56), Steiner ends with:

> We must make sure we do not try to turn out children who are copies of ourselves, and that we do not forcibly and tyrannically impose ourselves on those who will naturally develop beyond us. Each child in every age brings something new into the world from divine regions, and it is our task as educators to remove the bodily and soul obstacles, so that the child's spirit may enter with full freedom into life. These must become the three rules in the art of education. They must imbue the whole attitude of teachers and the whole impulse of their work. The golden rules that must be embraced by a teacher's whole being, not as theory, are these: first, reverent gratitude toward the world for the child we contemplate

---

[1] See Rudolf Steiner, *A Psychology of Body, Soul, and Spirit*.

every day, for every child presents a problem given us by divine worlds; second, gratitude to the universe and love for what we have to do with a child; and third, respect for the child's freedom, which we must not endanger. Since it is this freedom to which we must direct our teaching efforts, so that the child may one day stand at our side in freedom in the world.

What struck me about this description was that the teacher's ideal attitude is described given in relation to the *world*, to *work*, and to the *child's freedom*—instead of in her direct relation to the child itself. This gave me much food for thought. I tried it on:

"I am grateful to the world for this child I contemplate every day."

"I love what I have to do with the child, my work and my relationship with the child."

"I respect the child's freedom."

Yes, I could work with these thoughts every day of teaching.

As I studied the content of the lesson blocks year by year and taught the blocks (twice), I began to see how the "gesture" or "image" of the teacher's relation to the student changes from kindergarten through high school. From kindergarten through grade two, when the mood of the fifth prevails, the teacher stands behind the child, protecting and guiding. This is when I held the student on my lap to guide her knitting: we both face the world but I provided a protected place. From grade three through grade six, the image is one of the teacher and student facing each other. The student sees the world reflected in the expressions on the teacher's face and in the "tone" of her gestures. The final step begins in grade seven and progresses from there: the teacher and student gradually come to stand side by side, both facing the world they are engaged in, with their attention focused on the work. Ideal configurations.

As the curriculum is a course, a path of movement and change that the teacher and child progress through together, one asks, "What is the course of change, the way of change?" Here what is important is the spiritual world that coexists with the physical, living world we encounter with our usual earthly senses. In a lecture given on January 2, 1915, (*Art as Seen in the Light of Mystery Wisdom*) Steiner touched again on the work and attitude of the teacher in the ideal teacher-student relationship. In our day and age, we think of the teacher as knowledgeable and of education as a process of imparting knowledge, "filling the head" of the student, who is empty, a sort of "blank state." But Steiner gives a very different description of teacher and student that is based on understanding the whole human life, and even of the times before and after an individual's life. He makes the startling (to some ears, anyway) statement that the teacher's own next incarnation converses with the previous incarnation of the pupil! The teacher could say to herself: "The very best in me that my spirit can think and my soul can feel, and which is preparing to make something of me in the next incarnation, can work on the part of the child that is sculpturing her form out of times long past" (*Art as Seen in the Light of Mystery Wisdom*).

The teacher as an adult is moving forward and is on a course toward the spiritual world after this life, whereas the child has more recently left the spiritual world and is on a course toward the earthly life. Recall the verse in chapter two from *At the Back of the North Wind*. "Where do you come from?" asks the adult of the infant. But what the adult teacher has to offer the child, as these two courses meet and mingle, is the will to think and speak and feel in such a way that in the course of her lessons what comes from the past of the child will learn to love what reaches out to the future in the teacher. The teacher is reaching toward something in the future and the child is receiving something from the past. If the teacher can choose and prepare her lessons out of that reality, the child's higher self can come to love what the teacher is reaching toward, and in the process will be educated for life on earth. And, even more, the student will be able to develop according to his or her individual destiny and goals. We usually think of the teacher's past experience and education giving something to the child, for the child's future, yet this is the exact opposite of what Steiner portrays. It took me a while to readjust my thinking in this regard, but I eventually found these thoughts invaluable in approaching the children with the lessons I prepared for them.

The final "broad stroke" in relating to the curriculum pertains to children's changing consciousness over the time they are growing and developing. In one of a series of lectures given on education (Dornach, April 17, 1923) Steiner reiterates his work on the changes in consciousness that we all experience from infancy into childhood, adolescence, and young adulthood.

In infants and very young children, sensing and imitating are the important processes that lead to walking, talking, and thinking. These processes begin to transform when the permanent teeth come in. They gradually transform into an inner "soul habit" of imitation, which develops into memory. Steiner makes the analogy that the child's "memory" before and after the change of teeth are to each other as the wolf is to the dog. The two memory abilities are related, but they are not the same thing. From ages seven to fourteen the child is developing this inner imitation which is memory, and the teacher "works upon the child" through the medium of language. An image-like element pervades the child's speaking and thinking, and activities in the surroundings are transformed into pictures. All soul life takes place in pictures at the lower school ages, and the rhythmic systems of breathing and blood circulation are closely related to this pictorial tendency. At the midpoint in this age period, at around nine to ten years old, the breath and heart rate begin to come into the ratio of four heartbeats to one complete breath. This ratio is clearest in dreamless sleep. At this age, trochaic rhythms—that is, rhythms with a ratio of four to one—in music, speech, and movement, are of fundamental importance to the child's healthy development.

Steiner points out that the teacher must be aware of what is budding and germinating in the child, and he notes that this is only possible when there exists an inner bond between teacher and student. Here the parent as teacher has a distinct advantage. Such an inner bond is developed from the child's birth (or even before) and it continues and sustains the adult-child relationship through radical changes in the child's being, development, and education. And here is the crux: all education is a matter of self-education. The teacher must be able to teach, in content and in process, what is "welling up and flowing out of the organism." Thus the lesson content should be given in harmony with the pupil's rhythmic system, and to do this the teacher is required to work on their observational skills and moral attitudes. To paraphrase an old idea: "The children in themselves are alright—it is the adults who are not!" But this does not mean that children will grow and develop on their own—quite the contrary. It is critical that the teacher form a close connection with the student and give her just the lessons she needs at the appropriate time. Steiner calls for teachers to "strive toward knowledge of how we as teachers and educators ought to conduct ourselves. In other words, we need forces of the heart."

So the teacher finds her relation to the Waldorf curriculum: her heart is in it.

How to Get Started, or Study Is Hard Work

When our older daughter, Claire, was four years old and our younger, Sara, was nine months old, I began taking the girls to a playgroup at a Waldorf school. The playgroup was held in a kindergarten classroom, so I saw and felt the surroundings provided for young children: open space, neatly organized toys made of natural objects and materials, and a nature table with seasonal and festival elements—with soft fabrics and colors predominating. I sensed the work that went into creating and maintaining that space. This experience, and the experience of songs, circle movements, snack with grace, handwork, and an overall rhythm showed me it was possible to get through the day in a way that was enlivening rather than draining—for both myself and the girls. What a radical thought!

I began to read and go to lectures and meetings about the kindergarten and about young children. In the Waldorf kindergarten, I attended, over the course of a school year, an in-service training course on the senses and child development and teaching, and I also attended a workshop on music for your children in their mood of the fifth. I was also a member of a study group that focused on books written by Rudolf Steiner. This included reading aloud and paraphrasing as part of the method of study. My steps toward the curriculum, the classrooms, and the festival celebrations led me into a study of child development from an anthroposophical perspective, and, finally, into the content and methods of teaching. On each of these steps I was accompanied by teachers and parents experienced both in teaching with the Waldorf curriculum and in watching children grow and develop.

The year before I began teaching at home I was not directly working on the curriculum, but was involved with two important elements: study and seasonal festivals. Our study group consisted of mothers with young children who were interested in anthroposophy and Waldorf education. We met once a week, often in a park, and hired someone to watch the group of children there while we studied. We read basic works by Rudolf Steiner (*Theosophy* and *How to Know Higher*

Worlds) with a structured study format. Once the children were settled in playing and we were all seated at a table, we took five minutes for a concentration exercise. In silence, we each kept our thoughts on one object in front of us on the table, often a candle. This is an exercise that Steiner gives as the first of six "supplementary exercises." (See Steiner, *Six Steps in Self-Development*). Then we worked on the text by reading, in turn, one paragraph and then paraphrasing it. Any comments or questions were entertained and then we went on to the next person and the next paragraph. Of course, there were interruptions from the children, but mothers became very adept at persisting through interruptions! We studied for about an hour and then, with the children, had a snack, initiated by singing grace together.

We alternated between studying a basic written work and studying lectures related to the festivals that corresponded to the time of year. About six weeks before a major festival, we chose appropriate lectures and studied them. At the same time we created a plan for a festival celebration that we then carried out with the children and other family members. We didn't see the seasonal festivals as religious (either Christian or pagan), but rather as celebrations that were being renewed through Steiner's spiritual science. We used several resources, including *The Festivals and Their Meaning*, *The Four Seasons and the Archangels*, and the *Archangel Michael*. Our task was to understand the cycle of the seasons (at least as they exist in the temperate zones in the northern hemisphere), and to follow in our thinking and observation Steiner's indications on the spiritual aspects of this. We had the further task of bringing about festival celebrations that spoke to and nourished the whole group, which included parents and ten to twelve children with ages from two to five years. Quite a task!

We worked in this way for five years. This proved to be a wonderful preparation for school at home, because it was there that I learned, after the first year or so, that every day is a festival day. Thus, I already had the basis for understanding the quality of the time of each school day, lesson, and sequence of lesson blocks by the time I started kindergarten at home. And our festival group continued and became part of school as well as home life.

Each festival took place at least partly outdoors in nature, in a wilderness or nature preserve. We prepared activities, food, and stories that embodied the meaning of the festival and guided everyone through the celebration with a written program. Each festival included free play in nature for the children, verses, singing, a story, and eating together. For example, our St. John's festival on June 24, just after the summer solstice, usually took place at the beach. We met there in the late afternoon with chairs, blankets, food, and instruments, and we let the children play. After running free with the waves and the sand, we gathered together to light a beach fire. Sometimes though, before we lit the fire, one adult carried a torch and led a parade of marching children to the wood laid for the fire, while another adult drummed a beat. Once the fire was lit, we gathered in a circle for a reading of the St. John's verse from *In the Light of a Child* by Michael Burton (*Calendar of the Soul* verses rewritten for children). The verse for St. John's reads:

> The light filled beauty all around me everywhere,
> It calls to me to leave my earthly dwelling.
> On wings of fancy sweeping, swooping, soaring light as air
> Where sun rays glimmer and where waves of warmth are welling.
> My angel calls—his love I shall not shun.
> For in the sparkling light and glowing warmth of the sun,
> With joy we fly together—and are truly one.

Then we would sing a song about summer and maybe one about St. John's Tide, and hold hands in a circle to sing grace before our meal. We experienced all this to the rhythm of the soughing of the waves, the sight and smell of ocean breezes, and the bright shining of the late afternoon summer sun. After dinner the children would play, sometimes running with streamers up and down the beach, while the adults tidied up. By then the sun was low, and the fire had burned down enough that we could gather round to sing. In the dusk we sang folk songs, especially about birds as creatures of the air, that element that so predominates at the height of summer when our consciousness is expanded and dreamy. Accompanied by a wooden flute or guitar, we sang folk songs and campfire songs as we held the smaller children on our laps until it was dark and the fire was reduced to embers. Then it was time for the height, literally, of the festival: we took turns jumping over the coals of the fire. But we only did this after we had stood in a circle around the fire's embers and spoke the verse that Steiner gives at the end of his lecture of October 12, 1923:

> *Es werden Stoffe verdictet*
> *Es werden Fehler gerichtet*
> *Es werden Herzen gesichet*

Which we translated as:

> Substances are densified
> Errors are rectified
> Hearts are sifted.

With this serious contemplation in mind we each braved the heat and jumped over the fire, with dads or moms going again to carry over the little ones. It was almost as exciting to watch as to do, and I always felt a certain kind of confirmation and purification afterward. Then came the final challenge: to pack up and get everyone back to the cars in the dark without breaking the quiet festival mood on this one night a year when everyone stayed up so late into the night. We always kept it quiet in the car on the way home—only singing or listening to the children—in order to carry the festival mood back home and into sleep.

There were always unexpected events and challenges during our festivals. For one St. John's we had a musician with us who sat in a beach chair at the edge of the waves to play guitar and lead us in song. The problem was that her back was to the water and the tide was coming in. We watched as the waves came closer and closer, and finally came up under her chair. She just lifted her feet and kept playing. Intrepid! On another occasion, when we were walking down the beach in the dark, watching phosphorescence appear with each of our steps in the wet sand, we came to a place where a stream ran into the ocean. Earlier, when we'd come down to the beach in the afternoon at low tide, it had been shallow and easy to cross. Now in the pitch darkness and the high tide, it was too deep for the children to wade, and they had to be carried across on the shoulders of adults, all of whom got really wet! A festival is always a great adventure. (See Appendix 1 for a more detailed description of our family festival group and our celebrations.)

Study methods: rhythms of preparing and teaching. All this may seem far from the Waldorf curriculum and distant from studying to prepare for teaching. But once I started teaching, at first in kindergarten and then in the grades, I found the festivals to be a wonderful foundation for the school day and the lessons. It slowly dawned on me that *every day is a festival day*, and, therefore, the lesson material always takes place in the context of the festival that continues in the background, depending on the time of year. The seasons and related festivals guide the activities of school and even, to a degree, the content of the lessons.

Summer, meanwhile, is the time to be outdoors in the long days, playing and exploring. It is a time to travel to new places and to familiar places in order to renew connections with family and friends. Summer is a time for having dreamy, expanded consciousness, for being open to experience, and for taking in the warmth of the sun. Most people find it relatively difficult to concentrate and to do intellectual thinking in the summertime. Thus, we never had school or academic work in the summer.

But as the days grow shorter and cooler, we near the traditional beginning of the school year. We feel more wakeful and the teacher begins to turn toward forming lessons and choosing the sequence of lessons for the year. When my older daughter was in kindergarten at home, I began teacher training, first at the Waldorf Institute for Teacher Training (in Southern California, covering kindergarten and the early grades) and continuing with teacher preparation courses in the summer in Colorado and New York. So I, as the teacher, couldn't take the whole summer off from thinking! I also took workshops and courses on painting, modeling, handwork, eurythmy, spatial dynamics, and music throughout the time I was teaching.

When autumn approaches, the coming festival is Michaelmas, on September 29. This festival is much more familiar to Europeans than it is to Americans. There are many paintings of St. George slaying the dragon, and St. George is an earthly representation of a higher spiritual being, Michael. Steiner is very clear that human consciousness correlates to earthly seasons: in summer we become immersed in a nature consciousness, a sympathy and empathy with flowering, fruiting nature, but in autumn we are called upon to become *self-conscious*. As he says in *The Four Seasons and the Archangels*:

> If a person enters thus into the enjoyment of nature, the consciousness of nature, but then also awakes in themselves

an autumnal self-consciousness, the picture of Michael with the dragon will stand majestically before them, revealing in picture form the overcoming of nature-consciousness by self-consciousness when autumn draws near.

Figures 8a, 8b, and 8c: Progression of Michaelic figures in our homeschool blackboard art. 8a (above): Michael, from grade two

Connecting with the Curriculum

Figure 8b: St. George, from grade eight

THE GENIUS OF HOME

Figure 8c: Michael, post high school

As the teacher studies for the first school lessons and plans an overview of the year, she must be self-conscious and awake. She must prepare for the children to be more awake than they have been in the summer, even though their consciousness is not yet that of the adult. If school starts at the beginning of September, the songs, verses, nature stories, and even fairy tales can all be chosen to express the fading of summer and the coming of winter. And, naturally, some of the material can be related to Michael legends, in order to prepare for the coming Michaelmas festival. Thus, autumn holds the teacher's hand as she takes the plunge into being the children's loving guide.

I recall a story that relates to this. When my daughter Sara was three and a half years old, we were leaving the nature preserve where we had just celebrated the Michaelmas festival. The golden sun loomed large in the western sky as it approached the horizon. She said, "The sun has a face. Everything has a face; we just don't see it." I replied, "Yes, everything has a face." This wonderfully precise imagination can actually be a guide to the teacher in reminding us that the world is a place of living beings, whose presence we strive to bring to the children who are gradually losing their inherent connection to the world as they "wake up" and become more and more self-conscious. We don't just destroy the dragon (nature consciousness), we transform it.

Balancing Polarities, the Teacher's Likes and Dislikes

Across the wide range of topics taught in the main lesson blocks from first through twelfth grades, and even in the specialty courses on art, music, handwork, and movement, the teacher will inevitably find aspects that she is drawn to, and, also, the opposite—topics or activities she dislikes or feels intimidated by. For instance, I never heard live, unrecorded singing as I was growing up, and I don't have a natural affinity for tone, melody, and rhythm. How was I going to learn songs and provide the critical musical aspect of the circle in kindergarten, let alone in the more advanced years? Gulp. I had to swallow past the knot of fear lodged in my throat. I decided to play the Choroi wooden flute, especially the small, five-tone (pentatonic) flute, as part of the circle in school. The flute is easy to play and is designed to provide tones with the warmth of a human voice. I also used the flute to learn songs to then sing in school. I then went on to purchase a Choroi lyre, a new stringed instrument based on indications given by Steiner. That meant I could play the tones and match them with my voice. I used the lyre both when we gathered in the circle and when we gathered in the Rainbow House to light a candle and have the story that ended the school day. On a five-tone lyre, any simple sequence is enlivening—and it is easy to compose simple melodies to verses such as "Fire fairies burning bright, thank you for this golden light." Also, there are many songs available in the mood of the fifth, such as "Quintenlieder" by Julius Knierim and "I Love to Be Me" by Channa Seidenberg. It is important that the songs are repeated, though, and not just improvised each time, as repetition is "nutritional" and strengthening for young children. I gradually moved on to the diatonic flute and the larger lyre, and the girls and I started taking lessons from music teachers on these instruments. Eventually Claire and Sara took part in youth lyre workshops as well as the youth section of the World Lyre Conference. By that time, we were playing as an ensemble for Advent Spiral Walk festival celebrations in our homeschool family community and at a Waldorf school. Anything is possible!

Meanwhile, if I thought singing was bad, I was absolutely terrified of painting! Every time I confronted a blank white paper, I was filled with terror. And yet I had to overcome this reaction because I had to learn to paint before the children did. As young children grow and develop through imitation, the adult is called upon to provide movements, tones, and gestures that are worthy of imitation. Imitation is not copying, though, not in the way a Xerox machine works. Imitation means joining in with and continuing an ongoing process or action that is outside of one's self. Infants smile when they see other people smile. The tendency to imitate is powerful in human life, and strongest at young ages. Imitation can happen immediately in time and place, or removed in time and place, but it always has the quality of matching or tuning oneself to the outer world. So I had to face the blank paper with equanimity and force myself to put paint on the brush and put the brush to paper. It helped that the very earliest painting with young children is done with a single color: red, yellow, or ultramarine blue. (See the book *Painting with Young Children* by Brunhild Mueller). Also, the songs we sang to prepare for painting helped to set the mood.

By the upper grades and high school, students are ready for more complexity in their approach to color and bringing form out of color. To prepare the painting verse, I started with the description of the soul's correspondences with the colors of the rainbow that Steiner gave in lecture 14 of his *Speech and Drama* course (p. 323). I put this description into a verse that we could say before painting:

> When I see you, violet,
> My soul must pray.
> When I see you, blue,
> My soul becomes calm.
> I descend from the violet-blue
> And approach the green arch.
> I pour myself out
> Into everything that sprouts.
> Shining yellow gives me strength
> To be myself in the world.
> Orange gives me my own warmth.
> Red leads me back to heaven
> Bringing forth
> My overstreaming joy,
> My courage to give,
> My love for all beings.

Academic topics present different challenges to the "activity" or specialty topics. Steiner gave many lectures to teachers about different academic topics and about children of different ages. The list of books compiled from these lectures is too long to list. Even the secondary literature by Waldorf teachers expanding on Steiner's material is extensive. How does one find one's way? And what about the topics that are easy and those that are a challenge in some way? The writings are organized by grade, so one can locate one's area of study in relation to the grade for which one is preparing. And the regularity of the seasons and festivals provides an overall structure to the year. In the late summer the teacher is planning the sequence of blocks for the year, and researching and gathering materials for the first blocks. And this material has to "ring true" to the teacher, or the children will learn nothing.

Steiner sets the bar high for the teacher. In a lecture of February 24, 1921, he gives the example of the image of the fully formed butterfly coming out of its cocoon. He says:

> For only those things that we ourselves believe [of which we are convinced, my addition], in which we ourselves stand, will have an effect upon the child. Anthroposophically-oriented spiritual science allows one to say: I personally believe in this image; for me,

this emergence of the butterfly from the cocoon is not something I have made up, but what nature itself presents in a more simple way for the same fact which is represented at a higher level by the emergence of the immortal soul from the body. If I myself believe in this image, if I stand within the content/meaning of this image, then my belief will awaken the child's belief, representation, and perception.

The teacher's sense for the truth awakens the same in the child, and also awakens her images and perceptions. So, whatever the likes and dislikes of the teacher in relation to the topics taught in school, her truth sense and feeling of conviction are key. This relation of the teacher's conviction and the children's learning pertains most to the second stage of life, from the seventh to the fourteenth or fifteenth year—that is, to grades one through eight.

Personally, I encountered several challenges in relation to the material required for various blocks. Since my childhood, when I had a repeated nightmare about Roman soldiers, I have had an aversion to Roman history and culture. Also, I'm not gifted with mechanics and find it difficult to think in those terms. On the other hand, I am too aware of the logical problems with neo-Darwinian evolutionary theory to accept that theory "whole cloth" and have been interested in alternatives for years. Steiner's description of the relation of the human being to the animal kingdom (e.g., in *Man as a Symphony of the Creative Word*) provides a much more encompassing understanding of evolution than does Darwinist theory. The challenge is to be able to interpret and critique mainstream science. For example, I had to make myself study the Roman period in history in order to find what was positive in it. I had to work with machines and the mechanics of the human body in order to teach mechanics in physics. And I also had to have a clear vision of the relation of the animal world to the human world—and the changes that have taken place therein over long periods of time. At least my dislikes gave me guidance in what I had to study!

The goal is to bring balance to the teacher's sympathies and antipathies so that neither predominates and, ultimately, so that they are not the focus in the classroom. Balance means not dwelling too long on one topic and thereby giving another short shrift. And it also means keeping the focus on the presented lesson material with conviction and enthusiasm! Thus, one gains faith in the curriculum the longer one sees the effects on the children—and on oneself as teacher, too. Over time, we are all enlivened, confirmed, and strengthened.

The Individuality of Teacher and Student

If the child is a riddle, a message, a conundrum given to us by the spiritual world, then who is she? All children are in the process of becoming themselves. They are on a path toward themselves as developed beings, and the path has a destination, a destiny. The overarching questions for the teacher are: Who is the child now? Where is she going? How can I help and support her in her journey?

There are two rhythms that are important in answering these questions, and sleep turns out to be key for both—the sleep of the student and the sleep of the teacher. I will now explain this in relationship to the lessons being taught in school.

A lesson is not just the minutes or hours devoted to it in the formal school day. Each lesson draws on experiences the child has already had, including experiences in sleep, and each lesson projects forward in time to what is coming. When I prepared at night for the material to be given in school the next day, I was doing intellectual work—memorizing, practicing songs and movement activities, etc. But the last thing I did before going to sleep was to take a few minutes to concentrate inwardly on each child. I brought her face, her gait, her skin tone and emotional tone before my mind's eye. This inner work was echoed the next day when I greeted the child at the door to the classroom. Then I looked on her in her bodily form and movement, met her gaze, and shook her hand. But between those two moments I had slept, woken, begun the day, and, importantly, inwardly prepared for the school day. While the girls dressed and just after I had prepared the classroom, I took the time to stand facing the nature table and say a preparatory verse to myself. I began with the word "hallelujah" in eurythmic movements, and then, with hands crossed over my heart, I thought: "May the children's souls be guided by me into spirit worlds." Here I thought of the beings who were helping me teach. Then I did the eurythmic movements for "Amen."

After the routine of greeting at the door, entering the school room, and working in the circle on movement, verse, and song, we sat, ready to concentrate. The first thing I then said was: "What did we do in the main lesson yesterday?" The first step in working on the main lesson is to recall what has already been done, to link with conscious effort the present to the past, following the hiatus of sleep. We performed this recall together, as it is not a memory test. Rather, it is the work of building up the understanding and perceptions that have already been arrived at in order to establish the foundation for moving forward. My question was not a test question to which I already knew the answer. Yes, there were certain points I wanted brought out, and if they weren't mentioned, I would bring them up. But the mood was one of working together to reestablish previous ground before going on. This is not a rote type of work, of course, as the children often realized something new, either in their sleep after the last lesson or in the process of remembering. And sometimes the realizations come after the lesson. For example, when Claire, the older girl, was in the fourth grade she had several main lesson blocks on Norse mythology, including one on the Finnish epic poem the *Kalevala*. The description of creation at the beginning of the *Kalevala* involves six golden eggs and one iron egg, laid by a bird, that break apart to create the sky/heaven, the sun, and the earth. Then one of the three hero figures, Vainamoinen, is born from an egg. Later he sings the landscape and animals into existence. When he is wounded from a crossbow, there is a long section of the poem that describes the incantation about iron that will staunch the flow of blood. The incantation describes the creation of iron as well as the birth of another hero, Ilmarinen, the Smith Eternal. When Vainamoinen wants Ilmarinen to go to the far north and create a magic mill, the Sampo, Vainamoinen sings a great fir tree into existence:

> Then old Vainamoinen sang,
> Sang his songs and cast his spells:
> Sang a fir tree flower-crowned,
> Flower-crowned and golden-leaved;
> Stretched it high into the air,
> Through the very clouds he sang it,
> Till its leafy branches reaching
> Spread its foliage high as heaven. (Rune 10, 31–38)

Vainamoinen gets Ilmarinen to approach the tree, and it flies them to the far north, the land of the Great Bear constellation. In that land the witch wants to find out whether Ilmarinen is the smith, and he says that he is:

> Since I hammered out the sky
> And clinked out the lid of heaven
> When the world was uncreated,
> Not a thread of string yet made. (Rune 10, 267–270)

I combined this description of creation and the singing-into-existence of the tree in a painting lesson. I also painted the golden egg, then surrounded it with Prussian blue, then painted the tree by stroking from the yellow into the blue. I removed paint to create the white moon and clouds, and also removed small points of paint to create the stars. The constellation was then painted in golden stars on the tree. As they then painted, I read the verse above. As Claire painted the blue I said, "Now you are doing heaven." And she answered with real joy, "I'm Ilmarinen! With my hammer." I said, "Yes, and your tongs. You leave no mark." Painting brings a true experience of creation, and the rhythms of the *Kalevala* clearly speak to the fourth grader.

Yearly rhythms. I followed the practice of writing or finding a verse for each child to be given in honor of their birth. But as I was also teaching them in school, I focused on what was coming in the year ahead, often relating it to the content of the school year. This meant that I had to contemplate the child in her development, and also keep in mind an overview of the curriculum for the school year. Claire, who had a fiery constitution, turned six in November of her kindergarten year. I wrote the following verse for her and gave it to her on her birthday.

> Boldly I go
> My Angel above me
> The earth below,
> To find my way
> In each new day.
> Gently I fly
> To the stars
> Each night.

Three years later, her younger sister Sara, with her airy constitution, was given this verse:

Butterflies and birds and fairies
Fly high in the sky
And so do I.
We kiss the Earth with our feet,
We bring the Heavens the Earth to meet.
I knit and weave and play
Day after day after day!

I wrote the verses in color on a card and illustrated them to give as a gift. Because these verses were a combination of birthday and school verses, I decided to give Claire her verse on her birthday and then to have her memorize it to be presented once a week in circle. Once Sara started kindergarten, she also received her verse in November (though it wasn't her birthday), so that it could also be part of school. On the first school day of each week, the circle ended with the girls taking turns walking to me from across the room in a movement that matched their level of development. They then stopped in front of me and recited their verses.

To give a sense of the transformation of these verses over the course of the school year, I will share Claire's verses from first, fourth, and seventh grades. I will then provide her eleventh grade verse as a contrast.

First Grade
I have started on my journey
Traveling near and far,
Always on my path
Guided by me star.
What all shall I see?
Sun and Moon and Stars,
Plants and animals,
And all people dear to me.
The letters and numbers
And rhymes and songs
To help me grow tall and strong.

Fourth Grade
Boldly I come and boldly I go,
Strong my heart, my work to do,

Clear my thoughts like light in my head,
Free my hands to do my will.
Swords I cross with all life's tasks.
Lord I thank you for strength and skill;
Heart I have to walk my path.

Seventh Grade
(poem by Christian Morgenstern)
Let me behold thy inmost life, o world…
Let me pierce slowly through the sense's seeming…
As, in a house, brightness is slow unfurled
Until the wings of day wing through it streaming –
And then, as if this house could sacrifice
Even its roof and walls to heaven's gleaming –
So that at last, gold brimming, it might rise
Wholly transfused, a spirit building standing
Like to a monstrance, radiant spirit-wise.
So also might my rigid walls, expanding,
Let thy full life find entry into mine,
And, unto thy life my full life remanding,
Let life in life twine purely, mine and thine.

Eleventh Grade
(St. Patrick's Breastplate, traditional Irish)
I bind unto myself this day
The strong name of the Trinity.
I bind unto myself this day
The power of Heaven
The light of the sun
The whiteness of snow
The force of fire
The power of the resurrection with the ascension.
I have set round me all these powers
Against the incantations of false prophets
Against all knowledge
That binds the human soul.

The verses capture something of the individuality of the child, as well as something of the challenges they will face in the coming year. I wrote or found each at the beginning of the year, but as the year progressed the full meaning unfolded for all of us. Similarly, each lesson and each year built on the previous ones—and foreshadowed the new one to come. Just as life is a whole, what we study is a whole that changes and grows.

For comparison, here are the verses for the first, fourth, seventh, and eleventh grades for our younger daughter, Sara, who was airy to her sister's fieriness.

First Grade
The butterfly lights on the flowers so bright,
She brings the light and warmth of the sun
To her sister, the flower, the pretty one.
I lightly dance in the world today,
Seeing the letters and learning to say
My verses and counts, the names of things,
More beautiful gifts for me to sing.

Fourth Grade
To the earth I find my way
On my way I find the sunlight
Shining to me in the daytime,
Moonlight showers down at night
Earthly pathways to illumine.

Songs of heroes guide my footsteps,
Counting, swaying, to their meter.
Kantele and Sampo stories
Guide my steps, my wanderings,
Through the world of light and shadow.

Lion charges then she rests,
Courage glowing in her breast.
Eagle soars and sees the mouse,
Of the birds the most far-sighted.
Bull stamps heavy on the ground,
Strong and willful he is bound.

Connecting with the Curriculum

*Figure 9a and 9b: The classroom, early and late:
kindergarten and grade two (above); grades seven and ten (below)*

Numbers fall apart in pieces
Far too many for to count,
As the stars above in heaven,
As the grains of sand on earth.

Seventh Grade
(After the sonnet by Dante Alighieri, titled "To Guido Cavalcanti")
Friend, I would that Beauty, thou, and I,
Led by some strong enchantment, might ascend
A magic ship, whose charmed sails should fly
With winds at will where'er our thoughts might wend,
So that no change or any evil charms
Should mar our joyous voyage; but it might be,
That even satiety should still enhance
Between our hearts their strict community:
And that the bounteous wizard then would place
Goodness and Truth and my gentle love,
Companions of our wandering, and would grace
With passionate talk, where'er we might rove,
Our time, and each were as content and free
As I believe that thou and I should be.

Eleventh Grade
(Shakespeare, Sonnet 116)
Let me not to the marriage of true minds
Admit impediments. Love is not love
Which alters when it alteration finds,
Or bends with the remover to remove.
O no! it is an ever-fixed mark
That looks on tempests and is never shaken;
It is the star to every wand'ring bark,
Whose worth's unknown, although his height be taken.
Love's not Time's fool, though rosy lips and cheeks
Within his bending sickle's compass come;
Love alters not with his brief hours and weeks,
But bears it out even to the edge of doom.
If this be error and upon me prov'd,
I never writ, nor no man ever lov'd.

Embedded Rhythms

The school year is made up of embedded spiraling rhythms that approach but never return to their starting point. No two Septembers are exactly alike, the seasons are not mechanical, and neither is the curriculum. But each time we spiral back near a point in time experienced before, there is a sense of familiarity, and the possibility to prepare a little more ahead of time. After each Michaelmas I know that something intense is coming by the end of October/beginning of November. I do not know exactly what will happen, but I can be attentive in a way that allows me to be more conscious and to more fully participate. The curriculum provides a vehicle and a path through these spirals.

Chapter Four

Making the Lessons Your Own

Making the Curriculum Your Own—
the Teacher as Student

In order to teach, one must first study. What is the attitude of the student? That is, what is the attitude of the adult student who chooses the subject they want to study? One must be open to learning, eager to work, ready to listen, and, of course, aware that one doesn't yet know. To whom is one listening? Who are the teachers? What should one study? "Facts"?

In English we have the phrase "food for thought," meaning ideas or information that require mulling over, working on, working out. Our word "student" comes from the Latin *studere,* which originally meant to beat toward, strike toward, smite, and eventually meant to be eager to apply oneself. Food nourishes, but only if we break it down and build ourselves up again with it. Perhaps we have to smite or strike the food in order to make it our own, in order for it to nourish us. And maybe some ideas and texts are actually nutritious and upbuilding for us if we can take them in deeply and "metabolize" them. As teachers, we lead the children, but we are also students, and, therefore, are led by others. This is where Steiner's lectures on the curriculum, and where written works by Waldorf teachers and others, become a guideline for *what* material to study for each year of schoolwork. But what does it mean to study in this context, where one is not just looking up "facts" and statistics and regurgitating them for the student?

Steiner writes in his book *How to Know Higher Worlds* that the book itself is a teacher. Interesting.... But how can a book be a teacher? This is a clue that we are working with a very different kind of text than the usual published book. Steiner wrote one book on education, *The*

Education of the Child in the Light of Anthroposophy, and delivered scores of lectures on the subject. Some of his lectures on the early grades are collected in the volume *The Kingdom of Childhood.* Quotes from Steiner for each grade were collected by Karl Stockmeyer early in the Waldorf movement and published in the book *Rudolf Steiner's Curriculum for Waldorf Schools.* Mark-Dominick Riccio has written a guide, *A Primer for Spiritually Thinking Educators,* for studying Steiner's book *The Education of the Child.* Riccio, in *An Outline for a Renewal of Waldorf Education,* also analyzes the method of Rudolf Steiner's thinking and curriculum. Riccio's work puts more emphasis on the structure or form of the curriculum—that is, the relation of the grades to each other in a specific whole—than other authors do. Although all this material was written with an institutional school in mind, it all can, at the same time, apply to school at home.

I read Steiner's *The Education of the Child* while my daughters were infants, but I wasn't thinking of homeschooling then, and I didn't study the book so deeply. I just read it. I did understand, though, that the sense experiences that infants have are involved in forming their bodies, that is, that genes aren't everything, as we tend to think and hear every day. And I also understood that free play with natural objects—and out in nature—is critical to healthy development at all levels. But I didn't start thinking about homeschool until just before my daughter's kindergarten year. Therefore, study that year consisted of immersing myself in fairy tales, nature stories, and seasonal songs and verses. This turned out to be the perfect foundation for the study of school materials for the grades.

Truth sense, the power of the image, and insight. Steiner says in many places that human beings have a "sense for truth"—just as we have a sense of hearing and sight. We see the world by means of light, and we sense the truth by means of our consciousness of our physical body (Steiner, January 19, 1923). When we think the truth, we are in harmony with the feeling we have of our physical body, but, importantly, also with our sense of the connection between this physical body and our pre-earthly existence. The delicate connections of the physical body with pre-earthly life are severed by untruthfulness. On the other hand, these connections are strengthened by a love of truth and wholeness. If one holds the truth as an ideal and endeavors to speak the truth, then the right connection to the physical body is strengthened, and so is the sense for the truth. The ideal of truth is certainly a worthy ideal for anyone, but especially for teachers who are responsible for the development of their pupils. Precisely because the curriculum is a formed whole, and not just a linear series of lessons like beads on a string, it can function to strengthen the teacher's and student's sense of truth. This sense of truth, just like any other sense that connects us to an open and evolving world, is never complete but always improving. It is not infallible, but it is, in the balance, accurate.

When I first read in lecture 2 of *The Kingdom of Childhood* that abstract letters on a page in black and white have no meaning to the young child, and are actually deadening to them, my interest was piqued. Steiner later describes that for a child, healthy lessons in writing start with simplified forms from nature, such as conceiving of a lower case "f" as a fish slightly curved in opposite directions at each end. From this children proceed to form individual letters. This whole idea struck me as true, based on children's living experience of nature. Remember Sara's comment that everything has a face, even if we can't see it. To young children, nature is a "Thou," even if, when they grow up in present times, it becomes an "It." Forms taken from nature and gradually made abstract on paper allow the child to learn to write without giving up too much feeling and interest.

The experience of nature also relates to imagination and the power of the image—another aspect of the teacher's relation to the curriculum. Imagination is often, in our culture in present times, thought of as something that "goes beyond" the real or adds to mundane reality. This limited, rather dry definition contrasts to Steiner's meaning of imagination as an, at least somewhat, conscious ability to perceive aspects of reality beyond the physical. True imagination is an ability to be cultivated and refined, not just a childish fantasy that is an escape from reality. In this sense, Steiner drew on Goethe's idea of "exact sensorial imagination" (see Goethe's "A Delicate Empiricism," in his book *Scientific Studies;* and Robbins' *New Organs of Perception*). In order that children not completely lose their early abilities with imagination and their early consciousness of living in a world beyond the physical, they should be given nature stories and fairy tales until their consciousness shifts toward more awareness of the earthly world. This happens around age nine.

Given all this, the teacher has the challenge not to remember her own experiences at young ages, but to "live into" the child's consciousness in order to give them the teachings they need about the world. The teacher's imagination can be developed by spending quiet, contemplative time in nature, and by developing an openness to the images in fairy tales and nature stories. This openness involves restraining oneself from analyzing, categorizing, judging, and otherwise distancing oneself from the stories. Instead, one practices a kind of study that involves concentration and even memorization. One might also heighten one's awareness of the stories by becoming conscious of their form, for example, by finding the midpoint and looking at what comes before and after that point. In time-tested material, form is part of the meaning, and enhances and even clarifies the content.

Nature stories, meanwhile, are distinct from fairy tales and also from fables in very particular ways. Steiner gives an example of a nature story in lecture 4 of *The Kingdom of Childhood*, where he contrasts the shy violet and the greedy, hungry dog. He draws on the character or "signature" of the two beings, the violet and the dog, to form the story, and it is told in very concrete images. The typical description of this type of story would call such content "animism" or "personification" based on the attitude that nature is just a set of physical objects and processes, and human qualities such as feelings, emotions, and intentions do not occur in nature. But Steiner shows the opposite: nature is not the origin of the human being, but it is a reflection of the human being. All living beings—plants, animals, humans—share the level of existence called the "life body," which sets them apart from the nonliving, the mineral. Life includes growth and reproduction and a "style" of development, that is, metamorphosis. To this end, different types of plants have different "styles" of developing and maintaining their forms. Violets, for example, are small, stay close to the ground, and they are often slightly covered by the other plants around them. Who is to say this is not "shyness"? The challenge for the teacher is to discern the images of plants and animals and to let them develop in her mind, and then to see what the images tell about the phenomena in nature. She has the further challenge of putting these images into simple stories that will delight and nourish the children. It helps if the stories are timeless and universal—any linear, focused, patiently stalking egret that suddenly strikes the frog trying to hide in the mud is just like any other egret-frog pair. Nature stories, as much as fairy tales, can begin with "Once upon a time..."

Fairy tales form such a contrast to nature stories precisely because they are not about earthly nature. They are about spiritual realities and the human relation to these realities. They are pointedly didactic. But they teach by means of images, and this is what makes them such good tools for teaching young children. The fairy tales involve complex, powerful images that certainly have the power to catch one's attention. But the realities these images portray seem to be able to actually influence events, if one is attuned to this. These "synchronicities" are an indication of the power of the image one is working with in telling a fairy tale. And they also give an indication that the teacher is on the right track.

The first time I taught kindergarten, we worked with the Grimm's fairy tale of "The White Snake." This story tells of a wise, all-knowing king who always eats a special dish in secret at each meal. The servant who brings the dish, overcome with curiosity, defies orders, opens the dish, and finds a white snake. He takes a taste of the white snake, and suddenly he can understand the language of the animals. What he learns from overhearing the animals saves his life when he is wrongly accused. The king then gives him a reward of a horse and money—so he can see the world. In his travels he saves the lives of animals: first fish, then ants, then ravens. He then finds a kingdom where the princess wants a husband, but her father, the king, has set impossible tasks. Yet the servant is able to carry out these tasks because the animals he has saved come to help him. The story ends with the servant and princess, who becomes his bride, sharing an apple from the Tree of Life, at which point "her heart became full of love for him, and they lived in undisturbed happiness to a great age."

For one of the Nature Days when we were working with "The White Snake" in school, the girls and I went, along with another mother and her children, to a nature preserve. The children could play and explore at their own pace, but there was also a nature center with exhibits. They had a few live animals there to show the children, and one of them was a white snake! I had never seen a white snake before, and I haven't since.

Making the Lessons Your Own

I noticed this "coincidence," and I marveled at its timing in relation to the fairy tale. But what is the significance of the timing in encountering this animal? Is it chance, or something deeper—as suggested by the idea of "synchronicity"? In the fairy tale, something connected with animals and the wisdom of animals is "digested," that is, transformed, and the resulting human wisdom, when combined with goodness and courage, leads to love and new life. In seeing the white snake at the exhibit—an albino—at a time when I was so focused on the fairy tale with similar content, was I simultaneously experiencing different levels of existence? Was this a clue that the story was coming at just the right time? One such event could be overlooked, and chalked up to chance, but as I went on with the school lessons, I had further experiences like this one.

At the end of that first kindergarten year, we were hearing, acting out, and preparing to stage the Grimm's fairy tale "Cinderella"; this was to be Claire's end-of-the-year play to act out for an audience of friends and family. This story is well known, at least in some approximation. In it, an evil stepmother favors her own daughters over her beautiful stepdaughter Cinderella, whom she tries to keep from going to the prince's ball. She does this by demanding that Cinderalla first pick up, within two hours, every lentil that has been scattered in the ashes. Cinderella goes out the back door and into the garden and calls out: "You tame pigeons, you turtle doves, and all you birds beneath the sky, come and help me to pick

> The good into the pot,
> The bad into the crop."

The pigeons help her, and she is able to go to the ball. After three balls she finally is found by the Prince, but the pigeons had the role of alerting him to an attempted deception on the part of the stepmother and her daughters. And at the end, after the wedding, they peck out the eyes of the lying sisters and the story ends: "And thus, for their wickedness and falsehood, they were punished with blindness all their days."

Again, on one of our Nature Days, we were in a small park in a suburban neighborhood with trees, grass, and a small pond. This was a new place for us, and we were there by ourselves. As the girls played and explored, suddenly a flock of pigeons appeared above us, landed near us, and began pecking in the grass. I said: "See, Claire—'You tame pigeons, come and help me to pick the good into the pot, the bad into the crop!'" She took notice of the birds, but didn't say anything. It was almost as if such an occurrence were obvious to her. Again, I had never seen a flock of pigeons before (I'm not a city person), and I haven't since. Events in our lives seemed to be reinforcing the images we were working with in school. Or perhaps the images were organizing events in our lives?

Another experience comes from the next year when I was teaching Claire first grade at home. One day a week she went for German language immersion at the home of a family friend, and I took Sara to a Waldorf school where I led a playgroup for preschool children and their parents. In the playgroup we had a circle time with songs and verses, and then I would tell a story—fairy tales and nature and seasonal stories. In late autumn I liked to use the story "Star Money" from the Grimm's collection. This is the story of an orphaned girl who has only her simple night clothes when she goes wandering in the woods. Along the way she meets those even more needy and gives them what she has. When she is completely naked, suddenly the stars begin to rain down as gold coins, star money, and "although she had just given her shirt away, she had a new one which was of the very finest linen. Then she put the money into it, and was rich all the days of her life." I told this story sitting cross-legged in the circle with three-year-old Sara on my lap. I was wearing a long, smooth, silk, wraparound skirt, and when I stood up while telling the story to enact the moment of looking up and receiving the "money" from heaven, my skirt fell away! Wiggly Sara had somehow untied the skirt! Luckily, I was wearing leggings underneath, and I just went on with the story. I quickly gathered up the skirt afterwards and got it back on sheepishly. Later I told the parents how embarrassed I was, but they all thought I'd done it on purpose, as part of the story. Amazing!

We had similar experiences in later grades with material from the Old Testament. Both times that I had the painting lesson in grade three after we had studied the story of Noah and the Flood, there was a long and powerful rainstorm. The first time, in Southern California, such a thunderstorm—with strong lightning, no less—was an extremely rare occurrence. Yet when the same thing happened three years later, after we had moved to Pennsylvania, I was even more convinced. Even the opening of Ridley Scott's movie *Noah* in London had to be canceled because of heavy rains and flooding! And my advice if you work with *The Tempest* by William Shakespeare is to leave yourself extra time for all kinds of "interference." When we did this play we had illness, weather, cancellations, and more. I really felt I was pushing through a powerful force to direct and produce that play for Sara's eleventh grade play.

The sense of truth and the power of image are both guides to the quality and appropriateness of lessons. But there is a further phenomenon that is important, and that is insight—the "aha" moment when one realizes something new and real. Because the material we work with for the lessons is so fitting for children in their development, these insights, these "aha" moments, are fostered and supported by study. I go into detail about one such moment of truth I came to in exploring the difference between colored shadows and afterimages, something that Goethe studied and Steiner disambiguated. I share about my exploration of this in detail in Appendix 2 at the end of this book.

Working through the Lessons—the Grades in Relation to Each Other

As I said earlier, child development is not a linear "assembly line" process, and, consequently, the lessons are not just a linear sequence. Steiner describes the human life as consisting of a kind of "punctuated equilibrium" in which certain moments in development involve rapid changes. These moments occur at seven-year intervals, with the midpoints and thirds existing as important transitions. This means that different grades can relate to each other with similar progressions and "mirrorings." To this end, pedagogical studies based on the Waldorf curriculum have related the grades to each other in different ways. The main point for the teacher to realize is that although the lessons for any given grade are presented to the child at his or her developmental level, these lessons will be later intensified and enhanced in the lessons provided in other grades. I'll give some brief examples of ways to move through the sequences of lessons just to pique interest.

As I was teaching children three years apart in age, I was teaching *grades* three years apart—but *at the same time*. Of course, the second time I taught a grade I was more practiced and didn't have to start from the beginning with each block. But studying and presenting the material for two grades at the same time made me more aware of the "resonances" or connections between them. Here are some examples of the resonances I noticed in several pairs of grades separated by three years.

Animals are an important component of both grades one and four. In first grade they are a part of the nature stories that unify literature and science. They can also be very helpful, as stated earlier, for providing the child forms for learning the alphabet and learning to print letters. Grade four students, meanwhile, have learned print and cursive writing with pencil and are beginning to learn to write with ink. They also have a zoology block which covers the whole organized animal world in relation to qualities and aspects of the human being. Here their observation of animals, though, takes a step away from literature and instead lays the foundation for future scientific study of zoology.

When Sara in first grade was observing crabs at the beach, with their "C"-like claws, Claire was collecting gull feathers to take home and sharpen for quill pens. Sara saw the crabs scuttle sideways, opening and closing their pincer claws. And later in school she drew the claw, and simplified it to a "C." Claire saw the birds in flight and then, when we had the feathers at home, she could see how each central rib was hollow, and also how the barbs interlock to keep the feather smooth. She felt the feather's slight oiliness, which sheds water and keeps the bird warm and dry. But most importantly, she could whittle the end of the quill to a point, and, because it was hollow, dip it in black ink and begin the experience of writing on paper. Quite a responsibility! Then in the Animal block, she learned how the birds are creatures of air, clumsy on land, and how they are like human thoughts that can have an "overview" and can travel "unencumbered" from one point to the next.

Part of the reason that children learn about the animal kingdom in relation to the human being when they are nine to ten years old is due to the relatively sudden change in their consciousness and awareness at that age. They become much more "awake" to earthly existence and life than they were as young children. One day in school when Claire was in grade four, and we hadn't even had the Human and Animal block yet, we were having lunch. She started imagining how it would be if people shed their skins all at once, like snakes. She envisioned a big skin in the shape of a person. This was a little gruesome to imagine, but I'm sure it was related to her experience of some kind of transformation within herself—leaving behind an old way of being.

Three years later, when Sara was in grade four and Claire in grade seven, Sara studied the Norse myths and Claire studied human physiology. One wouldn't think there would be a connection between these two things. But what are mythic images actually about? This is a big question, and many people have taken a shot at an answer. I found Steiner's portrayal of the Norse myths—as depictions of humanity's development over long ages and of the evolution of consciousness—to be quite compelling. In grade four the students turn ten. Steiner characterized this age as a turning point in consciousness, a time when the child becomes much more aware of earthly life, of time, and, thus, of finiteness and death. In some ways, the Norse image of the Twilight of the Gods, in which the powerful gods must fight for their existence against the giants, captures the consciousness of this nine-year change. An old order or old way of being is going out of existence, and a new world will arise, but in between is the "twilight," the battle.

I didn't directly bring Norse myths into the grade seven Human Physiology block. But as I taught about the heart and the circulation of blood, and the function and qualities of blood, I remembered a link between Thor and blood circulation. In the Norse myths, Odin, who is the god of breath and who brought language to human beings, is the father of Thor, who brings thunder and lightning, and who has a magic hammer that always returns to him no matter how far he throws it. In teaching about the blood and circulation I used several books—*Living with Your Body* by Walter Buhle; *The Dynamic Heart and Circulation*, edited by Craig Holdrege; and *Functional Morphology* by Johannes Rohen. These works build on Steiner's point that the heart is not a pump, but a place where the circulation is interrupted, in order that the blood, both pulmonary and venous, can be "sensed" and sent on to the farthest reaches of the body, first to the organs and then to the finest capillaries in the extremities. If the heart is not a suction pump, but an interrupter of the circulation, then it does not cause the flow of the blood. The *blood itself* maintains the quality of movement. This is how Thor's hammer becomes a particularly parallel image. The blood returns to the heart, moving in a "circle," not because it is forced to but because that is its inherent property. And I could mention this parallel to Claire as part of the lesson because she had studied Thor three years earlier. Thus, simultaneously teaching these two grades that are three years apart brought into focus the connections between them.

My final example is a resonance between seventh grade Human Physiology and tenth grade Bible and Literature blocks. Again, one might ask: "What could those two possibly have to do with each other?" The topics in the grade seven Physiology block include the senses and the nervous system related to thinking and knowing, the heart/lung rhythmic system related to feeling, and the metabolic/limb system related to willing. But physiology also includes the topic of the reproductive system, in which we cover those specialized cells from the two sexes that come together for conception to take place—the formation of a new individual. This is a process of genesis—of origin, creation, and birth. Is there anything more than a metaphoric connection between human embryology and those accounts of earth creation and evolution from Genesis in the Talmud and the Old Testament?

If the human being is a microcosm of the macrocosm, then the answer to this question should be "yes." In *Occult Physiology* Steiner portrays the human being as forming the locus in which cosmic and earthly forces combine to transform physical warmth into compassion for all beings. Several medical researchers have worked on the correspondence of processes on the six days of creation in Genesis with those of very early embryonic development (e.g., Appenzeller, König, Weihs). From this material one can teach the physiology of reproduction in a way that broadens its significance beyond the mere physical. In some ways a human individual being conceived, developing, and being born, recapitulates the planet being born. This type of understanding counters the feeling that human beings are small, insignificant "specks" in the vast material cosmos that modern mainstream physics promulgates. The grade seven student has studied the Genesis stories in grade three, and even if they don't remember them consciously, the images will live again for them easily.

In grade ten the Bible is studied in relation to literature, to the structure and processes of literature, in order to gain skills in reading and understanding the ancient and classic texts that are included in the Bible. And since the grade ten student already had physiology in grade seven, the teacher, when presenting the creation story from the first chapter of

Genesis, can highlight the parallel stages of human physiological development. The student can see that the second chapter of Genesis tells a different creation story, and this can highlight another process basic to physiology—that of cycles. Human functioning is cyclic in many ways: waking-sleeping, breathing, eating, and reproducing. Likewise, there are certain points in the Bible where cycles are emphasized, either by the use of the Old Greek words *aion, ainos,* or *aeon,* which mean "cycle of time" or "by the listing of generations." There are specific places in both the Old and New Testaments where this quality comes to the fore, especially in Genesis and Ruth in the Old Testament. And in the last book of the New Testament, Revelation, cycles predominate, showing the spiral form of the Old and New Testaments as a single whole. Steiner's lectures on Genesis are key studies for the teacher, even though they are not presented directly to the student. They can be taken in by the teacher and transformed in the context of lessons given to a sixteen-year-old.

Various relations of the grades. Different relations of grades are highlighted depending on how one sees the sequence of grades. The traditional lower school in Europe and America has eight grades, but if the course of human development takes place in sequences of seven, then the grades would seem to be out of synch with development. Riccio (p. 41) provides a quote from Steiner (GA 301) describing the ideal teacher who "teaches in such a way in the first grade, that in this way of teaching (of first grade), the way is also given in which the pedagogue must teach in the eighth grade." If the grades are part of a form that is in sequences of sevens, then the eighth grade is a repetition, but at a higher level, of the first grade. At least that is one interpretation of Steiner's meaning. Then grades one through seven are related in a way, and grades eight through fourteen (that is, the second year of college) would be related in a similar way. Thus, in the first seven grades, grade four is the turning point, and the others "mirror" each other on either side of it, i.e., grades one and seven; two and six; and three and five.

If one takes the system as it is, that is, with twelve grades, then the grades could be related as mirrored "sixes." Grades one and twelve are both about the "present," but in different ways. Grade one children are in the timeless present of the "once upon a time" and grade twelve students are becoming adults who are appropriately aware of their present historical, social, and physical reality. Second grade and eleventh grade students are both presented with strong moral choices. The second grader is shown the two starkly contrasting paths of the saints and the animals, as if to say "these are the two possible paths." Eleventh graders are at the point where their choices will start to significantly affect their future. Third graders are awakening to the earth, so they learn about farming, house building, and measurement, along with Old Testament stories of what is required of human beings on earth. Tenth graders also study these stories, but in a way that is conscious of their form and intention. They need the moral courage to stand up to internal and social pressures. Fourth graders going through their change of consciousness feel more on the earth, but also more alone, and they need the rhythms and images of the Norse myths to strengthen them. Ninth graders, meanwhile, study the gritty reality of the Industrial Revolution, geology, and thermodynamics to help them get hold of intense swings of emotion. Fifth graders and eighth graders are both focused on the subject of time, but at different ends of the spectrum; grade five covers the ancient cultures and grade eight comes into modern times. Grade five ends with the Greeks just before Christ, when the first glimmers of conscience, that sign of the inner individual, become apparent and constitute the beginning of history. Grade eight is the culmination of history in present times. Grades six and seven are the turning point in this structure. They are similar in content, with grade six covering the Romans and geometry, grade seven the Renaissance and algebra. These two grades are in some ways the most similar.

Many other relational structures are possible. The accuracy or relevance of one does nothing to negate the same qualities of others. Such structures can be guides, though, to the teacher who may easily feel overwhelmed by the complexity of the task of preparing and presenting lessons. There is help available!

Finding Oneself in the Flow of Time—Teaching More than One Child at Once

Each year builds on the last one, and also forms the basis for the next one. The opposite pole of preparing for the lessons is actually carrying out a school day, a season, and a year. When Claire, our older daughter, was ready for kindergarten, our younger daughter, Sara, was only two-and-a-half. On Mondays, which were exploring days, I carried Sara in a backpack for our walks, and she toddled along when she could. I always referred to this day, when talking to Claire, as a school day. That is what it was. She knew that we had school on Mondays and that we went exploring. We usually had a packed lunch, or went out for lunch, and then went to a library to look at books and listen to me read to them. Because it was a school day, this structure prevailed, though the locations and durations of our explorations varied.

On school days at home—that is, Tuesdays, Wednesdays, and Thursdays—Sara played alongside Claire and me as we did school activities, or she joined in where she wanted to—usually with circle activities, painting, and story time. I often had her in the backpack while I was working with Claire. Seasonal activities and fairy tales set a mood that is appropriate for young children, even before they are ready for school. Claire knew she was in school, and that put her in a more "advanced" stage than her younger sister. As the older child, this seemed completely appropriate and right to her.

Fridays were also school days, but usually away from home for horseback riding lessons, music lessons, study groups, playgroups, or visiting with friends. Again, Sara was observing, playing by herself, or joining in with others for the ongoing activity. This general approach worked for us because Sara, even though she was three years younger than Claire, never needed as much sleep as Claire. Because sleep is so important for general health and development, not to mention for learning in school, it takes priority, especially for younger children. One of the great advantages that school at home provides is the possibility of honoring each child's need for sleep without sacrificing the focused time needed for school. Here the Genius of Home is deeply at work.

Rhythms are the signature of the living; sleep restores order to the rhythmic systems after the stresses of the day, and involves experiencing, albeit unconsciously, a very differentiated spiritual world (see *Sleep* by Audrey McAllen). Even medical research is becoming aware of the qualities of sleep and how they relate to waking life. In coordinating school for more than one child, therefore, especially when they are young, sleep is a critical factor.

Because the reality of sleep is related to the Waldorf curriculum, I want to go into some detail here about the sleep world, and then come back to the topic of teaching differently aged children together. Audrey

McAllen's book *Sleep* has a chapter on "The Child's Relationship to Sleep." When a child falls asleep, all her day experiences form the "sleep world" in which she lives at night, "all the day experiences echoing in [her] soul, these form the content on which the body of formative forces works in the upbuilding of the physical constitution" (McAllen, p. 25). This applies at all ages, but particularly before age seven. From seven to nine fairy and folk tales that describe the "elementals," that is, the spiritual beings that work directly with the earth—fairies, gnomes, undines, sylphs, etc.—especially prepare the children for sleep "work." From nine to ten into puberty and beyond, what matters most is the adults' conscious use of speech, such that spiritual truth and knowledge shine through. Although it took me years to grasp these ideas and put them into practice in our family life, I could endeavor to relate to the spirituality of sleep from the time the girls were very young, precisely because I could see how critical sleep was to maintaining physical and emotional health in daily life. They showed me clearly and directly.

So, when it came time for Sara also to have school, that is, kindergarten, I had a rhythmical basis to family life and a school day that I could adjust to include two grades in one day. Sara had kindergarten for two years, starting the first year when she was four and Claire was in grade two, turning eight in November. I continued with the practice of letting Sara "sit out" or play or draw by herself while Claire was having her main lesson at her desk and I was working on the blackboard. But what was new was that Sara participated in the circle and I kept kindergarten material in the circle, as well as adding more advanced work that I did only with Claire. Practical handwork and artistic work were tailored to each child. Sara's kindergarten painting, drawing, modeling, handwork, and musical instrument lessons were variations on the ones I had given Claire three years before. Here is an example of a circle from the beginning of the school year that combines kindergarten and grade two:

- Song with movement—"Autumn winds"
- Morning verse—for second grade, k-student stands and watches
- Song with movement—"Wake up! Wake up!"
- Song—"Che che 'Kule"
- Body geography, with verse
- Beanbag tossing, with verse
- Four little pumpkins verse, with actions

Autumn verse
Hark my child a breeze doth blow
Winds bear seed corns to and fro
See, how gently one drops down,
Seeking rest in earthly gown—
Softly softly hark my child
For your angel hovers mild,
Lays into your heart's warm shrine
A seed corn, too, both small and fine.
And it sinks in silence slow—
Wait oh wait for roots to grow,
Till a flower like a star
Lightens all the earth afar.
(from *Journey Through Time in Verse and Rhyme*)

We end with a recitation verse—Steiner's bell-ringing verse from *Truth Wrought Words*. We recite it standing, while holding hands:

Guarded from harm, cared for by angels, here stand we,
loving and strong, truthful and good.

With children of different ages, it will usually be the case that the younger child watches the older child's school before she has school herself. She sees the older child doing what she can't and learns to look up to her and look forward to when she herself will be able to take part in more advanced activities.

The first class day of the year always started, after the bell-ringing and greeting at the doorway, with a small ceremony to mark the first school day of the year. In first grade, I gave Claire one flower, rang the bell one time, and said, "Now you are in first grade!" I then gave her new crayons that she would be using that year, stick crayons in seven colors in a roll-up cloth holder. And, of course, the big change was her very own desk standing there in the classroom. Each year, Sara saw this ceremony. When Claire was entering grade four and Sara entering grade one, Sara got to be in the ceremony, too. Such a big step. Then Claire got four flowers and four rings of the bell—fourth grade!

And Sara took her own place coming into first grade. That day when we started the main lessons, and Sara as the younger child always went first for the main lesson, Sara wasn't fully concentrating. Claire caught her up short and said sternly, to show her the seriousness of the occasion, "This is school! This is work!" Sara sat up straight and paid attention.

The children's relationships, clearly, will change as they grow and mature. When Claire was fifteen, she didn't want a little sister around who looked up to her. And Sara had to develop her own friendships and interests away from Claire. And when Claire was in grade eleven, she decided she wanted to go into an institutional school. She applied and was accepted at a nearby small, private preparatory school and went into their grade eleven and stayed for grade twelve and graduated from there (with honors). So that meant that Sara had High School at home alone with me, as Claire had had her first years of school alone with me. Sara also decided to go into an institutional school for grade twelve. She boarded with a family who was friends of ours, and finished at a Waldorf school in a nearby county.

I found that it was stimulating to return after three years to material I had previously studied, and it was encouraging to have a base to build on—and to be able to improve on the lessons the second time around. At the same time, I was learning new material for the new lessons, and that was always very exciting. As each year prepared the children for the next year, it also prepared me. I became better at studying and at being open and at sensing which material was important to include in the rhythm of the school year. And all these years, my husband was playing with and reading to the girls in the evening, and taking care of them while I was at training courses. He was our school's Co-Chair of the Board, Chief Financial Officer, Janitor, and Child Care Expert. If it doesn't take a village, it at least takes a family.

And families come in all kinds of configurations. Our family of two parents and two children is a traditional "nuclear" family. We don't live near our relatives, so it is not an extended family, and support for homeschool had to come from other homeschool families. My mother did come to our house for a couple of weeks in the summers when the children were younger and I was far away at teacher training classes. But otherwise, we were on our own. Families with other configurations have similar challenges: how to live in rhythm and manage the time to teach, parent, and prepare for teaching. Here the parent's and the child's natural circadian rhythms are all-important. My husband, our older daughter, and I are all "morning people," up and alert early, and early to bed. Our younger daughter is the opposite. Therefore, Sara, the younger, did better later in the school day and Claire did better earlier. I had to go to bed early, but I could get up at 3:00 AM when everyone was asleep, work on the lessons, and go back to sleep until the children woke up. We all have our own rhythms to work with—and the freedom we have to structure our own school day, block, and year allows these rhythms to be used in a strengthening way.

Challenges for Each Grade—Who is the Child Becoming?

The thing about children is that they grow and develop. They don't just grow bigger, or mature into different proportions and abilities, they actually transform. The child we have before us, even through adolescence, isn't the individual they will be when they are an adult. This individual is coming to their life path all during childhood. The word "destination" contains the word "destiny" in a way. Destiny is the path to the destination. And just as Aristotle (in *Physics*, Book III) solved Zeno's paradox (that an object would never reach an end point because the distance to the end can always be divided in half, infinitely) by pointing out that the end point is contained in the force that propelled the object in the first place, human beings already have a destination when they incarnate. But this isn't the same as the idea of predestination. Rather, the idea that we have a destination allows for the possibility of sensing whether we are on the path toward it—or not. And parents and teachers can come to sense this for the children for whom they are responsible.

Although all children have their own unique destinations and evolution, they all share certain stages and progressions on the path to becoming individual selves. As a teacher I found that I couldn't tell what the school year was really about until the whole year was done. At the end, especially after performing the final play, I would say "Aha! That is what grade __ is about!" So, I know that for the second time around I can use this knowledge to guide my lessons, but I don't know ahead of time what it is about *for this child*, the one I'm teaching now. For that I have to wait and see. And I couldn't say anything in this regard about any child I hadn't taught. But as for the general developments for each grade, I do have some observations.

In grade one each child is coming into a clear, consistent social form. And it may take most of the year for that transition to take place.

Qualities are important—the qualities of letters and numbers, even of the arithmetic operations. Nothing is broken up into parts yet, neither time/space, nor self/world.

In grade two they get a glimpse that there is more than one path for them, a hint that a decision will have to be made. But that decision is still far in the future. This is the year of saying "no"! They will say it all the time and in response to anything, because it isn't really about anything specific. It is just trying out a distinction between self and other. I usually didn't reply, unless the situation was critical. Once Claire said "no" to something and I said, "You always say 'no,'" to which she replied, "No I don't!" Point taken.

In grade three the awareness of earthly life is increasing and it is important that the children experience the fact that earthly life, though good, is hard work—continuing work. They actually do the work of gardening, caring for animals, building a structure. The preeminent task of the teacher here is to show joy in the work. The children are being *welcomed* to earth. Even math lessons are in the context of earthly work, that is, they involve measurement of quantity, distance, and size. The history of measurement, which shows how human beings only gradually moved away from the human form as a basis of measurement units, fits with the stage of children here. They don't yet have the idea, which is so pervasive in our culture now, that the universe has nothing to do with the human being.

In grade four, when the nine-year change comes to an end (see chapter two), something of a young childhood consciousness is ending—and the children have a bit of an apocalyptic feeling. The feeling is valid, and it is met with stories of the Twilight of the Gods, and with fractions in math. Something is coming apart, breaking into pieces. The whole animal world, as an image of specialized aspects of the human being, is also an image of parts "fallen away." All this schoolwork supports, rather than exacerbates, the process of leaving young childhood.

When, in grade five, the child encounters images and stories of the ancient cultures—India, Persia, Egypt, Chaldea, Greece—they are experiencing a recapitulation of the development of human consciousness. In some ways they are also experiencing, unconsciously, a recapitulation of their own development in consciousness since birth. That is why these stories and images are so powerful. However, I would advise against covering Egypt at Eastertime. The double concentration on death is just too powerful then. When I did that the first time, I taught grade five, and both Claire and I got sick with very high fevers at the Easter break. We both had strange fever dreams involving animals and death. But Claire did seem to have a particular affinity to Egyptian culture. Children are beginning to find themselves in time by this age. The study of plants helps to "purify" the feelings in some ways and can be a kind of guide in balancing the emotions and human relations (see Goethe's poem "The Archetypal Plant").

For grade six the image of the wise child teaching the elders can be helpful for the teacher. The children are coming into their own thinking more, and they begin to question teachers and authorities. They are, as it were, standing in a doorway, just about to step out onto the path of their own individual destiny. The study of minerals and physics can give them a mental clarity that they appreciate and need.

In grade seven the student works on descriptions in history of the emergence of separate, characteristically different, nations. This parallels the development of their separate, individual personalities. Their temperaments become more consolidated, and, we hope, more balanced. They are stepping into adolescence, about to embark on a rough sea, but they haven't yet been overwhelmed by internal changes. Joan of Arc can be a critical figure here—not so much as a martyr, but in terms of her internal strength of will and her physical stamina. These can be inspirational.

Grade eight is in some ways like grade one at a new level. The children are coming into wider social forms beyond family and school. Experience volunteering can be very useful at this age, especially in situations where people or animals need care. Giving freely to others helps balance a tendency to be inwardly involved and too focused on self. Values and ethics receive developmental support in relation to the larger society surrounding the family. Claire and Sara volunteered at Camphill Village workshops and farms, as well as in a kindergarten. These volunteer activities actually began earlier, and continued through high school, but they are particularly important at this age. The experience with special needs individuals living in community was invaluable to the girls in terms of their growing understanding of the wider world and their place in it. We also played lyre for Advent Spiral Walk

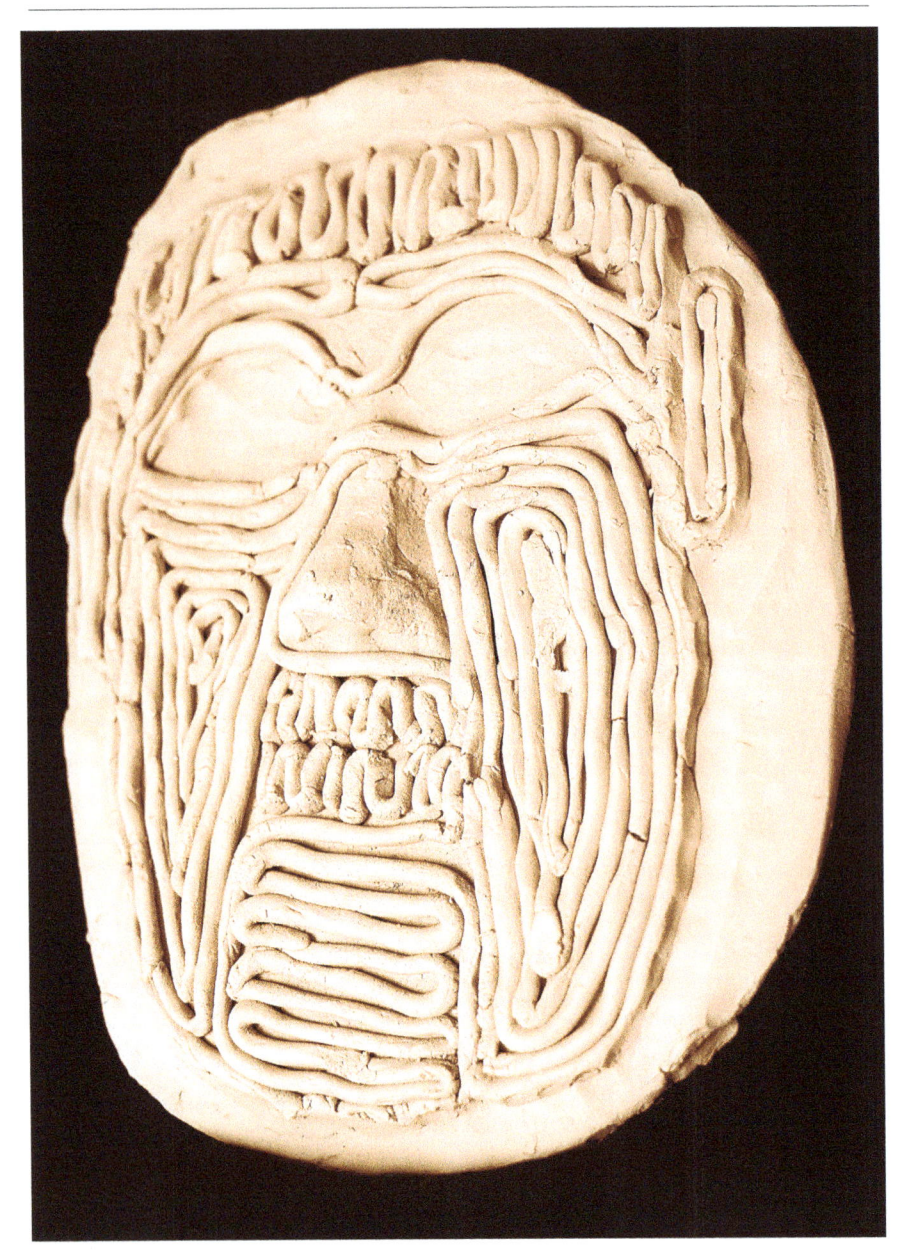

Figure 10: Sara's terracotta figure of Humbaba (from Gilgamesh*)*

festivals in Camphill and in Waldorf schools, and in that way supported the community celebration of festivals that keeps the "lifeblood" flowing in the group.

In some ways, grade nine mirrors grade six, so we start again with geology and minerals, and add thermodynamics in physics, but we are working at a more abstract and analytic level than at the younger age (without giving up the experiential-phenomenological beginning point of all science lessons). Physical bodily changes come to the fore at this age, and there are often mishaps, accidents, and broken bones. When Claire was working with a thin glass tube for a thermodynamics demonstration, it slipped, broke, and completely pierced through one of her fingers. That was shocking for both of us. I quickly pulled it out and put pressure on the wound—and then took her to the hospital. There was no lasting damage, so we were lucky, but these physical challenges seem to be part of grade nine and the full onset of adolescence. The Michaelmas festival with its emphasis on courage and meeting physical and soul challenges can be particularly helpful to young people at this age.

I have heard Waldorf school teachers describe, in an offhand way, grade ten as the year of "sex, drugs, and rock and roll." At this age, the young person's body is much more mature than before, but the awareness of self and others and the development of values and conscience still have a way to go. Botany is a part of the science curriculum, and it can have the same "purification" effect on self and social relations that it did in grade four, but this time at a more conscious level. If the plants are taught in a way that stays true to their qualities, rather than projecting animal "sex" onto the plants, the young people can be afforded inner ideas and images to balance the animal side of life. The ancient cultures are taught again, but this time in view of the whole progressions of cultural evolution and human consciousness as a whole, which contributes to the children becoming whole. The Epic of Gilgamesh, from the ancient Sumerian culture, comes to the fore as an archetype of the beginning of earthly consciousness of death and sex. And, of course, it is also archetypical of the consequences of transgression and of the meeting with evil. The monster Humbaba in the depths of the dark forest is an image of what the tenth grader is up against.

In grade eleven the theme for the whole year can be captured by the word "transformation." Here the study of chemistry, with its balanced equations and physical transformations, is very important. Grade eleven is a difficult age because such radical change is occurring at all levels of the individual, and, at the same time, the young person is starting to make more of her own profound, life-affecting choices. She is stepping out, away from family and school. Such independence is laudatory, but it can also be dangerous. Chemistry experiments can explode. Electricity and magnetism in physics can be such strong forces that one ends up burned or shocked. Here the Parzival epic is so important because it shows a young person sent out into the world unprepared, and having to face the consequences of his mistakes. But it is also important because the story itself contains "prompts" to remember the spiritual world, and thereby to avoid being completely lost in the material world. All this is much needed at the age of seventeen.

Grade twelve is a culmination the traditional school system. Here students stand on their own feet, and are beginning to exercise judgment—and make their own choices. In other words, they begin to take up their own destiny. I didn't teach grade twelve at home, although I trained for it in physics and English. And I did teach an optics lesson for a grade twelve class in a Waldorf school. But both our daughters chose to go into institutional schools for this grade. So, from my own experience, I can only say something about that transition from home to institution, and that comes later in this book.

Chapter Five

Individualizing the Lessons and the School

What to Keep, What to Let Go

Every teacher who is choosing the content of her lessons uses many resources and guides in the process. Steiner's lectures on education and on other topics related to specific lessons provide the core of the Waldorf school lesson material. But Steiner was often presenting "indications" and "hints" that required the teacher to conduct her own research into the phenomena and into the material to be taught. Previous Waldorf teachers, over the past seventy years or so, have researched and written on many of the topics, and their work forms a kind of "secondary literature" on the topics relevant to each grade. Summaries of the lessons for each grade have been written in German and in English, and some Waldorf homeschool compendiums exist. Yet what in all of this is to be included in an individual lesson for an individual child? This highlights the basic questions of what relates specifically to each child's level of development and interest, and also what "rings true" for each individual teacher. What I want to do here is give examples of ideas that I tried and changed, and also those I discarded.

Mood-of-the-Fifth Music

It took me awhile to understand what music in the "mood of the fifth" is; indeed, I'm still working on it. But I benefited from Steiner's lectures on music (*The Inner Nature of Music*), as well as from articles by Waldorf teachers, from attending conferences for music teachers in Waldorf schools, and from teaching history through music in grade ten. As I learned more about music in relation to human consciousness, I became much more aware of what we experience through music, and how music affects everyone, including small children. As I found out more about the mood of the fifth and its importance for young children, I had to make decisions about what music to use in school, and also what to include in daily life. Some of the music included in the Waldorf training materials was not in the mood of the fifth. So here was a contradiction. Contradictions are always a call to wake up and make our own decisions, as painful as that sometimes is.

In a lecture of March 8, 1923, Steiner describes the experience of the musical interval of the *fifth* as an expansion into the vast universe. The "fifth" is defined as a distance of five tones, so that if D (the tone above Middle C) were the first tone, then the fifth tone above it is A. Try listening as someone else plays these tones, especially on an instrument that allows the tones to resound and last, such as a lyre. Just focus on your experience, especially if the person is playing two different intervals randomly, for example, a fifth and a fourth, or a fifth and a third. The fifth is very open and expansive. This can give us a clue as to the prevailing consciousness of young children before the nine-year change, that is, the time when they become more conscious of earth, present surroundings, and present time. In Steiner's description, the experience of the fifth is an expansion into the cosmos, while the experience of the third (e.g., C and E) is the return of the human being into the structure of his or her own organization.

This open character of the interval of the fifth can be maintained in a melody, if certain tones are used and if certain sequences are maintained. In a lecture to Waldorf music teachers (March 7, 1923), Rudolf Steiner stated that the best tones for young children are the D, E, G, A, and B above Middle C, along with the D and E an octave above that. If these tones are seen as radiating out from the central A, then the movement out from the A and back to it can be seen as a kind of "breathing." This breathing can be maintained in melodies, which can be sung or played on simple instruments. This is music in the mood of the fifth and it supports the harmonious breathing out and in that is the life of the young child. (For more on this, see Sheila Johns, "Music, Mobility, and the Mood of the Fifth.")

How does this translate into music for school? We use singing as part of the circle in the grades, and to open the class day in the upper grades. If music in the mood of the fifth is important for young children because it matches their open, "timeless" experience of the world and does not lead them to a prematurely "awake" and self-aware consciousness, then how do we find and play and learn this music? There are presently several songbooks based on mood-of-the-fifth music, for example, *Quintenlieder,* by Julius Knierem and *I Love to Be Me: Songs in the Mood of the Fifth,* by Channa Seidenberg. These songs are based on the seven tones ranging above and below A, but leaving out C and F, because this pentatonic series retains the qualities of the interval of the fifth: openness and a flowing beauty, with no discordant combinations. But pentatonic scales are the basis of much of the folk music in the world, and this music does not exist in the mood of the fifth. Rather, it exists in the third, that is, with a definite beginning and end. This is the opposite of the mood-of-the-fifth's timelessness, of that sense of "once upon a time." Thus, the teacher has to develop a discerning ear. She must also develop a sensitivity to how the children live into the music. Are they joyous and rosy-cheeked after the singing and movement? Or are they a little stiffer, a little paler?

But in our current culture we can't provide only mood of the fifth experiences for children, either in school or in daily life. We can't take Steiner's indication as the only approach to music—but we can make sure that the mood of the fifth is at least part of the infant's and young child's experience as they are growing up. They will be stronger for it later. Folk music in grades three, four, and five, with rounds starting in grade four, lay the basis for the study of the physics of acoustics in grade nine, where ratios of string lengths correspond to intervals of tone. And this all comes to fruition in the History through Music block in grade ten.

Festivals: Blocks and the Time of Year

Each year in the curriculum includes blocks of lessons on certain topics (although variation in the years increases somewhat in high school). This pattern of lessons is provided both by indications from Steiner and from the experiences of teachers in the first Waldorf schools. After teaching kindergarten through grade eleven twice, I am thoroughly convinced of the wisdom of the curriculum. However, the order of the blocks in the year can vary, and this is one of the ways the teacher individualizes the curriculum. I found that the seasonal festivals can provide guidance in choosing the timing of lessons. The festivals provide the background for each lesson, just as, from the perspective of earth, the zodiac configurations are the background to the moving planets between the fixed stars and the earth. We can experience the lessons with the festivals "shining through them," as it were.

School begins in autumn after a long summer of rest, fun, and "breathing out." Because of the rest, and because of the changing light and length of day (again, in temperate regions), one can be more "awake" and ready to study and think in autumn. So school begins slightly before Michaelmas (September 29). But what is important to realize is that festivals build gradually, peak, and then fade into the building of the next festival. Although Michaelmas is celebrated on September 29, it has been building since August 1, the day halfway between the summer solstice and autumn equinox. Here it is necessary to say something about the relation of the seasons to the festivals—a huge topic! The seasons are natural phenomena based on the movements of the earth in relation to the sun. The festivals are celebrations for which the dates are set by human beings, either based on ancient tradition, the ecumenical church, or on new spiritual research such as that conducted by Rudolf Steiner. In 1912 Steiner published the *Calendar of the Soul*, which has fifty-two meditative verses—one for each week from Easter of one year to Easter of the next. In a lecture on the *Calendar of the Soul* (May 7, 1912), Steiner describes the Calendar in the context of the relation of cosmos and earth, and states that the Calendar expresses the objective fact of the birth of the highest human aspect, the I or conscious self. Therefore, the Calendar marks the year from Easter to Easter, which is the celebration of Christ's transformation through death in the physical body into birth in the resurrection body in the etheric sphere of the earth. This new sequence is of variable length, because the date of Easter is calculated based on the Sun, the Moon, and the Earth. Therefore, the solar year, which has fifty-two weeks, must be reconciled with the "Easter year," which can have a different number of weeks. As Steiner says: " ... in what is unequal there is life; in what is uniform and fixed there is the impress of death, and our Calendar is intended to be a creative impulse for life." Using the *Calendar of the Soul* one can find one's place in the outward flow of time, and also experience the timelessness in rhythmic alternation. The teacher can use the meditative verses of the Calendar at the beginning of each week to experience what is heightened in the lessons because they are given when they are. I'll give some examples below.

School begins just before Michaelmas, when crystalline forms in nature and as qualities of thought are just beginning to appear. From grade one through grade five, I used Form Drawing as the first block of the school year. Thus, the school year was "formed," so to speak, by the Form Drawing block that began the year. It set the mood of concentration and work, yet did not overwhelm the students with too much content at the beginning of the school year.

Black lines on paper are abstract, deadening, and meaningless to young children, but forms themselves are hygienic and enlivening when they are experienced as the result of flow and movement. The very first lesson in form drawing introduces the two primal forms: the curved line and the straight line. I introduced these as figures in a story about an old, bent woman and her straight, strong staff. I first told the story, then drew the forms on the blackboard in white chalk. Then, standing beside each other, we drew the forms in the air, the student and teacher together. Then we drew the forms with our fingers on each other's backs. Next, we went outside and drew them in the sand tray. Finally, we walked the forms in the classroom, the student following in the teacher's footsteps. All of these experiences provide awareness of the forms as the result of movement, and thus are free and open. There is no possibility of "mistakes." The next day, after the review, the student would draw the forms on the board, and then try them on paper with crayons, or later, pencil. Here they could go over the lines to gradually bring them closer to the ideal. After practice on paper, on the third day, the child would then draw the forms in her main lesson book, which always requires the best effort. It is the permanent record of the student's work. As the grades went on, I dropped the ongoing story, and then the sand drawing, but we always kept the drawing in air, on our backs, and also kept walking the forms. By grade six the form drawings become geometry lessons, at which point the transition to mathematics had begun. Clearly, forms go beyond mathematics, and they are a core part of eurythmy, which applies in specific ways to all lessons in all grades.

High School Main Lesson Blocks

Grade nine calls for a Physics block focusing on thermodynamics—the actions of warmth. In autumn, warmth is rhythmically withdrawing, and in spring, rhythmically returning. I taught thermodynamics in the spring because direct experiences with warmth are important, and there was time before physics to have an Algebra block to prepare for the math. In spring we are in the festival of Easter and the beginning of the Soul Calendar year. All this brings to the fore the difference between warmth in the outer world and warmth in the human being, where the blood is the carrier of warmth. And what happened on one of our first days of experiments in thermodynamics? As I mentioned previously, Claire broke a glass pipette, which pierced her finger and left her bleeding! This certainly brought to our attention that the experience of warmth is actually the perception of the difference between outer and inner warmth—carried by the blood.

In the first classroom experience in thermodynamics, the student is presented with three bowls of water: one cold with ice in it, one as hot as they can stand, and one at room temperature. They put one hand in the cold water and, simultaneously, the other hand in the hot water. After a few seconds they transfer both hands into the room temperature water. What do they experience? The hand that was cold now feels hot and the hand that was hot now feels cold. Warmth itself is not something physical, even though we can sense it. We sense it as a difference between inner and outer warmth. This is the same difference that the thermometer measures (and indicates on various scales that have a long history of development). This relation of inner and outer is the basis of all thermodynamics and corresponds to the relation of the centripetal (compression) forces related to matter and earth and the centrifugal (expansion) forces of the surrounding cosmos. After learning about the history of measuring warmth/heat as temperature, and realizing that the registering of warmth was never direct, but always based on changes in a material substance, Claire said about warmth, "It's not physical!" Regardless of whether she meant that warmth is not material or that it is beyond the physical, this was a major realization.

An example from the opposite pole of topics, the literary, comes from the block on Poetry in grade ten. In History for grade ten one covers the ancient cultures. The Poetry block covers the topics of meter and rhythm and different forms of poetry. It begins with ancient epics and moves through historical time to the modern era. I chose Victorian poetry for in-depth study because the poets of that time and place retained a sensitivity to the spiritual, as well as to nature. Sensing the spiritual aspects of the world, the Victorian poets expressed various related soul moods. In eurythmy—the relation of movement to speech, tone, color, and other phenomena—Steiner explored movements that correspond to movements in speaking, singing, and moods of soul. These soul gestures include happiness, devotion, and despair (see Steiner, *Eurythmy as Visible Speech*).

Meanwhile, in our schoolwork we did an in-depth study of one poem from January through March, that is, from Christmas toward Easter. Before I describe our work with one poem, I will digress into exploring the importance of circle activities in academic work. In the lower grades every class day begins with singing and rhythmic movement activities in a group. These activities allow the teacher and student to come together in rhythmic in-breathing and out-breathing as a transition into sitting quietly and concentrating. In the traditional classroom, these activities continue through the first few grades and are usually reduced to just singing as the students get older—and then are dropped entirely by high school. I continued the age-appropriate full circle activities through grade eleven, the last grade I taught at home. I found that rhythmic physical activity helped to prepare for mental concentration through all the grades, from first grade all the way through high school. This also meant that I could include activities that either complemented or enhanced the main lesson block. In the case of the in-depth poetry work, I was able to extend a block by working over a period of months on one aspect of the subject. Here are the circle activities we were using when we started the poetry work:

- Sing the tone of the day
- Sing choral warm-up (various intervals and chords), two parts
- Sing Alleluia in two parts
- Recite morning verse in German
- Practice German conversational phrases
- Bat ball with paddles, move in circles, walk, skip, run, while counting in German
- Poem: "By the Margins of the Deep" by AE—Speak a line, find eurythmy gestures, feel the form and begin choreography
- Sing "Harmony of the Stars," two parts
- Recite the verse "Guarded from Harm"

In order to choose the poem we would study, I read Sara several poems from the Victorian period and she chose the one she had the strongest connection with. She chose "By the Margins of the Great Deep" This is a poem in four stanzas, each one sentence long, in hexameter rhythm:

By the Margins of the Great Deep by AE

1 When the breath of twilight blows to flame the misty skies,
2 All its vaporous sapphire, violet glow and silver gleam
3 With their magic flood me through the gateway of the yes;
4 I am one with the twilight's dream.

1 When the trees and skies and fields are one in dusky mood,
2 Every heart of man is rapt within the mother's breast;
3 Full of peace and sleep and dreams in the vasty quietude,
4 I am one with their hearts at rest.

1 From our immemorial joys of hearth and home and love
2 Strayed away along the margin of the unknown tide,
3 All its reach of soundless calm can thrill me far above
4 Word or touch from the lips beside.

1 Aye, and deep and deep and deeper let me drink and draw
2 From the olden fountain more than light or peace or dream,
3 Such primeval being as o'erfills the heart with awe,
4 Growing one with its silent stream.

First, we worked on the overall structure of the poem, paying special attention to the mood of soul for each stanza. I followed Sara's lead, but made suggestions as we went along. It seemed that the first stanza was a kind of introduction, but that the next three each had an overarching soul mood. The second stanza seems to be centered on faith, that is, the peace and quietude of the human heart "rapt within the mother's breast." The third stanza emphasizes love in the phrase, "From our immemorial joys of hearth and home and love." The fourth stanza centers on hope, as in being in awe and growing one with being's silent stream, that is, becoming one with existence.

Steiner gave several lectures on the particular human qualities of faith, love, and hope (e.g., Nürnberg, December 2-3, 1911). He describes faith as the forces of the astral or soul body, love as the forces of the life or ether body, and hope as the forces of the physical body. These are the forces that form and maintain the various levels or bodies of the human being. We therefore choreographed the poem's first stanza as an introduction, while each of the other stanzas included the soul gesture at the beginning and end of the movement. Steiner gave gestures for love and hope, but not for faith. Working with a Waldorf high school eurythmy teacher, we developed a gesture for the soul mood of faith. As a rough description I would say it has elements of a greeting or acknowledgment, an obeisance, and an opening to offer or receive. The right hand is vertical with palm out at about face level, the knees are bent with the right foot slightly forward, and the left hand is extended to the front with palm up. Both hands are barely curved, as if resting on or just touching a huge sphere. The gesture for the soul mood of love, developed by Reg Down and described in his book *Color and Gesture,* is such that the feet are together, the arms are extended straight outward at shoulder height, with the palms facing upward, so that the whole figure forms a kind of cross. Hope, finally, is formed when the feet are apart and facing forward, the arms are outward but lowered, and the palms are facing upward. This description is, of course, only of the outer physical level of the gesture; the more fundamental etheric and astral levels are described in Steiner's *Eurythmy as Visible Speech* and Reg Down's *Color and Gesture.* Here is my own poetic description of the soul mood of hope:

> *Hope*
>
> My breath released flies from its cage,
> Heavenward into the blue ether.
> The dome of heaven holds
> The whole world.
> Purple veils of evening cascade
> To the great circle of the horizon,
> As I take one dusty footstep
> After the other:
> Walking into the unseen,
> But not the unknown.

In order to choreograph the movements to AE's poem, I spoke the poem and we worked out the movements according to what we sensed.

Did the movement in the line of the poem suggest forward or backward? Right or left? Up or down? Curved or straight? Expanding or contracting? The poem moves from the twilight misty skies to becoming at one with the silent stream of being. The poem is, at one level, about the change of consciousness in evening, going into sleep. Along the way the moods progress from quietude and faith to calmness and love and finally to awe and hope.

We worked on the gestures and movements for the poem during circle activities over the course of three winter months of January, February, and March. Winter is the Christmas festival and the time of deepest inwardness for human beings. Then, as we move out of winter and toward spring, we move toward the Easter festival. The soul moods are referred to explicitly in the Soul Calendar verses: Christmas—hope, January—love, February—joy, March—certainty and love.

To deepen her understanding of the poem, Sara did pastel color studies for each stanza as she listened to me speak the poem. And at the end of the work, Sara wrote her own poem:

Twilight

In the breathing evening air,
In the twilight's gloom resounding,
Comes the call of twilight's people,
Comes the silence ever sounding.

Out of the mist, the silver mist,
Out of the rainbows darkening shades,
Raises her head, the gleaming moon,
As sunset's splendor slowly fades.

Soon will come the night time darkness,
Soon will come the guardian star,
But now the moment of twilight rules,
Misty magic whispers far.

Turquoise calmness draws to a close,
Violet's flowing veil falls,
Slowly peach blossom ebbs from the sky
One more time my beating heart calls. (2010)

At the end of her main lesson book on poetry Sara wrote: "The certainty of what poetry truly is still escapes me." And I would say that is a good thing—the question is still open.

My final example of a main lesson in relation to the season is that of optics for a grade twelve Physics block. One of the topics that can be covered in that block is colored shadows, as described by Goethe (*Farbenlehre*) and explained and demonstrated by Steiner in *The Light Course*. Goethe first describes his observations of colored shadows in snowy mountains in the evening, when the sun is darkening and setting. He then describes his systematic observations of them in experimental situations designed to highlight their aspects. We often have the abstract idea that shadows are black, but if one sees snow in the golden light of late afternoon, it becomes clear that shadows are actually blue. And they are blue to the extent that the sunlight is golden yellow. This complementarity of color is what Goethe noticed, but he jumped to the (speculative) conclusion that this complementarity existed because the shadows were afterimages, in other words, that we are seeing afterimages when we see the shadows. This complementarity points out the practical reason to cover this topic in winter, that is, when the sunlight is more golden and less white. But what is the relation of this to the festival in winter? This is in the realm of Christmas and Epiphany, and starting with Epiphany the Soul Calendar refers to the "light of cosmic Being," and the "fire of the cosmic Word." (It is noteworthy that Steiner's lectures on optics, *The Light Course*, were given at Christmas, 1919.) This means that as we study light and optics in physics, we remember to stay awake to its dimensions beyond the physical. In his lectures to teachers from April 29, 1924 (*Faculty Meetings with Teachers*, Vol. 2), Steiner states that light does not exist in rays, but rather, in expansion and contraction. Light creates a visual space or contracts when it meets matter. The latter is usually called refraction. This quality of light should be foremost for the teacher of optics in both the lower school (grade six), and in the high school (grade twelve).

I didn't teach grade twelve at home, but I did give the colored shadows lesson as part of the Optics block in a nearby Waldorf high school. I used the Socratic-experiential method of teaching that I used with every lesson. We started with remembering personal experiences of the phenomena or topic, then we moved to structured demonstrations in class. In both cases my role was primarily to ask questions to draw out the student's experiences and thinking about the experiences. In the Optics lesson, once we had observed colored shadow, and observed those I created with different patches of colored glass in sunlight, we moved to the demonstration Steiner (after Goethe) had used.

Meanwhile, the fact remains that every lesson takes place during a festival time, and that each season or festival can be a guide for the teacher in understanding and preparing the lesson. Some blocks are closely tied to the season, for example, the Farming block in grade three, which is best presented in fall for harvest and spring for planting, at least in the temperate regions of the northern hemisphere. And then there are some blocks that require others to precede them as preparation. For example, the Physics block on mechanics in grade ten requires a certain amount of algebra first. I also found that the demands on the teacher and student were so different with the math and science blocks versus the letters and humanities blocks, that it helped everyone if we alternated them. Science and math blocks are so pure, in a way. The physical materials will always be strict taskmasters for the teacher—and will present endless possibilities for observation for the student. Math can be frustrating, but it is a complete and coherent system if one just has patience. Eventually this kind of work begins to wear on one, though, as if the mineral world is too predominant—even in the biology blocks. When the lessons switch to the letters and humanities, one feels the relief of not having to work so much with the material, and can instead enjoy the gift of delving into the complexity and richness of the human worlds of language, literature, and history. But eventually the complexity and endless openness of these topics brings back the hunger for the concreteness of math and science. I experienced the value of alternating these topics, and I think the students did too. In addition, I used complementary material in circle and main lesson work. That is, when the main lesson was math and science, the circle concentrated on language, and vice versa. This continued right through high school.

Tests and grades

In lecture 13 of the series *Foundations of Human Experience* (September 4, 1919, p. 203), Steiner says the following in relation to tests:

If you are cramming for a final exam, you are learning much that does not interest you. If you were to learn only what interests you, then, at least under today's conditions, you would fail the final. The result is that cramming for a final disturbs your sleep and brings disorder into your normal life. We must pay particular attention to this with children, and it is best and most in line with the ideal of education to let the congested learning that precedes final examination fall by the wayside—that is, drop final examinations all together. In other words, the end of the school year should be just like the beginning. As teachers, we might ask ourselves why we should test children at all, because we have had them in front of us and know very well what they do or do not know.

When I studied this as part of my high school teacher training, I had been homeschooling with the Waldorf curriculum for years, and had long ago decided not to use tests and grades. But this passage in Steiner's lecture made me become more conscious of why I had made that decision. I taught at university before I began homeschool and I already had seen the destructive aspects of grades, that is, the attempt to put individuals on one scale of comparison, and then to determine their futures based on that kind of evaluation. Individuals don't belong on mathematical scales of comparison—this is a contradiction in terms. And, as Shakespeare says: "Comparisons are odious." What struck me in reading Steiner's suggestion to do away with final exams (the only exams in the European system at that time) was that this had an implication for grades as well. If there are no exams, there could also be no grades. Yet how are grades used in education now? They can be used as rewards or punishments, or as a purported comparative measure of ability or accomplishment, or they could be dispensed with entirely because the teacher is able to see and discern the students' abilities and performance in the course of teaching. I did not want my daughters to experience school as frightening and stressful, but as a source of interest and encouragement. So I didn't use tests or grades. In grade ten, my older daughter, Claire, asked to have quizzes and tests because she wanted that experience. So, I gave her quizzes and tests, which I corrected and went over with her without assigning a grade. She continued through grade eleven at home and then went into a traditional preparatory school near where we lived. There she contended with shifting class schedules, long days, overt ranking of students, and, of course, tests and grades. She survived. She went on to graduate with honors and to win a Presidential Scholarship at the college of her choice. But she had been spared these stresses until she was seventeen years old. Sara did her grade twelve at a Waldorf school (where she boarded with a local family), and there she encountered tests and grades. But at least the daily rhythm, the curriculum, the method of teaching, and some of the students were already familiar to her. She fit in well and did well in her work and graduated from that school.

Inclusive Language and Narratives

If the teacher is aware of the bias in our culture to evaluate the male and men more positively than female and women, then she might want to counter this tendency in the language she uses in teaching. She can also be more conscious in her choice of material presented to the students. I personally am not convinced that the pronoun "he" or "him" in English can stand for all of humanity. That is, I'm not convinced that hearers and readers are not affected by the use of the male pronoun to refer to a group that includes women and girls.

As a reader of science fiction since seventh grade, I read everything of Ursula LeGuin, and her work sometimes deals with sex and gender roles (e.g., *The Left Hand of Darkness*). I eventually read her essays, as well as her fiction, and I was struck by the evolution of her thinking regarding the male pronoun and its effects on a narrative (e.g., her book of essays *Dancing at the Edge of the World*). Because I was convinced that girls begin to feel left out and marginalized if they always hear the male pronoun, I was careful to use the feminine pronouns when women or girls were the subject, and the plural when a group was referred to. This means using some nonstandard forms of English, but I think this allowed their consciousness of language to stay more open as a result. So, take for example the following quote by Steiner: "Adam and Eve disobey His Commandments and thus become the forebears of man who has to sustain himself by reaping the fruits of the earth" (in *Education Towards Freedom*, p. 96). Some maintain that the word "man" in this context means "human" and that "himself" means himself and herself. But if that were the case, changing those nouns and pronouns to be more inclusive would not change the meaning, or our understanding, of the sentence. Let's try it: "Adam and Eve disobey His commandments and thus become the forebears of humanity who have to sustain themselves by reaping the fruits of the earth." Here there is no possibility that girls feel themselves left out, unless they already don't feel completely human. (For more on this topic see Dorothy Sayers' book *Are Women Human?*) I should note that I didn't change any sacred text that I used in class, be it Hindu, Buddhist, Hebrew, Christian, or Islamic. Therefore, God remains "He," but we can only progress so much at a time. Teachers of boys might ask themselves the effects on boys of excluding girls in language and narratives.

Whenever possible, I also chose narratives in the lessons that either concentrated on, or, at least, included women. For example, I used a book of paintings called *The Women in the Bible* when I taught the Old Testament in grade three and the Bible and Literature in grade ten. I also used a book, surprisingly slim, called *All the Women in the Bible*, and another called *Not Including the Women and Children*. One can't cover all the narratives and stories in the Bible in either of these grades, but one can be sure *not* to leave out stories that focus on women. In History I used a book called *Women's History* to at least check on women as actors in various stages of history. In the science blocks I made an effort to look up women scientists, who are often very accomplished but don't make it into the standard texts and synopsis materials. For example, there are many books on women pioneers in science, including women Nobel winners.

Learning Means Digesting

We often use metabolic terms when talking about learning, such as "food for thought" and "break down the argument." Piaget developed a developmental theory of the origin of logic in thinking based on the digestive processes of assimilation and accommodation. When we digest food, we break it down—and eventually something new results. (For more on this, see Steiner, *Disease, Karma, and Healing*, lecture of June 17, 1909). In the case of the teacher, this something new is the lesson given to the child. In the case of the child, it is the change in their body or soul that results from the lesson—as well as the practical work and schoolwork they produce. In this context, I'll discuss here the role of sleep and child study in the teacher's lesson preparation and the children's production of main lesson books, as well as the relation of handwork and artistic work to certain main lesson topics.

Teacher Preparation

Breathing, in the very general sense of alternating flow from inward to outward and back, is a basic process of life. It is also, at our present time in human evolution, a process that is the basis of consciousness. When we breathe in we wake up a little, and when we breathe out we "fall asleep," i.e., become a little less conscious. Breathing air is a small cycle embedded in the larger cycle of waking and sleeping, in which the I and soul are drawn into the body or released from the body. In the case of sleep, the changes in consciousness are much more obvious. But what happens when we are asleep and, therefore, for the most part, unconscious? Our sleeping time, when we are "out in the cosmos," is a recurrent topic in Steiner's work, especially in his main work on evolution, *An Outline of Esoteric Science*. This book includes a chapter titled "Sleep and Death." The important phenomenon for our purposes in relation to teacher preparation is the possibility of something new arising through the teacher's conscious work with sleeping and waking.

Let's start with the rhythm of the main lesson. On the first day of a new main lesson block the teacher is presenting new material and the children are beginning to take it in. I would start with the title of the lesson block on the board, and, when the children were young, I would "unveil" a new drawing related to the lesson—a drawing I had created and covered on the blackboard the night before. The beginning of a new block can't start with recall of previous material, so I usually started a new block by asking the student to recall experiences she had had in the past with the phenomenon or topic at hand. I then gave the first lesson and outlined the whole block. The first assignment was to do a drawing or a piece of writing for the main lesson book—in draft form. Then sleep intervenes before the next school day. After roughly twenty-four hours we are in the same situation again, but much has changed. Now the lesson begins with the teacher asking, "What did we do or talk about yesterday in main lesson?" Then the teacher and student work together to build up the material that was covered the day before. But it now goes beyond that, because both have digested the material during sleep and now have new questions and realizations. These new ideas are the starting points for further work; and so the cycle repeats over the days and weeks of the block. Blocks are typically four weeks long, so about a lunar month. Within the block there are weeks with three

Individualizing the Lessons and the School

to four days of block lessons. Within the week there are two to three waking and sleeping cycles. How can the teacher consciously work with these rhythms to prepare for and structure a main lesson block? And how could she structure the main lesson blocks for the whole year?

As we lived in a temperate climate with four distinct seasons, I tried to schedule blocks that required outdoor work in the fall and spring. For example, grade seven chemistry focuses on fire and the carbon cycle, so fall is a good time to have a bonfire, to burn substances, and to work with a lime kiln outdoors. And I usually alternated math and science blocks with humanities blocks. These two areas require such different kinds of thinking and working, thus the alternation proved healthy. When we were working on science, the literary could "lie fallow" and "sink in," and vice versa. As I was teaching two grades at once, three years apart, I used the same block rotation of sciences and humanities for each grade. For example, when I was teaching grades five and eight in the same year, the schedule began with shaded black-and-white drawing for both students, then moved on to Geometric Drawing, Botany, and then Ancient History for grade five, whereas for grade eight the beginning sequence was Perspective Drawing, Physics (acoustics, optics), and European and American History. That way I could concentrate on the same type of work for each student for each block.

Certain resonances between the grades become more apparent when one is working on the grades at the same time. In this particular combination, of grades five and eight, it struck me that as the eighth grader is working in clay modeling to sculpt the five Platonic solids in their metamorphic sequence, the fifth grader is studying ancient Greece. As Claire formed the solids with the palms of her hands, I read from Plato's *Timaeus* in which he describes the elements and their forms—the solids. The final solid, the fifth one, the dodecahedron, is not given an element by Plato, rather just a very general statement that it is the "quintessence"—and that God used it up for the universe. It struck me that the dodecahedron is a transformation of all the other forms and that it corresponds in some way to the human being as a microcosm of the universe. Of course, I did not say this in any of the lessons with Claire in grade eight, but it did help me to understand the progression in human consciousness during the time of ancient Greece. I could use this understanding to structure my lessons for grade five Ancient

History, which ended with Greece and culminated in the development represented by Socrates of a conscious awareness of an "inner voice" or daimon. This "inner voice" is the connection between the macrocosm of the universe and the microcosm of the individual incarnated human being. The two can connect because the microcosm was involved in the creation of the macrocosm.

Through grade nine we had three consecutive days a week for the main lesson block, and usually four weeks for the block. We had Nature and Library Days on Mondays, main lesson on Tuesdays, Wednesdays, and Thursdays, and lessons, sports, and group activities on Fridays. In the higher grades we also began to have some practice sessions for math and language on Fridays. Saturdays and Sundays were social and festival days. This rhythm of three "thinking" days to four "action" days worked well for us from kindergarten through grade nine. After that, for grades ten and eleven, another schoolwork day was required. Then the ratio became four "thinking" days to three "action" days. This schedule meant that we all had the first day of the workweek to "breathe out," to be outdoors, and yet to be with a structure and general purpose—to explore. I used the time in the latter part of the day in the library to work on main lesson presentations, while the girls were free to read what they wanted. By Tuesday we were all ready to concentrate and get on to new material.

The beginning of the block requires more time for the teacher, and the end is more work for the student. I found that the three-day cycle for main lesson provided the right amount of new material, with two nights to sleep on it, and two chances each week to look back on previous work and to take in more. The first day's work planted seeds that somehow mysteriously developed during the night and blossomed into new questions from the student. Then on the second day, the teacher's work with the questions provided the impetus for the student's new realizations after the second sleep. I prepared at night for the next day's presentation, and that meant that I took into sleep not only the ideas of the lesson but also the questions the girls had brought up during the day. I had two types of seeds: my own questions and their reactions. I usually concentrated on an image of each child built up out of the details of the day, each night before sleep. This provided fertile ground for new material that I could bring into the lesson the following day.

Individualizing the Lessons and the School

Here is an example of a main lesson sequence from the first time I taught grade eight, the first History block. We started with a two-day introduction to England, its geography as an island, and, as a representative of the awakening of individual consciousness at that time, its famous playwright William Shakespeare. The next week we had a three-day sequence of main lesson presentations. I began by asking, "What did we do last time?" We then recalled the material on England's geography as an island, and how England developed on its own in some ways—and we also recalled how Joan of Arc had pushed the English back to their island. Claire said, "That was powerful!" And then, after a pause, "But that wouldn't work now because people don't believe...don't believe in those things now." I replied that yes, it is different now, people have a different awareness. This is a key insight in the study of history—that awareness and consciousness change over the span of history. I then proceeded in that lesson to cover the origins of the Church of England, and noted how this was important in its influence over some of the first Europeans to come to America. The next day the lesson was on Elizabeth I, and we recalled the Magna Carta. We then moved on to Wycliff and Luther—and how the English were separating themselves from the continent and from Rome. I ended with how the Reformation took place in England. On the third day I gave dictation of a description of how England moved toward the freedom of the individual: more on the Magna Carta, the formation of Parliament under Edward I, and more on John Wycliff and the attempted reform of the church. Claire's realization from the introduction to the block— that England had become isolated from the continent in a way that depended on a certain kind of spiritual awareness, but had then gone on to develop a different consciousness that revolved around the individual—was the basis of understanding the next lessons in the block. And my understanding of her insight guided me in what to emphasize in the lessons.

The most concrete "something new" that the children produce is the main lesson book for a block. The teacher makes assignments, and in the early grades demonstrates the work that the child copies, but as the children progress through the grades, they become more independent and creative in what they include in the main lesson books. The books represent hard work and show the course of a block as well as its conclusion. We always ended the school year by arranging the books in order and looking through them again to admire and comment on the work. Just as any portrait painter is always in some ways painting a self-portrait, each child—in making their book—is producing a reflection of their own unique person.

Inner and Outer Forces During Childhood

Human life is always an interplay between inner forces, such as experience, memory, and intention, and outer forces of the natural world, and other human beings, that surround the individual. The balance of these two types of forces changes from infancy and childhood, through adolescence and adulthood and into elder ages (e.g., Lievegoed, *Phases*; Steiner, *The Child's Changing Consciousness*). Here we are concerned with the school years, so I will describe three phases of development and give examples of Waldorf lessons that fit with the developmental dynamics of the child's stage and age.

From kindergarten through grade four the physical body is being formed and developed quite rapidly based on the workings of the life body and the metabolic-limb system. The life body is primarily working to form the physical from birth to age seven (the time of the change of teeth), at which point it is freed somewhat for thinking and memory. But until age nine to ten, the child is still immersed in a dreamy, action-based consciousness. Goodness in the child's surroundings relates to hope in the child, and eventually brings about the beginning of individualization, at which point, around age nine, the child becomes more aware of her outer world and of the transitory nature of life. So—goodness and hope. An adult's actions that are conscious, consistent, unhurried, reverent, and loving are good. Housework done in this manner provides a good surrounding for a young child. Likewise, in kindergarten and grade one the fairy tales they hear are all about good and evil—and the consequences of each. Nature stories that give plants, animals, and other aspects of the natural world a point of view or perspective also teach and surround the children with goodness.

In grade two, goodness is prominent in the stories of the saints. They are examples of human beings with extraordinary courage and conviction, though certainly the details of their trials are not presented to the children. In grade three, practical life predominates, with farming by hand as a way of relating to nature and creating whole landscape

Figure 11: Claire's grade three drawing of the first day of creation

"organisms." The stories of the Old Testament, again, are explicitly about good and evil. And the first story of Genesis parallels human embryological development (see Thomas Weihs, 2017), so when children hear these stories, they unconsciously are hearing out their own beginning, as well as the beginning of the world.

Grade four is a transition time between dreamy childhood and the rapid changes of adolescence. The lessons become more complicated as we study stories of the Norse gods who, although powerful, are not always good. This is when the children begin to wake up to the outer world, and begin to be aware of its moral complexities. The science lessons now focus on the animal world in its manifold wholeness, and concentrates on relating the animals to the human being, wherein each animal shows a specialization of a more general human aspect. Each specialization, for example, a horse's hooves instead of separate fingers and fingernails, allows for an exploration of certain advantages, such as strength and endurance, yet also limitations. In this case, hooves' lack of dexterity and flexibility of use are sacrificed, as it were.

The importance of goodness and hope for rapidly developing young children makes sense in general. But how does a teacher put these ideas into practice and tailor them to individual children? Fairy tales are universal, but they do have different characters and can fit different children's needs at different times. Saint's legends at the beginning of the year in grade two can be about Michael, as the Michaelmas festival is in the fall. These legends, in simplified form, are accurate stories for younger children, too, and provide an example of maintaining courage as the earth progresses into winter. When I was teaching kindergarten and grade two at the same time, I had told the legend of St. George, the earthly representative of Michael, in school. The next day in school when I presented a form drawing on the board to the second grader, and then while she and I drew it in the air, her kindergarten-age sister said, "Michael is an angel; he is not on earth—he is in the sky." I replied "Yes, he is." Then as her older sister and I went on with the form drawing, Sara started singing her own original song: "There is something new here. Have no fear of anything." She sang this over and over.

When Claire was in grade two and Sara in kindergarten, I gave Claire a main lesson on the alphabet, showing uppercase and lowercase letters in cursive. Sara was playing and drawing in the schoolroom at the time, as she did through kindergarten. When the lesson was finished, I left the room to prepare snack and I could hear them talking with each other in the classroom:

> Sara: Where did we get the letters?
> Claire: Adam gave them.
> Sara: Where did we get the order?
> Claire: Adam gave it.
> Sara: Where did *we* get it?

> Claire: Adam told Eve and they told their babies and their babies told their babies and now everyone alive knows.
> Sara (pausing): Where did Adam get the letters?
> Claire: God told him before he made him.

Thus, I had the privilege of overhearing them making the lesson their own.

In grades five through eight beauty in the child's surroundings becomes very important, and it supports the development of love for one's surroundings. This phase is the beginning of adolescence, when astral forces can become so strong they can overwhelm the individual. Interest in the outer world of nature and of other people counteracts this tendency, and beauty in that world helps support interest in and love toward the world. This interest and this love counter, in a balancing way, the inner awareness and forces that increase in adolescence. Grade five science lessons concentrate on botany, for a good reason. The purity and beauty of plants is a perfect antidote to overwhelming emotions, which can sometimes be destructive. Goethe's poem "The Metamorphosis of Plants" has an ending that is surprising in some ways. The poem is addressed to "my love" and ends with the following lines:

> Think how our tender sentiments, unfolding,
> Took now this form, now that, in swift succession!
> Rejoice the light of day! Love sanctified,
> Strives for the highest fruit—to look at life
> In the same light, that lovers may together
> In harmony seek out the higher world!

In some ways the poem is about a kind of love between people, but a love that allows them to seek a greater world together. Modern life has lost touch with the resonance between the forms of plants and the growth of love, and of love for the world, but lessons on the types of plants and their transformations can give students who are just beginning adolescence a natural order of growth that they can draw on later for strength. The lessons I taught on botany followed the same order for the two girls, and we did observations of the plants in our area over the three seasons covered in the school year. But the lessons were different for the two girls who were so different from each other. For Claire, who had an interest in science from the beginning, the lessons were about close observation—and her drawings aided that observation. For Sara, who knew she would be an artist at the age of five, the observations were a training of the eye, and her drawings an exploration of technique as well as a botanical record. Claire's grade five play was on Pandora, who is caught between forward-looking Prometheus and his backward-looking brother Epimetheus, and who can't control her curiosity—what a picture of the modern eleven-year-old, on the brink of adolescence! In this play, there is one quality left in the treasure chest or box when all the evils have flown out, and that is Hope. And in our play, Hope was little second grader Sara, who rose from the chest in gossamer white, bringing the hope of a young child.

By the time Claire was in grade eight, the end of the time when lessons help support love for the world, Sara was in grade five, at the beginning of the period. Claire's grade eight play was Goethe's version of *The Magic Flute*, which exists only as a fragment, without an ending. I wrote an ending and Channa Seidenberg composed some music for it. I also wrote transitional musical pieces based on correspondences with the planets. (A copy of the script for this play, as we performed it, is in the Rudolf Steiner Library.) In a scene of a kind of initiation, a treasure chest is opened and out flies a golden child, beautiful and free—and, of course, this was Sara (echoing Hope flying from Pandora's chest three years earlier).

Grades nine to twelve cover the period when the intellect is awakening, gradually, and truth in the surroundings engenders faith in the world and the self. In these post-deconstructionist times, truth is not a popular idea. It is the province of analytical philosophy and organized religion. And yet Steiner often described the "sense for truth" as a potential ability; he gave lectures on goodness, beauty, and truth—and he wrote *Truth and Knowledge* (1892). Steiner sees direct experience as the basis of true knowledge, and this approach informs all of the Waldorf curriculum. But it is most obvious in the science lessons, especially in the high school. Contemporary mainstream science has lost the emphasis on systematic observation as the basis of knowledge, and, instead, begins with a theory or model that is described as if it were reality (see Barfield, *Saving the Appearances*, for example). Steiner saw Goethe's method of nature study as the basis of an objective, idealist way of knowing, and so Goethe's experiential science forms the basis of science in the Waldorf school. This way of working brings about in the students a faith in their own powers of observation and cognition. All the science lessons in the Waldorf curriculum begin with direct experiences of the phenomena being studied, but in the high school these lessons take the further step of being systematized and organized in thinking and in writing and illustrating. Most importantly, this way of working, starting with the experience and moving to general statements, preserves the experience of the world as an open and eternally evolving "organism."

In grade eleven, Chemistry focuses on transformation of substances. After observing crystal forms, and growing crystals, students observe combinations of substances in precise proportions in chemical reactions. Then processes of oxidation and reduction are observed and tested. Oxidation was first observed by heating iron and copper, and then by burning metal powders such as zinc, iron, copper, and magnesium. The teacher gradually moves the student toward the generalization that oxidation is the process of oxygen combining with other substances—from which warmth and sometimes light result. And one also leads toward the inverse process of reduction in which oxygen is removed from a substance. Once a student has gained her own direct experiences with the phenomena, the teacher can provide descriptions of the experiences and explanations of early scientists. In discussing the nineteenth century idea of phlogiston, or fire as an element, Claire made the observation that "fire is always there—like God." I answered that yes, that is true, it just needs certain substances to be present. Science lessons are, potentially, a place where students can know truly.

The Individual Homeschool

In chapter one I described our own individual decisions about why and how to school at home. Here I return to the topic in both a wider and a deeper form. It is wider in that I want to cover more general topics of school and home, and deeper in that I go into some of the ramifications of the decisions in more detail.

Each school is different, has a different character, from any other school—all the more so for homeschools. A homeschool is usually made up of one family, although sometimes parents share teaching in a school. Some parents arrange tutoring for their children and don't teach themselves. Some children enroll from home in online schools and courses. In this book I am concentrating on a particular type of homeschool, one in which a parent teaches and uses the Waldorf curriculum. Even within this restricted category, homeschools differ widely, because the teachers and students vary so much in their abilities, interests, and purposes. They also vary widely because the curriculum explicitly supports the development of ethical individualism (see Steiner's *Philosophy of Freedom [Spiritual Activity]*). As each school grows out of the individuality of the teacher who works reciprocally with her growing and developing children, each school will vary in its form. But the Waldorf curriculum, sensitive as it is to the daily, weekly, monthly, and yearly rhythms that strengthen learning and development in children, calls for a structured method of teaching. In that, it differs from intellectually-focused curricula, or the unstructured, "unschooling" approach of John Holt.

Each parent or couple has to place their school within the context of their home and family life, and, beyond that, within the context of the larger community—and, also, of the state and its legal requirements. All these levels exist simultaneously and have to be considered in planning and developing a homeschool. I'll start with how our individual school developed. By the time I was pregnant with our first child, I knew that home birth was the right choice for us. I was able to find very competent support for birth at home, and we had a positive, intense experience with that. I remember a friend of mine who was helping us, and who was a professor in a university school of education, saying that many people who have home birth also have homeschool. I hadn't even thought of that, and put the thought out of my mind. I had learned about Waldorf schools by then and assumed our children would go to one. School seemed infinitely far into the future at that point. By the time we had our second daughter, a little over three years later, we were living in a different state (also with no Waldorf School near) and about to move across the country for my husband's new job. Decisions about school still seemed way over the event horizon.

In our new locale we were a forty-five-minute freeway drive from a Waldorf school and started attending play group there once a week. The summer before our older daughter, Claire, would turn six, it became clear that she would not do well with a long freeway ride to and from school every day. I put off facing the music until August, and then I knew that we should have school at home—kindergarten—at least for that year. My husband and I discussed it and explored what this would mean for our daily lives, and we decided together that it was the right thing to do. We saw the decision as pertaining only to that year, and that the decision about first grade would be made anew the next spring or summer. At that point, we were living in California, which has very liberal laws regarding homeschool. Homeschool is completely legal and doesn't require training for the parent. One can even obtain state funds for materials if one enrolls in the homeschool program and gives a report to a state-certified teacher once a month (which we did for two years). So, our decision to conduct school at home only affected our lives—and the lives of the other families that we cooperated with in various homeschool groups. And even in these groups, school activities consisted of festival celebrations, handwork, eurythmy, and singing, rather than main lesson work, which was carried by individual parents.

Just before our daughters entered grades five and two, we moved across the country again, this time to Pennsylvania. Our identity and rhythms as a homeschool were established at this point, but our relation to the larger community had to be developed. I quickly found other parents interested in Waldorf homeschooling through the Waldorf Without Walls organization founded and run by Barbara Dewey. And there was a Waldorf School about forty minutes away with which we could coordinate for festivals and events. The state laws were quite different from California, however. Homeschooling was not legal in Pennsylvania unless the parent-teacher was certified by the state. That was not a possibility for us, as the time it would have taken for certification would have interfered with the girls' education. We solved this problem by enrolling in a small, private day school that had a homeschool component supervised by certified teachers. The school, Upattinas (near Downingtown, PA, and no longer in existence), was founded by homeschooling parents who valued the right of parents to decide about their children's education. We enrolled for a minimal fee, went over the year's lesson plans with the supervising teacher at the beginning of each school year, and she evaluated the children's work at the end of each year. She marked their progress on the state-mandated form and kept records on the children. No grades were given in the day school (which went through high school) and none were required in the homeschool program. Once the children were in high school, a detailed transcript was kept for them by the school. The school also did not conduct standardized testing, nor require vaccinations. Although this school had been founded by unschooling parents, it provided the connection to the state legal system that our homeschool needed and didn't interfere with the basic values and procedures of our school. As an aside, I would add that the supervising teachers were always impressed with the work our girls showed them, and very positive and encouraging in their reviews of the work. In this way, Claire and Sara experienced an adult outside of our school taking a positive and supportive interest in their work, rather than experiencing the typical "test" attitude that endeavors to put individuals on one scale and to "grade" them as better or worse.

The individual character of our school grew out of the configuration of the leading adults and the developing children. Every family, as a group, has a certain "identity," and so does any school. But when the family also contains the school, the two identities coexist. You might say a family is a "stream" of individuals whose destinies flow together for at least some period of time. And here the idea or image of a river is helpful. A body of water is a river precisely because it consists of changing, flowing waters. The river remains one by changing what it contains. In the context of change the river remains the same, and those who encounter the changing water experience their own "staying the same" in contrast. That is, they experience their own continuing self, or identity. When we were in school, we entered the "flow" that was the structure, rhythm, and roles of school. When we were not in school, we were in the "flow" of family, our particular family. The fact that these two identities coexisted allowed me, as both the mother and teacher, to see directly the continuities between work and realizations in school and experiences and realizations outside of school. I, as the conscious, planning adult in both groups could work based on the continuities I saw. When Claire, the night before her first day of first grade, said, while having her bath, "I'm glad I'm not the child I used to be," I as the parent saw in her a dawning realization, consciousness, and self. The next day in school when I shook her hand, looked her in the eye, and greeted her at the door of the schoolroom as her teacher, I knew that I was leading her across a threshold, both materially and beyond, in a very specific sense.

Chapter Six

Rhythms of Teaching and Learning

In the last chapter the topic was making the curriculum your own. Now the teacher can put this into practice. To this end, one does well to coordinate lessons with the rhythms of life. These swing back and forth between certain polarities, such as waking and sleeping, listening and speaking, activity and quiet. Working with rhythms is a skill that improves with practice.

What is rhythm? It is stability within change, ordered change, not chaos. Why is rhythm important in teaching and in learning? These questions have different answers depending on one's understanding of time and the coordination of human life with time. In this chapter I will describe different levels of rhythms and how they aid the work of the teacher by supporting both the student's learning and the strength and life of the teacher and student.

We moved from Connecticut to Southern California for my husband's work. There we lived in three different houses over the course of seven years. When we arrived our girls were three years old and six months old, respectively. When we left they were ten and seven. At the end of the seven years we moved all the way back across the country to the east coast, and have lived in the same house since then. In both of these cross-country moves, we moved to a place with no friends and no relatives. But we started kindergarten for Claire in the first house in California, so even through all these changes of house and locale, we always had home and, in addition, we always had school. And the rhythm of school and the festivals remained a constant. These rhythms were a given in our lives and became a large part of how we met friends and fellow travelers in the homeschool world.

My guide in describing the rhythms of teaching and learning is a set of two lectures by Rudolf Steiner (given December 21, 1908, and January 12, 1909, in R. Steiner, *Disease, Karma, Healing*) in which he describes rhythms in the human body and the human being. I will progress through the grades starting with the daily cycle of twenty-four hours, then the weekly cycle of seven days, followed by the monthly cycle of four weeks. And I will end with the yearly cycle—which is roughly twelve months multiplied by four weeks multiplied by seven days. This pattern I apply first to the kindergarten, then to the lower grades, and finish with the high school.

Kindergarten

> Is play mere fun, or a serious matter for a child? To a healthy child, playing is by no means merely a pleasurable pastime, but an absolutely serious activity. Play flows in real earnest out of the child's entire organism. If your way of teaching can capture the child's seriousness in play, you do not merely teach in a playful way—taken in the ordinary sense—but you are nurturing the earnestness with which a child plays. What matters at all times is to observe life accurately.
> Rudolf Steiner, *The Child's Changing Consciousness*, p. 70

Daily rhythms. By the time I started teaching kindergarten at home, I had experienced the rhythm of a playgroup at a Waldorf school, and, in addition, I had experienced it in the way the seasonal festivals were woven into the daily rhythm. What is most important about young children is that their consciousness is perpetually somewhere between waking and sleeping. In an outer way they do sleep part of the day, and wake for the other part, with naps of short sleep interspersed. But they are never as fully awake as adults, and never as fully asleep, either. When our younger daughter, Sara, claimed at age four that "I never sleep! I'm awake all night," she was saying something about her state of consciousness. Her older sister was indignant at this statement and assured her that it was not true. What are the implications for kindergarten? Young children in their open, timeless consciousness, need a quiet, consistent, rhythmic world in which to "float"—and in which to eventually wake up. Time is really nonexistent for them, and the most directly experienced rhythm is the daily rhythm of waking, living, sleeping, and waking again. Gradual transitions and an overall mood of calm, positivity, and interest provide what the young child needs. In our case that translated to my rising before the children in the morning, but letting them sleep until they woke up on their own. After breakfast and dressing, we began our day—either a school day with me or a weekend day with both their father and me at home. Our school days began about an hour and a half after waking and continued until early afternoon. Then there was time for reading to the children, handwork, free play, and preparations for dinner. After dinner there was some free play, but mostly preparing for bed with their father by undressing, listening to reading, then listening to me playing the lyre and singing by candlelight. Then we recited the nightly prayer together—and after that it was time for the lights to go out.

The *Prose Edda* of the Norse myths describes a ship called Skipladnir:

> It is so huge that all the Aesir, with their arms and effects, could go on board. As soon as its sails are lifted, it has fair winds wherever it is directed. If it is not in use, one can fold it like a piece of material and carry it in one's pocket… In other words, sleeping Man takes a trip to the gods. He travels in the macrocosm with the ship Skipladnir and all the Aesir on board every night. The nightly trip to the gods renews the forces of the organism. That ship always has a fair wind as soon as the sails are lifted. The sails are lifted at the moment of going to sleep (Uehli, pp. 123–4).

It is as if young children, before the age of seven, have one foot on the ship and one foot on land, and they just shift their balance back and forth between the two. For this reason, the rhythm of the day and night cycle, the sleeping and waking cycle, is the predominant experience and "basic habitat" of the young child. So young children may not be as aware of their immediate surroundings as older children, but they may be more aware of the broader cosmos. Here is a conversation overheard between two young girls who are sisters:

> First: What's higher than the sky?
> Second: The sun.
> First: What's higher than the sun?
> Second: The stars.

The Genius of Home

First: What's higher than the stars?
Second: Heaven.
First: What's higher than heaven?
Second: God.
First: What's higher than God?
Second: (Pause) Here.

(As I recall this, I can't help but think about a short story with a very similar description by Ted Chiang, entitled "Tower of Babylon.")

When my younger daughter, Sara, was in her first year of kindergarten, I ended every circle with the same song, using gestures to express the meaning. The lines and gestures are below:

I came from the heavens to be here on this earth
   (starting with arms raised and gradually lowered)
To be good to my neighbors, to be good to my friends
   (we each take hands)
I came from the heavens to be here on this earth
   (same gesture as before)
To be good to the whole wide world
   (arms curved and joined into a circle)

Weekly rhythms. Although children are not conscious of the weekly cycle, a steady rhythm at that level can be confirming and strengthening for them, and for the teacher, too. At least since the Middle Ages, people have made correspondences between plants, metals, colors, tones, and other objects and qualities with the seven so-called "planets," that is, the movable celestial bodies as seen from Earth. These bodies, because they move in relation to the background of the "fixed stars" of the constellations, have been called "wandering planets." Over millennia of sky observation, various cultures have distinguished seven of them: Moon, Venus, Mercury, Sun, Mars, Jupiter, Saturn. These "planets" correspond to our days of the week: Sun day, Moon day, Mars day (*mercredi* in French), Wednes-day (Wotan's day in Old Norse), Thurs day (Thor's day in Old Norse), Fri day (Freya's day in Old Norse), and Saturn day. Why should any day be different from any other except for seasonal variations in light? Why should people group days into weeks? If we follow Rudolf Steiner's descriptions of the seven-day cycle, we see that the seven days relate to a rhythm of inner versus outer awareness (for adults). Is each day of the week the same, in terms of consciousness? Can we do anything on any day, without any effects on what we do? Certainly, there are social conventions regarding activities for different days, but beyond that, can we be conscious of the qualities of the days and of our own awareness? In my own experience, Saturday, Sunday, and Monday have a more "inner" quality, whereas Tuesday is a turning point and Wednesday, Thursday, and Friday are a time to be more outer-oriented. Steiner gave indications to various groups (eurythmists, music teachers, and others) regarding correspondences with the days. The particular correspondences found in various sources differ, but what is effective is the discipline of using them. Saturday: corn, blue, tone G; Sunday: wheat, peach blossom, tone A; Monday: rice, violet, tone B; Tuesday: barley, red, tone C; Wednesday: millet, yellow, tone D; Thursday: rye, orange, tone E; Friday: oats, green, tone F.

We had "scripted" indoor kindergarten days on Tuesday, Wednesday, and Thursday. On those days I would wear something of the color for the day and make snacks that included the day's grain. Later on, these correspondences—and others—appeared in more detailed ways, but these simple repetitions helped the girls to know where we were in the cycle of school days. Millet was probably the most challenging to make into a snack that they liked, but it did broaden their experience with grains! Meanwhile, I found some aspects of living with these correspondences challenging. Before this effort, I never wore certain colors (orange—yuck). Making myself wear certain colors changed my emotional "tone" for the day, and certainly educated my visual sense for gradations and compatibilities of colors. I also learned the look and feel and tastes of certain grains (which was a good preparation for grade three farming.) I bought a good quality hand mill so the children and I could grind whole grains and bake with them. I also used the musical tones for my own preparation for school days, but didn't use them systematically in the kindergarten teaching.

Seasonal rhythms. The only other rhythm that affects kindergarten is that of the seasons, or the cycle of the year. This cycle corresponds to the waking-sleeping cycle of the earth (Steiner, *The Four Seasons and the Archangels*), so the kindergarten teacher in working with the children and the seasons is working with the waking-sleeping cycle in the microcosm and in the macrocosm. The seasons were not very differentiated in Southern California, yet they definitely were in Pennsylvania. But there are always songs and stories that take place in particular seasons (see the Wynstones Press books of poems and songs for each season), and foods that can be selected as local and current. "Star Money," a simple and short Grimm's fairy tale, tells of a little girl, cold in the woods, who gives away her last scrap of bread. That can be a fall or winter story. Perhaps a snack of wheat bread made together with the children on Sunday could be included the day of the Star Money story. Beyond the weather and changing light of the seasons, there are festivals that have been associated with the seasons, and are being renewed through anthroposophy (see Steiner's *The Festivals and Their Meaning*).

The festivals as renewed by anthroposophy do overlap in some ways with traditional Christian celebrations. It is not my intention to go into the relation of anthroposophy with established religion, so I will simply say that Steiner's lectures on the festivals have been our family's and homeschool group's guide and inspiration in bringing seasonal festivals to our children. Of course, anthroposophy was never explicitly discussed or mentioned in any of the festivals, and, even more so, in any of our teaching. Anthroposophy is for the teacher to study; the curriculum guides what the teacher brings to the children.

Typical institutional schools begin in the fall. But there is more than a traditional reason to follow this practice. The plants, especially the deciduous plants, are "falling asleep" at this time of year; they are declining and becoming less active. In contrast, the earth itself is becoming more awake, according to Steiner (see *The Cycle of the Year*). And at this time, the human being becomes more conscious and capable of thinking. Before our younger daughter, Sara, began her first year of kindergarten when she was four, we were camping in late August in the mountains near Lake Tahoe in northern California. One morning she told me of a dream she had the night before, with a tone of voice that made it seem she was re-experiencing the dream, not just remembering it. In the dream Sara had several sisters, and a dragon carried off all of them except one—whom Sara had warned not to show herself. The others showed themselves because they thought the dragon was a young man, but, as Sara told me, "I knew it was the dragon." Hearing this dream made me remember that the day before I had felt the first of autumn in the air and light. The dragon is part of the image of Michael, whose traditional day is September 29. Songs and verses about autumn and songs about Michael make an energetic beginning to the kindergarten year.

After the Christmas festival at home (and the break from school), we went back for the second half of the school year, focusing on winter in our images, verses, songs, and activities. After the quietness and inwardness of Christmas, the children are more engaged and interested in school than they were before. Sara became more interested in the circle activities in kindergarten and more involved in the work as "school." One day after Christmas, my husband was sick and home from work, so he was a visitor to our school, and watched and listened as we went through the school day. Both girls were definitely aware of him as an observer and were on their best behavior. Sara said later, "I was shy of him." He said the girls were definitely different with me in school than out of school; in school I am the *teacher*!

The main festival in spring is Easter, with its preparations and after-events. In school we grew wheatgrass on the nature table—and we celebrated spring with songs and activities that embodied the return of warmth and the loosening grip of "King Winter." In Southern California the seasons show fairly subtle differences, so it was even more important than in more temperate climates for us to have school material that supported the children's awareness of the larger cycles of the seasons. We didn't see snow where we lived, but we cut out snowflakes and sang songs using the movements of snowflakes drifting to the ground. We did go to some low mountains where there was snow one winter, and when she saw actual snow falling, Claire said that she had always thought snowflakes were the size of the paper ones we put in the window!

One of the fall/winter handwork activities in kindergarten is finger knitting long chains of wool loops. We used very large yarn to make thick rope-like chains that could be used for reins. One child held the ends while the other had the "reins" looped around her chest. The one with the ends was the driver and the other was the horse. We used this for "ploughing" in the fall and then with bells sewn on as a "horse"–drawn sledge in the winter. Once when Sara was the driver, our dog, an Australian shepherd mix with herding instincts, wanted to get involved and he chased the girls around the circle, biting at the reins, and tripped Sara. She went crashing down and, of course, we had to save the day! I said he was a wolf tripping up the horse, but he wasn't really going for the horse, just for the reins! We all laughed and went back to it. Imagery is all-powerful in kindergarten, and it was important to continue our "scene"—even when the unexpected happened. To this end, Steiner makes an important distinction between children's play and adult's work—not in its earnestness, but in its source or cause. Children have an inherent, inner-initiated impulse to imitate adult activities in all seriousness in their play (*Child's Changing Consciousness*, pp. 70ff). When I gave Sara the task in kindergarten to carefully oil all the wooden objects in her small "kitchen," she was overjoyed and set to the task with zeal.

The warmth of spring was discernible, but it came in early February. That is when things began to bloom, although the hillsides had been green already for a while by then. We had songs and verses about squirrels and oaks, although they were extremely rare in our hills covered with chaparral. May and June are relatively cool months in California, so we could extend the feeling of spring until almost the end of school.

If there was a play to be performed, the preparations were always in spring and the performance near or at the end of school. The circle material gradually became mostly lines, songs, dances, and even scenes from the play—not only to lead up to the performance, but to make it easier to learn the play. All the plays we performed for kindergarten were adaptations of Grimm's fairy tales: Cinderella, The Frog King, and Snow White and Rose Red. In each case we joined with another family or two to have school days together, as we prepared for and rehearsed the play. In some ways the play encapsulates the whole school year, in its themes and challenges, and in the condensed moment of its actual performance.

The largest cycle in the kindergarten year was the school year itself: the first day of school to the closing day, in which the teacher and children presented a program for father, for grandparents, and for other families. The girls and I performed circle activities that we had worked on all year. Sometimes the girls also performed a small instrumental song or did a recitation. But at this young age, it is important not to single out individual students too much for separate attention, as their dreamy consciousness is important for developing a more wakeful consciousness later. Yet we all felt a real sense of accomplishment after the end of school performance, and a release into the out-breath of summer. I always kept a full three months for summer, with absolutely no school or intellectual work.

The yearly cycle. The only way the yearly cycle enters into kindergarten is in the child's birthday verse, which marks the cycle of a full year's change, especially in the physical body. We gave the birthday verses as part of our family celebrations of birthdays, but I as the teacher used the birthday verses as part of the circle in school. The verses always related to what was coming in the year, and, in a way, there was a full year to work on these challenges—until the next birthday. We celebrate the yearly cycle for each individual with birthdays because the year is a real cycle—a spiral. After a year we are back to the point we were a year ago, but on another level. But in relation to school, the birthday is not just one day. It is a time to look forward to all the developments and challenges of the coming year. In the grades the birthday verses became more explicitly part of school, which I will describe in the coming pages.

Teaching over the years. I taught kindergarten three times, once for our older daughter, and twice for the younger. It seemed to me that I improved with practice. I knew the stories and verses better, and I found that the flow of the day and year went more smoothly. But beyond that, each time I taught kindergarten I was able to enter more deeply into the mood of the fifth in everything I did in school. I was better able to enter into the consciousness of being open to whatever came. Steiner describes the child before the change of teeth as "an ensouled sense organ entirely given over in a bodily-religious way to what comes towards it from the surrounding world," and that, therefore, we should take care that everything in the child's vicinity is "suitable to be received through the child's senses, thereafter to be inwardly worked upon" (*Child's Changing Consciousness*, p. 75). Further, whatever the young child perceives with her senses, she also perceives with soul and spirit, and so she "also absorbs the inherent moral element of what is perceived." Parents and teachers have, by the change of teeth, "already set the scene for the most important impulses of its later life" (ibid., p. 76). This represents a heavy responsibility for those caring for young children! To learn to be open, to be positive, and not to hurry—these were the main lessons for me, the teacher, in my years of teaching kindergarten. The children also taught me that play is serious work, and that my responsibility to foster and encourage their efforts was paramount.

Rhythms in the Lower School: Grades 1 through 8

Daily rhythms. School days in the Waldorf curriculum have an overall rhythm that works with the extreme changes of consciousness that we all experience in a twenty-four-hour or full-day cycle, that is, the changes from waking to sleeping. Most approaches to education say nothing about the relation of schoolwork to sleep (other than maybe the overall idea of efficiency or tiring from work), but the understanding of child development underlying the Waldorf curriculum lays great importance on the *activity* of sleep. We lose consciousness when we go to sleep and gain it when we wake up, and, mysteriously, this regained consciousness is continuous with the last cycle of wakefulness. We know who we are when we wake up and we remember the previous time awake. But what happens when we are asleep? Is there continuity with that time, too? Most people have the experience of having a new insight into something they have been wrestling with after "sleeping on it." The Waldorf teacher takes seriously this type of experience, and uses it in planning and presenting main lesson material. Steiner said the ideal day for children would be mathematics in the morning, practical work in the afternoon, and stories in the evening (Steiner, *Practical Advice to Teachers*). What an ideal that would be! Lessons in school, however, are given in blocks that work with the day of the week and the season, so the ideal cycle for each day is modified to fit within the block structure.

School day and main lesson rhythms. Consistent with Steiner's indications, in the lower school, grades one through eight, most school days generally have the following structure: greeting, circle activities, main lesson, recess, finish main lesson, lunch and recess, handwork/artwork/movement, (perhaps practice academic classes in the higher grades), and ending of the day. Thus, children are concentrating on thinking work that requires close attention in the morning, but only after physical and musical activities that "bring them into the space" and act as a transition into it. After that, they breathe out with lunch and recess, and return to work, but this time of a practical or artistic nature. Each day ends with a quiet closing. Waking consciousness changes over the course of a day, coming and going in waves, before finally going dark in sleep. The school day acknowledges and uses these "waves" from clear wakefulness to dreamy semi-wakefulness.

The main lesson has its own very important rhythm even at the daily level: each main lesson begins with recalling what was done in the last working session. Clearly, the first day of the block cannot include this type of recall, but I always drew on the child's direct experience of the topic of the block in introducing the first lesson. In that sense they are recalling their own experiences and the contexts of the experiences. When we were starting on the letters in grade one for Claire, I asked her to remember how she had first noticed letters on signs, and started to get the words on the signs without anyone pointing them out. She could remember specific times she had done that, and I said, "Now we will learn all the letters and you will write them!" This was a new world opening up. In grade three when we began the Farming block, they could each remember what they had done in the children's program at a nearby living history farm. There the children were involved in farm activities as they had been carried out in the late 1800s. They saw horses pulling plows and wagons, they saw grains planted and harvested—and they helped scare wild geese off the newly planted fields—and they took care of lambs in spring. I as the teacher worked with them to recall these experiences, and I emphasized the aspects relevant to the lesson.

Once we were into a main lesson block, the first step in each lesson was to recall the last main lesson period. That means the children had slept at least once in between, and their understanding had been changed in the process. So, they understood more now than before, and their recalling formed links to the previous work and made a continuous thread through all the lessons in the block. In grade four with Claire, when we began the block on the Norse myths, I began by telling the creation story of the Giant Ymir—and how his body became the earth. When we recalled the lesson the next day, Claire said, "We already know about the creation (from the Tanakh in grade three), but these are different people." Then she paused and exclaimed, "They're all true!" And when we got to the description of the Norns, the three women who weave everyone's fate, she asked, "Are they over the gods?" I said, "Yes, they are." And she said, "They are not our God, though, are they?"

After that first introduction, every main lesson began with me asking, "What did we do last time?" Without looking at any materials from previous work, the student and I together built up a description of what we had worked on so far on the topic of the block. This was mutual, reciprocal work in which each thing that was recalled sparked a memory in the other person. As the teacher, I wanted certain things to be stated as a foundation for the coming lesson that day, and I could make sure these ideas and pictures were part of the recalling. This work of remembering was a small and short part of the lesson in the first grades, but became a longer and more detailed part of the lesson as the children grew and the lessons became more complex and related to broader spheres of experience and of the world. For example, in grade one, as I mentioned earlier, my form drawing lessons were in the context of an ongoing story about an old woman with a curved back and a straight stick. The story developed over the school year, and events happened that developed the picture of the form I presented to the child. We always recalled what had happened in the story previously, that is, one week before, as we had form drawing once a week. This is a gentle exercise of memory because there is no evaluation and the process is a cooperative one, and it is focused on pictorial, or imaginative knowing. By the time we got to grade four, form drawing became much more complex, with braided and woven Celtic and Norse forms drawn, sometimes with color. In this case, we would recall either the Norse myth narrative to which the form related or the previous form if they were closely related.

After I presented the new material in the block lesson, the student would work with it in class to practice, write it out, or make drafts. They would then work in their main lesson book on the material from the previous lesson to put the lesson work into their book in final form. Thus, they have "slept on" the lesson for at least one night before they recall it, and then for another night, at least, before they put it in their book. I didn't give any homework until grade ten, so they were never doing schoolwork in the evening, rather, only during their alert and quiet time in the late morning.

Figure 12: Claire's grade four form drawing of knot forms

After the main lesson work, we all needed to breathe out, so the children had recess, outdoors or indoors, doing whatever they wanted while I prepared lunch. Then we had grace at the table and ate lunch, and they had a rest afterwards. In the afternoon we did painting, handwork, or music. As they got older and were given longer and more complex lessons, they sometimes did some practice or main lesson bookwork in the afternoon in addition to art and practical activities. We then had our closing verse, and school was out! Yay! They usually wanted to play outside at this point, but would come back in and want me to read to them. We sat on the couch and I read from favorite children's book authors, or seasonal material, either something for each age, or something that both girls could enjoy. They worked on handwork while I read. When we finished that, I was exhausted!

Teaching More than One Grade at the Same Time

What I have described so far pertains to teaching one child at a time. The picture is a little more complicated if one is teaching more than one child. I only had two children to teach, and they were three years apart in age. So that meant that I didn't have two main lessons to teach at once until the older child, Claire, was in grade four, when the younger, Sara, began grade one. Before that, Sara just played while Claire had school, or I worked kindergarten material into the grade structure of the school day, with, of course, lots of free play for the kindergarten child.

When I was teaching two main lesson blocks at a time the daily schedule was similar to that described above, but with a few changes. The circle verses, songs, and activities were always a mix of material from the two grades I was teaching. For example, when I was teaching grade one and grade four at the same time, the circle would include mood-of-the-fifth songs (see chapter two), but also some folk songs with a clear beginning and ending, such as the "Skye Boat Song," from Scotland. If some of the activities were too advanced for the younger child, she would sit out and watch. The older child could be enlisted to help with activities for the younger—for example, to be the horse when the third grader acted out plowing for a farming song. We always began with the schoolroom cleared for circle activities. We then said the morning verses—and on the first day of the week they took turns saying their own birthday verse, with the younger child going first. Then we had circle. After circle, we moved the desks into the room, with the younger child in front. Her lesson came first, while the older worked on her main lesson book; then the two switched activities. The blackboard was large enough to accommodate two lessons. In the afternoon, we had art, music, or handwork, with each student working at their level. I modeled painting, more simple for the younger child and more complex for the older one. Interestingly, though, in our family the younger child was so talented with visual art that she was sometimes beyond her older sister.

Sometimes one child's work would enlighten me about the other child's lessons. For example, while I was telling Claire the end of the Kalevala in grade four, the rune entitled "Marjatta," Sara was doing a free drawing with crayon. She drew a plant with a large red berry and a sky behind it. In the "Marjatta" story, Marjatta swallows a red berry, and then becomes pregnant and bears a special child. Later, after school, Sara was talking about her drawing and said the berry was the sun. And it was true that in her drawing the berry was very large in relation to the plant, and it was positioned so that it would be on the "horizon."

When she said that, I immediately realized that the red berry in the story *was* related to the sun—Marjatta had taken in something from the sun. I would not have understood the rune nearly as well without the first grader's crayon drawing!

The Weekly Rhythm

All through the lower school grades we kept the same weekly rhythm: Monday, nature exploring day; Tuesday, Wednesday, Thursday, class days at home; Friday, lessons or group activities away from home; Saturday and Sunday, family time. The qualities of the days of the week were important for the activities on that day. Modern life is dissociated from nature and nature cycles, so the awareness of different cycles of time requires hard work. Why societies organize time into seven-day weeks is not obvious. Daily, monthly, and yearly cycles based on observations of the sun and moon in relation to the earth are relatively clear, but why weeks? And why seven-day weeks? Does this matter to our lives, other than in coordinating with others in scheduling?

The fact that the days of the week are named for the planets that can be seen with the naked eye, and that move in relation to the background of the fixed stars of the zodiac, is a clue that the days are not arbitrary, and that they do have a relation to the cosmos. The seven-day cycle seems to date to the ancient Babylonians, and, whereas other lengths of weeks have been tried, none has persisted. (See Buhler, 2017, p. 41.)

Once students are in the lower school, they gradually spend more and more time in study and in engaging with main lesson subjects. Can't this work be done on any day of the week, especially if one has school at home? One could give lessons to children any time of day and any day of the week at home, but if rhythm is based on natural realities, and does affect human beings, then it should be better to be aware of rhythm and to work with rather than against it.

What are the qualities of the number seven? It is only divisible by itself and one, so it is a certain kind of whole in and of itself. It can be broken down into three plus four or into six plus one, but in a certain way those two become equivalent if we think of seven as a living movement through one, two, and three, to a turning point of four, and a completion through the final five, six, and seven. Steiner characterized seven as the number of the living, and gave detailed descriptions of the movements involved in the seven form (Steiner, *"Freemasonry" and Ritual Work,* pp. 12–19). Steiner describes the seven form as the form of the living, and as related to two processes critical for development and evolution: evolution and involution. In evolution, movement outward into the world of nature, physical reality, action and activity predominates. In involution, the opposite movement, inward, involving memory, re-experiencing, inner awareness predominates. Between these two is the turning point of stillness—nothingness. He also says that every involution must become an evolution, and that development takes place in a spiral. So, applied to the seven-day week, this form gives us three more active days, a turning point, and three more inward days. The qualities of Saturn, Sun, and Moon seemed more inward to me; Saturn is traditionally associated with memory, Sun with reverence, and Moon with dreaminess. So, I tried to orient our week accordingly.

Starting with the inward days, Saturday, Sunday, and Monday, we had our family days and nature exploration. We did active things as a family, spending time outdoors, eating out, and participating in festival activities. But the focus was inward—in the sense of being in our time together as a complete family. I always experienced Monday as a transition out of this inward time. It took some energy to begin the week, but we all had a need to have a gradual transition into mental work. So we went exploring in nature without talking or teaching, had lunch, and spent some time in a library or bookstore. This was a school day, but the children were relatively self-directed in "nature's classroom." By Tuesday, we were ready for the structure and focused activities of school. Tuesday was the day of introduction to the topics of the week, as well as the day for recalling the active period from the previous week. Wednesday, meanwhile, was a day for the elaboration of the material—and Thursday marked the consolidation and writing of the material of the week. These were all outward, or evolutionary, activities. Friday was the turning point, wherein we had lessons, but mostly in the arts or in movement/athletics and in a setting away from home and with teachers other than myself. Then, again we could return, in a spiral fashion, to the new set of three inward days: Saturday, Sunday, and Monday.

The Monthly Rhythm

In the lower school the monthly rhythm is basically the main lesson block rhythm, as blocks are usually three to four weeks long. So how does one decide the order of blocks in a year? For most of the grades, I worked with the polarity of Math/Science and English/History, that is, I alternated blocks of these types, but kept the same type across the two grades. Also, I used the circle as a complement to the main lesson block. That is, when the block was Math/Science, I used riddles and other narrative work in the circle. When the block was English/History, I used math practice in the circle. In addition, sometimes blocks build on each other (e.g., fraction topics before Business Math), or are closely related to the season (e.g., Farming).

The Yearly Rhythm

The yearly rhythm in the lower school took place only in anniversaries, for example, in birthdays and in annual festivals. We did have a program at the end of each school year in which the students showed their circle activities and some schoolwork to parents and friends, and we had plays near the end of the school year as well. Due to the content of the plays, and the intensity of working together, this became an encapsulation of the whole curriculum for the year. For example, in grade three there are several blocks on the Old Testament. Our play that year was a simplified and shortened version of the Oberufer Adam and Eve Play, with songs. The plays, once finished, released us into the final academic work and preparation for our end-of-the-year assembly. Here I presented each student with a bouquet of flowers, and officially welcomed each to the next grade. This was a very big day, and they walked tall afterwards.

The High School

The Main Lesson between Teacher and Student: Awakening the Intellect

> When the child has reached puberty, the astral body, which has been working through language up to this point, now becomes free—free to work independently. Previously, the forces working through the medium of language were needed for building up of the inner organization of the child's body. But after puberty, these forces, which are also working in many other spheres—in all that is form-giving, both with regard to plastic and musical forms—these manifold forces are becoming liberated, to be used for the

activity of thinking. Only now does the young person become an intellectualizing and logically thinking person

One can clearly see how what is thus flashing, streaming, and surging through language delivers a final jolt to the physical body before becoming liberated. Look at a boy of this age and listen to how his voice changes during puberty. It is a change as decisive as the change of teeth in the seventh year. When the larynx begins to speak with a different undertone of voice, it is the last jerk the astral body, that is, the forces flashing and working through speech, make in the body. A corresponding change also occurs in the female organism, only in a different way and not in the larynx. It is brought about through other organs. Having undergone these changes, the human being has become sexually mature. (Steiner, *The Child's Changing Consciousness*, pp. 70f)

The last four years of school—the high school years—bring many changes to the structure of the school day and year. The main lesson becomes much more of a focus, and basic academic subjects are strengthened through practice. The arts and movement arts, too, continue at a more and more advanced level. But the overarching transformation in these years is the awakening intellect that leads to the beginnings of individual choice and responsibility. The teacher in these years is preparing all along to send her students into the world with love.

The main lesson. Starting in grade nine, the main lesson begins to take up a larger part of the school day, that is, most of the morning session, including time for the student to work in her main lesson book. In a way the rhythm of the main lesson for the day and for the whole block is similar. In each day and over the course of the whole block the form of the main lesson develops *between* the teacher and the student. Each main lesson session begins with recalling what was done in the previous session (except for the very first day of the block, of course). And this recalling is a joint activity of the teacher and student, each adding what she thinks of, yet always guided by the teacher, who emphasizes certain points in relation to the greater topic. The teacher then presents new material, and this can include back-and-forth conversation and questions. Afterward, the student has time to reflect and work in their main lesson book, and then the school day progresses to other activities, giving the student "inward" time with the lesson. Meanwhile, the teacher has a plan for the whole block, and each lesson has a place in that plan which has been worked out and fleshed out ahead of time. In presenting this new material she is "giving out"—bringing something she has worked on inwardly out into the world. In that sense, this is what Steiner would call an evolutionary process. While the teacher is "evolving" the main lesson, the student is taking it in, which is an involutionary process. The teacher and student complement each other. As the block progresses, the teacher presents less, the student becomes more active, putting material in the main lesson book, becoming more proficient, asking more questions, and, thus, the balance shifts and the student is engaged in an evolutionary process. The teacher then must take in and comment on the student's work, which is more on the involutionary side. The teacher and student are engaged in a continual process of complementarity in the course of each main lesson. In the high school the students gradually become more capable of individually meeting the teacher and the lesson.

Below I will cover the contrast between history and physics lessons in grades nine through eleven, the grades I taught at home, and then conclude with some points about grade twelve in order to show the contrast between language-oriented and science-oriented blocks. I will also show the progress and evolution of the lessons over the course of high school. One way to view the relation of the grades is that grade nine is working primarily at the physical level, grade ten at the etheric or life level, grade eleven at the soul or astral level, and grade twelve at the I or individual level. Let's see if any of this becomes clearer with specific examples of lessons.

Grade 9

Physics in Grade 9: Thermodynamics

I always looked forward to teaching the Physics blocks because the thinking involved was so clean and pure and constrained by the physical. And the demonstrations required careful working with physical objects, even though the actual demonstration was creative and open. Almost anything could happen. Not everything in physics is predictable! (This is actually an important lesson about science for both the teacher and the student.) One of the main Physics blocks in grade nine is Thermodynamics. Consistent with Goethean science methods, one emphasizes systematic, direct experiences with warmth and cold, which the student must then think clearly about in order to distinguish patterns. We began with the dictionary definition of the term "thermodynamics": the "energy, force changes, or actions of warmth." (My background preparation for this block included study of Steiner's lectures in the collection *The Warmth Course*, which makes a clear distinction between the phenomenon of warmth and the abstract, material-based idea of heat. I also prepared by reading about the history of measurement and studying suggestions for Waldorf physics lessons.) We then studied the history of how people had thought of warmth and the progression of steps in trying to measure it and develop scales for degrees of warmth. The reason the history of the measurement of temperature is important is that it shows that warmth is always measured indirectly by means of changes in some physical material (water, alcohol, mercury, solid metal). At a certain point in learning this history, Claire exclaimed about warmth, "It's not physical!" I thought, "Yes!" This is a major insight. The next step was a systematic set of direct experiences with warmth and cold designed to lead to a general understanding of the phenomena.

The Thermodynamics block progressed from the history of measurement of heat and warmth in the eighteenth and nineteenth centuries to the direct experience of warmth and cold—and then to the materialization and mechanization of warmth into heat. This included making calculations for "specific heat" and making observations of state changes and transitions with graphs with Cartesian coordinates. To start the process of direct experience, I set up the demonstration of three bowls of water at varying temperatures that I detailed in chapter four—one bowl of hot water, one of cold water, and one of water at room temperature. Through this, Claire, as the student, learned that she could sense the same water temperature differently in the two hands if they had each previously been immersed in water of different temperatures. What do we make of this? The next step is to measure this temperature change directly. So we carried out the same steps, with the same three bowls of water, but now made observations with a yogurt thermometer—which is large, easy to read, and has the necessary temperature range. And what do we find? We see that the thermometer, which is based on a dual metal strip, that is, two metals that are affected by warmth at different rates, rises when placed in the hot water and experiences a slow lowering when placed in the water at room temperature water, etc. Isn't that the same as what we experienced with our hands? Thus the thermometer is used to place our sensory experience on a measurable, reproducible scale.

We then worked with the expansion and contraction of liquids, gases, and solids. This set the stage for a better understanding of the nineteenth century ideas of specific heat and state changes, which form the basis of our modern ideas on thermodynamics at the non-quantum level. This mechanization of warmth fit perfectly with what Claire had already covered in her history blocks on the Industrial Revolution—the mechanization of work and the stratification of society based on wealth, and the misconception that work could be equated with money. When we finished the Thermodynamics block, which was the last one of the year, we reviewed the topics and discussed the general ideas. On the topic of one's ability to perceive differences in warmth, Claire understood that it is related to what the thermometer does, but she said the difference is that the thermometer shows specific degrees. I agreed, but also pointed out that some people have a more natural ability in their bodies to point out exact degrees of temperature—without a mechanical thermometer.

This is why thermodynamics is taught in grade nine: It has to do with warmth and movement and interest in the world. Love *is* inner warmth going out to meet the warmth in various aspects of the world—this is the deed of love, and there are laws to it. This is what the awakening teenager needs to learn about and learn to do.

History in Grade 9: The Industrial Revolution

Hand in hand with studying thermodynamics in physics, the curriculum covers the Industrial Revolution in history blocks. History is the study of the evolution of consciousness. (See Steiner's *From Symptom to Reality in Modern History*.) Therefore, written texts from the past are not windows into the past, but are symptoms or indicators of the consciousness of human beings in that period and in that place where the texts were produced. In grade nine the students are roughly fifteen years old and are just waking up to their intellectual capacities. That is, their thinking begins to be applied to thinking. So they are beginning to understand the world through concepts. In some ways this development parallels the development of thinking in Western culture usually referred to as the Enlightenment—the time period in which inductive thinking and a certain type of scientific method come to the fore. Not coincidentally, this period precedes and includes the major political revolutions in Europe and America. To illustrate this development in thinking, I will briefly describe some history lessons in grade nine, and some of Claire's own generalizations and realizations arrived at in the course of the block. The literature to accompany this block was Charles Dickens's *Hard Times*, which I read aloud.

Early in the year we began with material on rebellions in general, and then on the events in Europe that formed the setting for the French Revolution. I concentrated on European history in grade nine because we had covered United States history in grades seven and eight as we live in the U.S. But European history is closely related to that of our own country, and therefore important for students to know. When we got to comparing the Covenanters in Scotland and the Cavaliers in London—that is, the group that emphasized the law or covenant in religion and one that emphasized enjoying earthly life—Claire said, in a very intense way, "Neither is right." And then (I'm paraphrasing here): "God wouldn't make all that is beautiful and not want us to be pleased by it, but we aren't here just to play and amuse ourselves. The Protestants thought we were here to pass a test to get into Heaven and that's the only reason. That's not enough: we come here to improve the earth, to make it better, then we go to Heaven and then we come back to work more. We are working to make the earth paradise, Eden again." In these ideas she had gone beyond the (admittedly simplified) conflict between the Protestants and the Catholics.

A little further on, when she was entering her writing on King Louis XIV of France into her main lesson book, she got to his statement: "*L'état, c'est moi*." (The State, that is me.) And she said: "Did he really believe that?" When I said, yes, she said, "It's like the Pharaoh in Egypt; he was Egypt." I said, yes! She had noticed a very important parallel there, in that the European kings in the time of revolution were degenerate forms of the idea that the king was divine, to some extent, or at least had a divine right to rule. Steiner does point out that our current cultural period is a reflection of the Egyptian epoch which preceded the Greco-Roman period just before ours (*Outline of Esoteric Science*). But a divine king and a true state cannot coexist, and this is what Rousseau and Voltaire were pointing out in their different ways.

When we had the History through Drama block, we went all the way back to ancient theater in Greece and worked forward from there. We explored the Middle Ages in Europe, the Renaissance in Italy, Shakespeare in England, and then worked our way into modern times. Claire noticed on her own the parallel between the dramas for the public that first came out of the Mystery cults in Greece and the way the Medieval morality plays had come out of the formal Christian church service. Then with Shakespeare we covered the beginning of modern consciousness, which involved questions of who knows what—and of individual conscience. Steiner points out that the change from ancient to modern drama involves the transition from the workings of destiny to the existence of character types that have consequences for the story (*Speech and Drama*, Lecture 16). At this point in the year we were reading the play that we would perform with our homeschool group for grade nine: George Bernard Shaw's *Pygmalion*. As we were covering the ideas about moving from destiny to character in the Drama block, Claire thought about *Pygmalion* and reflected, "At the beginning of the play Eliza (Doolittle) is a character—at the end she is an individual." This she experienced herself in preparing for the role, where she learned Cockney and then Received Pronunciation, and went through the story of the professor giving her the manners of the upper class—which she ultimately rejects. Perhaps this further transition from character to individual is one our age of consciousness is working on—a work in progress.

Our last grade nine History block was on the Industrial Revolution, and we read about its beginning in eighteenth-century England. Then we thought of all the descriptions from the literature we had studied, including *Hard Times* by Dickens, which I was reading to them in school, and also *David Livingstone's* autobiographical description of his childhood in *St. Nicholas Anthology* and Richard Llewellyn's *How Green Was My Valley*. All of these pieces present the time from the worker's point of view. This was a good lead-in to discussing the organization of social life, and how many parts of it have three aspects: head, heart, and hands; thinking, feeling, and willing; culture, law, and economics; freedom, equality, and mutuality. We covered Robert Owen in England and America with utopian social ideals, and Marx and the beginning of communism. This led naturally to the Russian Revolution, the communist social order, and the path by which Lenin became a dictator.

In all the material on revolutions, I emphasized the ideal of freedom in cultural life, equality in rights, and mutuality in economics. And we saw how in each revolution this three-part social "organism" was misunderstood or malformed in some unbalanced way. These lessons at least plant the idea that these three spheres exist and have their own inherent regularities. At the end of this block, we performed *Pygmalion* and Claire experienced for herself something of the poor worker existence, the rigidity of upper-class English life, and the individual qualities needed to find one's own way. We cross our fingers that some of this will stand her in good stead for the coming challenges of adolescence and young adulthood.

Grade 10

Grade ten is a turning point in the student's development of independent thinking—and also a growing point in independence of feeling and action, too. The process is not simple, and it is not easy—there is sadness at a loss of innocence, but, also, an excitement and anticipation of abilities and events to come. Mechanics in Physics emphasizes the reality of the physical world, and how its laws provide limits we can trust. Ancient History takes the student through levels of consciousness in a kind of review to prepare them for the adult consciousness of the present time on earth—the beginning of individual consciousness based on one's own intention and effort.

Physics in Grade 10: Mechanics. We began with observations of bodies at rest and of dimensions that covary or not, and then of bodies in motion. Direct observation and then thinking through what was observed is critical at this age, both as a foundation for science in general and as a support to the development of intellect which is moving toward a certain kind of "materialism," that is, an awareness of the physical world. We would build up to an understanding of bodies in motion, but it was important to start with direct experience of bodies at rest and dimensions that covary before going on to mechanical motion, or kinematics. The mechanics of motion we studied by perceiving moving objects, and working out the "laws" of movement by timing the movements and perceiving the forms of the movements. The best way to carry out this sequence is to replicate some of the experiments performed by Archimedes, then to cover Aristotle's reasoning on motion, and, finally, to perform for ourselves the experiments on bodies in motion that Galileo described in his *Discourse on Two New Sciences*.

Physical realities are grasped best when they are experienced directly; measurement procedures can then be demonstrated, but the measurements have an experienced bodily meaning for the student. Finally graph representations of measurements and algebraic formulas can be demonstrated and explained based on the experiential foundation of the ideas. By grade ten, students are developing a new kind of abstract thinking, but such thinking is most meaningful in relation to experience. With these ideas in mind, the first lessons in Mechanics involved direct observation. So, we began with Archimedes' observation of the difference between weight and size in relation to the displacement of a liquid, in which case it might be somewhat of a surprise to find that a heavy and a light object displace the same amount of liquid—if they are the same size. The separable dimensions of size and weight can begin to be seen as abstract qualities. We also worked on length and weight by using a yardstick balanced on a counter, half on and half off, and then added weights to the overhanging end and moved the fulcrum to show that length from the fulcrum affects the amount of weight that can be held. Because the yardstick is a standard measure, we could relate length and weight numerically, that is, by measurement. But we could also directly perceive the amount of pressure needed to hold up the weight depending on where the fulcrum was placed. Finally, we watched a ball rolling on an inclined plane, and varied the angle of the incline. Here the dimensions are speed and angle, but we were also seeing acceleration. We then dropped a ball off the roof and watched it fall, and then dropped a ball and a feather at the same time. With all these experiences Claire first watched, then described the events, and then we discussed the qualities of change in each case, and she made notes on her observations.

In the next lesson we recalled these observations and then built up to the idea of measuring using quantities and dimensions. Why should we do this? Because it can make our observation more specific and it is critical to communicating about the physical world. What are scales ("scala," Latin for ladder)? She eventually realized: "Something we make up!" Yes, that is true, but they fit nature—an amazing phenomenon. Finally, I read to her from Aristotle's description of motion in *Physics*, Book III, Chapter 1. Here Aristotle begins:

> Since nature (Greek *physike*) is a source of motion and of change, and our pursuit is for nature, we must not let what motion is remain hidden. For it is necessary, being ignorant of it, to be ignorant also of nature. And once we have drawn a boundary around motion, we must try in the same way to advance upon the things that follow in succession.... Being in relation to something is attributed...to what moves (something) and to what is moved... what changes, changes in place.

As Sachs (2011) points out, Aristotle is perhaps the only thinker to try to define motion, rather than just assuming or denying it. He also points out that physics since at least Newton has concentrated on "space" and in (mathematical) space there is no place. He writes (in *Aristotle's Physics: A Guided Study*, p. 19):

> Aristotle has considerable interest in change of place, but such a thing is possible only if there are places. Motion as mathematically conceived happens only in space, and in space there are no places. Underneath the idea of motion prevalent today, lurks this other idea—unexamined and taken on faith—that there is such a thing as space.

Of course, we don't make these ideas an explicit part of the lesson for the students, but the teacher is aware of these shifts in thinking and what is assumed by scientists, and must work to keep these realities in mind in presenting material in her lessons. The realities that Aristotle was aware of in his thinking can be "rethought" by the teacher, and she can guide the student in this thinking.

And then we move on to cover the next key steps that happened in the history of physics, that is, Galileo's work on mathematicizing nature—and the step from "place" to "space." The paradox here is that this type of "materialism" is a step *away* from nature and away from direct observation and thinking about nature. Abstract thinking moves away from certain realities in the world, and grade ten students must go through this step in order to eventually develop their own free thinking.

In the next steps we reviewed trigonometry concepts and facts, and then moved on to dimensional analysis, in which physical events are measured in units, e.g., time, weight, distance. The next lessons led up to the ideas of vectors and vector analysis. In order to make direct observations of speed and direction of movement, we carried out demonstrations based on movement. I had Claire walk slowly across the lawn with a bucket of white stones so that she could drop a stone every time I called "now," which was every three seconds. Then she walked quickly doing this, and we could see the difference in the intervals between the stones. Then I had her sit in a chair on wheels while her sister and I pushed at the same time from opposed sides. We saw the resultant motion, which was "between" the two angles of push. We were pushing at right angles to each other and the chair moved forward in a third completely different direction! When we pushed from the front and side, the chair went sideways. We then imagined swimming across a river with a strong current. Finally, we defined speed and velocity with symbols and formulas, and began discussing vectors mathematically as a way of representing velocity, that is, speed with a direction. When we were working on the graphic addition of vectors, I tried to get her to think about vectors in general. I said: "There's a point you leave and you are aware of it even if you go away from it, right? You're still advancing on a line related to it and eventually you'll get where you are going?" She replied, "A life? That's what it sounded like you were talking about." This really struck me—our lives have destinies (destinations?) and they are vector-like in some ways. Or perhaps vectors are life-like.

The final steps in the Mechanics block were to carry out Galileo's experiments on acceleration, to measure the dimensions, and to work with the formulas for speed, velocity, and acceleration. We watched a ball roll down an inclined plane that had been divided into four equally distant sections from the starting point. We could see that the ball was speeding up and I asked her to remember the ball dropped from the roof. What did it do? It was speeding up. Yes, and it had a direction, so it was velocity and not just speed. Why is it doing that? Again I read in Aristotle that objects with "earth" quality move toward earth, that is, downward. But what is it about the ball that makes it speed up? Claire replied: "Its weight? Its shape?" Here is where I brought in Galileo, beginning with the story that he saw hail balls of different sizes hitting the earth at the same time. In his time, people thought that Aristotle had said that weight determined acceleration. Yet this was not what Galileo observed, and what was real to Galileo was what could be measured. And what could be measured was distance and, more and more accurately, time (because of changes in the instruments). Thus I read the beginning of his "Dialogue III, Of Motion Naturally Accelerated." Here Galileo stresses that demonstration and observation by the senses are critical to understanding. He can see that a stone falling from a roof acquires "continually new increments of velocity." He considers the "great affinity there is between time and motion" and this affinity is of increments of time and space. Here we see the shift from Aristotle's thinking, in which motion is primary and time a part of it, to the beginning of modern thinking—in terms of abstract dimensions that relate to each other mathematically. We replicated Galileo's experiments and timed the ball as it rolled a quarter of the distance, and also the whole distance.

The final lessons in this block bring all the observed motions into mathematical description with the formulas for speed (distance divided by time), velocity (change in distance divided by change in time), and acceleration (change in velocity). The important point to get across is that *increments* of time are chosen and the average change during those increments is computed and used in calculating the variables for uniform acceleration (such as in free fall). We stepped through this very carefully in the calculations, showing that neither time nor distance is taken as continuous in these calculations. We used increments of seconds and as we were working through an example on the board, I said: "Time in the physical world is very complex." I wanted her to think about the difference between Aristotle's conception of time and Galileo's, and I said: "Time is not a string of instants, no—it is a flow." Claire, with a pained look, said, "Time is relentless." I said, "It is a movement." She said, with dread almost, "Anything can happen in a minute..." (This is true—think of all the things that can happen in a minute: conception, death, a wrong turn of the wheel.) After working many problems on vectors, velocity, and acceleration, some as assignments on her own,

Claire had a final discussion with me on Galileo's thinking related to which events can be taken apart into their physical constituents, and which can be seen as measurable dimensions. I asked her what kind of thinking would work this way in order to do this kind of analysis. She said "earth"-type thinking and I said yes, crystallized distinctions and exclusive categories.

The Mechanics block was the last block of grade ten, and in some ways it encapsulated the overall arc of the school year, that is, the change from ancient awareness to modern, materialistic consciousness. Mechanics is hard work to think through, just as it is hard work to carry out in the physical world. This aspect of physics exercises the thinking that students are coming to, and even though it means the loss of a certain kind of awareness, it is a step forward in their lives.

History in Grade 10: Ancient Cultures.

The usual approach to history involves using written sources from the past to create coherent narratives of past events and to speculate about causes and motivations, cultural factors, geographic and economic influences, and so forth. But the Waldorf approach goes beyond those "symptoms" to work on the forces beyond the physical that have affected human beings since ancient times. This latter approach is based on Steiner's lectures on history (*From Symptom to Reality in Modern History, World History in the Light of Anthroposophy*) and on specific time periods (e.g., *Wonders of the World, Trials of the Soul*). And Waldorf teachers have themselves written resource books (Christoph Lindenberg, *Teaching History*; Charles Kovacs, *Ancient History*) while anthroposophically knowledgeable historians have also written on the subject (e.g., Stewart Easton, *The Western Heritage*). The resources in the mainstream literature seem endless, but I found several basic works very helpful (Will and Ariel Durant, *The Life of Greece*; Kramer, *History Begins at Sumer*; Ernst Gombrich, *A Little History of the World*). The amount of material to be "digested" by the teacher and presented to the students can seem overwhelming. But the guiding principle is that history is not about documents but about the evolution of consciousness among different groups of people at different places on the earth over a long time span. In grade ten the emphasis is on ancient history, so it goes as far as classical Greece in approaching the present. Why this topic in grade ten? The students had this material in a simpler and also a less reflective and analytical way in grade five. There they were given imaginative descriptions of the various ancient cultures from India, Persia, Egypt/Chaldea, and Greece, and they worked on rhythmic recitation and movement activities related to the various cultures and their specific consciousness. Now in grade ten these aspects are encountered again, but with the addition of much more material, more discussion and reflection, and more reading of ancient texts. It is as if, now when they are waking up to modern materialistic thinking, they must review how they got to this point, that is, review the development of their own consciousness since childhood, and review what has been sleeping for five years in school. In some ways every block in grade ten embodies this "review" quality; we saw how the Physics block moved from the classical Greek thinkers and experimenters, through the Middle Ages, and into modern times with the concepts of mechanics. The History block goes back further in this review, all the way back to prehistory.

We began by imagining how people lived before there was writing. They lived in groups and traveled to hunt and gather and build temporary shelters. We looked at pictures of cave drawings and did some painting with earth pigments and drawing with charcoal (which came from the bonfire which was part of Claire's younger sister's grade seven Chemistry block), the materials people at that time would have had to use. Then we moved on to the first building, rock foundations and walls, doors that closed off caves in a cliff or hillside. We recalled seeing the Paleolithic sites in Scotland—a tunnel, a circular rock foundation, to illustrate that the first building consisted of minor enhancements to natural formations. I want to record a conversation Claire and I had at the beginning of the History block, in the first main lesson session because it illustrates how at this age the students are not only ready for this material but are almost "hungry" for it; they are thinking about certain questions and trying to find their way into the world as it is now.

I will start with two conversations Teacher (I) and Student (Claire) had at the beginning of the Ancient History block in order to give a "flavor" of how a fifteen- or sixteen-year-old approaches this material (as opposed to the ten-year-old who experienced the material imaginatively and pictorially):

Teacher: (After looking at maps of Europe during and after the last Ice Age, and discussing settlement and agriculture) After settlement and farming, what is the next big step?
Student: (Thinks about it—no answer)
Teacher: What if the settlement gets bigger?
Student: Cities!
Teacher: Yes! And what would it take to build cities? (We looked at the maps of the Tigris and Euphrates rivers and the ancient cities of Enridu, Ur, Uruk). The rivers would flood and then later there would be a dry season. Canals would be wiped out unless they were made of stone. What would that take?
Student: Time?
Teacher: Yes and lots of people. And how can lots of people work together, do they all make decisions?
Student: Oh! A leader—they had to have a leader.
Teacher: Yes! Now "Uruk"—does that ring a bell?

So one can see that the Ancient History block consists of a condensed review of the consciousness of human beings from early beginnings to the beginnings of history in the Middle East and the Mediterranean. In a way this is a kind of "practicing" of the material from grade five, but now with a different level of thinking ability. Now the students are more aware of the passage of time and of linear sequence. And they are beginning to think about causes and effects, and to ask questions about the past, and how people have changed. This thinking and practicing is supported by the History through Poetry block which goes back to ancient texts, and up to at least the Romantics, and then also the Bible and Literature block which goes over texts from ancient Hebrew and Greek, starting from before the time of philosophy in Greece and extending over a hundred years into the Christian Era. Grade ten involves a repeated passage through levels of consciousness and changes in consciousness from ancient to modern times.

Grade 11

The Physics of Electricity and Magnetism

This block gives students contact with powers that can be dangerous and challenges them to think about phenomena that are difficult to perceive. Both of these qualities prepare them for life experiences that are coming as they approach the end of adolescence.

There is some variation regarding the grade in high school in which Electricity and Magnetism are taught in physics, but I chose to teach it in grade eleven after Geology, Thermodynamics, and Mechanics. These topics are very interrelated and therefore previous material can be used in new lesson blocks. For example, the earth's magnetic field as it affects layers of rock was a key part of developing the idea of plate tectonics in Geology. Those ideas can be reviewed when magnetism is studied. Electricity and magnetism as phenomena have certain qualities that resonate with the point in development that children in grade eleven have reached. That is, they are beginning to think about what cannot be directly sensed and observed. As Sara wrote in her main lesson book:

> What is electricity? From natural observation alone that is a very hard question to answer. It is an invisible force that we can only see the effects of; it is also dangerous, powerful, and can be lethal. Electricity must be dealt with carefully.

Although we have no sense organs for electricity, it can be experienced to a certain extent. We began with recalling experiences with static electricity: children, after jumping on the trampoline and then sitting in a circle and touching fingers in sequence, can send a shock around the circle. Similarly, we can sense electricity when we get clothes out of the dryer in winter—or pet the cat in the dark. Sparks of light and little shocks can be directly perceived. And the sight of lightning is a vivid experience of electricity. As Sara wrote in her book:

> Looking at photographs of lightning, it reminds me of root tendrils or veins that branch off of one main stem. Although we most often see lightning striking from cloud to ground, it also dances cloud to cloud, and even sometimes ground to cloud. Lightning is also seen around volcanic eruptions.

Here, for contrast, is the beginning of her sister Claire's main lesson book on Electricity and Magnetism:

> Electricity surrounds us in the natural world, but usually we are unaware of it. (Unless there happens to be a lightning storm!)

One day out on our trampoline though, it was quite obvious, and I received many shocks. I noted my situation, and found several factors which were contributing to the thriving static electricity. Most importantly it was a cool, extremely dry day, and this, along with the fact that my wool socks were in constant friction with the woven plastic cloth of the trampoline, was causing the electricity to gather. My sister and I experimented with this phenomenon, discovering more of its nature. The most noticeable effect was that after jumping, our hair began to stand out from our heads. When this happened, we knew that if we touched each other, or the metal springs of the trampoline, a shock would occur. Also, we found that if a few people sat in a circle, a shock could by passed all the way around.

When I began my Electricity and Magnetism block, I recalled my experiences on the trampoline, and decided to make further observations. I had always thought that by jumping on the trampoline we caused it to create and store electricity, so that when a metal spring was touched it released a shock. This was not the case. After my sister and I jumped, my mother (who had not been jumping) touched the metal and nothing happened! Only my sister and I received shocks. Thus, we found that the trampoline was not the only thing affected by our jumping, we ourselves were affected. And it was the combination that caused a shock to result.

We can see interesting contrasts between these two descriptions. The first is more artistic, and the second a clear example of scientific thinking. Interestingly, Sara, the first writer, is now going into training for art therapy, and Claire, the second writer, is in veterinary school aiming to specialize in equine surgery. But what is similar is that both are describing effects of something only fleetingly perceptible. And, most importantly, the *location* of the phenomenon is unclear. This fact is the stepping-stone to the idea of fields, and the relation of fields to local effects.

But what does static electricity have to do with the "power" that lights our lamps, runs our appliances, and makes the car function? To get to the point of answering that question, we went through many carefully ordered experiments. We made systematic observations of materials with electrostatic properties, and then moved on to exploring ideas about "storing" electricity, and then we studied magnetism—and the differences and similarities between electricity and magnetism. I was careful to use neutral terms when describing the behavior of different materials, such as glass and resin after they have been rubbed with fur or cotton to bring out the polarities of attraction and repulsion. Terms such as "charge," "discharge," and "flow" do come in, but the teacher can keep them to a minimum. Terms such as "generators" and "capacitors" and "attraction" and "repulsion" are more neutral terms— and even more descriptive of what can be experienced. Lightning is a prototypical example of electricity in nature, which one hopes only to see and not feel. But it is possible to see how bright its light is, and how brief—and also something of its form, which is either branching or dendritic. In some of our experiments, especially with the van der Graaf generator, one seems to be in a field of disturbance, in which one's body hair responds to the field and radiates out. This seems to be a "signature" of electricity—a radiating field.

Magnetism also cannot be sensed directly, but it is not dangerous, except in some artificially enhanced situations, so it is somewhat easier to observe experimentally. Magnetism is more difficult to sense than electricity, but if one closes one's eyes and places a strong magnet on one side of the hand and a piece of metal on the other, one feels pressure akin to something pushing on the skin. In daily life we would not normally be aware of magnetism, although most children have played with magnets. We first built up observations of magnets in experiments with iron filings, to see the shape of the magnetic space. Magnets of different shapes and strengths showed different fields. And magnets interacted with each other in some ways similarly to electrostatically organized substances, that is, they showed attraction and repulsion. Then we worked with compasses to show that the whole earth is magnetized. We found the difference between astral and magnetic north, noting the difference between the sundial's reading and that of the compass. We then studied the *aurora borealis*—the northern lights—that sky phenomenon that corresponds to lightning but is related to magnetism. This phenomenon of undulating "curtains" of colored light occurs most strongly near the north pole in winter and seems to be related to earth's magnetic field. The usual speculation about its cause is that charged particles from the sun are interacting with the earth's magnetic field.

Steiner, however, in his lecture of October 13, 1923 (GA 351), says the lights are caused by electricity coming from the earth in the absence of sunlight. The point is to keep an open mind, and not to confuse theory and theoretical assumptions with fact. An ongoing and persistent effort is required!

History: The Background to Parzival

The indications for history in grade eleven show that it should cover the medieval period and be conjoined with the study of literature. I accomplished this in two ways. The first involved reading and assigning literature and history from the Middle Ages. The second involved concentrating on the history of the period leading up to and going into the ninth century in Europe and the Middle East. This led us into the study of *Parzival*, the epic poem by Wolfram von Eschenbach. Also, in conjunction with *Parzival*, we read about the late eleventh and early twelfth centuries, the period in which the poem was written.

Throughout the year, our reading at the end of the school day, or the reading I did out loud while the students worked on handwork, was from the medieval period. We began with a little-known German tale, *Gerhard the Good*, by Rudolf von Ems, who was a knight living in what is now Switzerland from 1200-1250. The hero of the tale is a knight, the son of a merchant, rather than the Emperor. The story's combination of historical description and legendary events, including interventions by angels, characterizes literature from the Middle Ages. *Gerhard the Good* consists of almost seven thousand rhymed verses in Middle High German, though I read a shortened, prose version by Rudolf Treichler (translated into English by Elizabeth Whyte). In the tale a successful but humble merchant tells of his rescue of English knights and tells of a Norwegian princess betrothed to the young English king. His moral judgment is tested twice: Should he trade all his goods to ransom the knights and the princess, even though he may never recover the money the goods are worth? And later, when the merchant's own son has married the princess because the English king was lost at sea, and the English king himself arrives at the reception, alive, should the merchant persuade his son to give up his love? This is a story of making difficult choices—and of looking to higher realms for inspiration.

Next, we read *The Return of Martin Guerre,* by Natalie Davis. This tale is a history of events from the early 1500s from a village in the hills west and south of Toulouse, in what is now southern France. The story provides a vivid picture of the life of well-off, agrarian peasants, living as they had for hundreds of years. The story has lost the aspects of legends, and deals instead with questions of individual identity. In the tale, Martin Guerre is betrothed and married as a boy to Bertrande, the daughter of a leading peasant family. When they marry, they live together, but not happily. After the birth of their son, Martin disappears without a trace. After eight years a man comes into the village and presents himself to Bertrande as her long-lost Martin Guerre. After this they live together and prosper, and love each other. He takes up his responsibilities and becomes respected in the village. But then the story develops a conflict when Martin asks Bertrande's uncle, the patriarch of the family, for an early inheritance of some land. Eventually Martin is brought to trial over this, as questions have arisen over whether he is the real Martin Guerre—or an imposter. Bertrande is caught between her love for him and her fear of God, as she seems to know that he is an imposter. She ends up testifying against him. Yet just as he is about to be acquitted anyway, the real Martin Guerre arrives in the courtroom. The imposter is then sentenced to death and executed by hanging. This leaves Bertrande inconsolable. This story brings up several important questions for students. What is true marriage? What is true goodness? These are questions people struggle with perennially. Also, the questions of identity versus false identity signal something important—a change in consciousness that arose at the beginning of the modern period that ended the Middle Ages.

Parzival is a story that may function to bring into modern times knowledge gained from an earlier stage of consciousness that otherwise would be lost. The events of the story are likely to have taken place in the ninth century, and, as I have said, the epic was written around 1100, at the end of the eleventh century. Historical events at both of those times would be important to understanding the setting of the poem as literature. Events in the ninth century include the origins of knighthood, the beginnings of powerful Frankish kings, and the eventual dominance of the Christian Church and the Holy Roman Empire, including interaction with the culture and religion of Islam in the East. There are several good sources for this material, including Stewart Easton's text *The Western Heritage: From the Earliest Times to the Present*, Charles

Figure 13: Sara's blackboard drawing of Parzival

Kovacs' *Parsifal and the Search for the Grail,* and Christoph Lindenberg's *Teaching History.*

The ninth century in Europe, from Britain through Russia, saw pagan migrations and invasions mixing with the beginnings of established Christianity. At the beginning of the ninth century, Charlemagne is crowned Emperor by Pope Leo III, and by the end of the century the Magyars have crossed the Carpathians into central Europe. The meeting of these two impulses forms the foundation for the origin of knighthood, which combines bravery and battle skill with an effort to control aggressive tendencies—and to show mercy and kindness. Here, Parzival as a character shows the development of an individual from an unlearned "nature" man of innocence, through a transitional period of doubt, and into his manifestations as an accomplished knight who is eventually purified by his own effort. This tale, along with those that tell of the Danish invasions of Britain and of the establishment of the court of Charlemagne, are full of stirring images that bring history to life for adolescents.

The eleventh century in Europe, at the end of which Eschenbach wrote *Parzival*, is characterized by the spread of Christianity and the Roman Church and the establishment of powerful kingdoms based on trade with the East. At the very end of this century the Crusades begin, which led to deeper interchanges of Western and Eastern culture. The Crusades were just beginning when *Parzival* was being written. Parzival, as a German knight, comes into direct contact with Firefiez, the Muslim knight. Brief accounts of the events of this century provide support for understanding the epic of *Parzival*.

The reason that *Parzival* is part of the curriculum for grade eleven is, once again, because of a parallel in consciousness between groups in the past and the individual in the present. Students in grade eleven are in between their childhood consciousness and what will become their adult consciousness. One would hope to somehow retain what was good about the openness and archetypal awareness of childhood into the more intellectual and rational period of young adult thinking. The epic shows this both in the character of Parzival as an individual and in the events of the whole story. It is noteworthy that we happened to be studying a Grimm's fairytale in German during the block on Parzival. The fairytale was "Der Sterntaler" ("Star Money"). We paraphrased in English the fairy tale's ending, in which "wealth comes down from the stars," as "wealth for the rest of her life." I then noted that the narrator of *Parzival* says that he got his story from someone who could read the stars. To this, Sara replied: "Parzival is wealth from the stars!" Yes!

Grade 12. I did not teach grade twelve at home, as both daughters chose to go into institutional schools for their last year of high school. I did, however, develop a lesson for grade twelve physics on colored shadows (see Appendix 2) and I taught that class lesson in Sara's grade twelve Waldorf school Physics block. We also had a completion ceremony at the end of grade eleven for each student, and for one of these I made a school-leaving speech that covered the whole arc of school up to that point (see Appendix 3). So although I did not teach the curriculum for grade twelve, I studied it, and I watched both daughters deal with the last year of high school and prepare for what was coming.

Conclusion. The Waldorf curriculum matches and challenges children's development at each stage and provides the possibility of practicing what is learned repeatedly at newer and higher levels. Rhythms of day, week, month, year, and whole school life are nested within longer and longer stretches of time. And over the course of this nesting, certain larger rhythms emerge. The time of kindergarten through grade three has a quiet, almost celebratory openness to it that ends with a real "coming down to earth" in the nine-year change. Mirroring this, grades ten, eleven, and twelve show a kind of opening up to the wider world and a "growing out" of a relatively known and familiar place—into something new.

Another overarching rhythm is that of the spiral. Several times the same material is returned to at a new and higher level in the curriculum. For example, grade five covers the ancient cultures in story and image, whereas grade ten covers these same cultures in the context of time, history, and the beginnings of analytic thinking. Five years after grade ten some students are in college, thinking critically about historical analyses. (Would that a Waldorf curriculum could be developed for students into their twenties!) Another rhythmic form is the great circle. Whereas touch is such an important sense to the youngest children in kindergarten and grade one, the sense of the awareness of another individual, another I, begins to be important to those in grade twelve. In between, students have been cumulatively developing all their twelve senses (see Steiner's *A Psychology of Body, Soul, and Spirit*). These overarching forms of rhythms can help the teacher place herself in the "geography" of time, and, thus, have a better sense of where she is and where she is going in her work of enthusiastically teaching these supremely changeable beings.

CHAPTER SEVEN

From Kindergarten to Grade Twelve: Growing New Faculties

Growing is a process that we all experience through our whole lifetime, but this force is strongest at the youngest ages. As we "grow up," the growth of the physical body transforms into the growth of faculties and abilities, and these never stop growing. As a teacher of children from kindergarten through grade eleven (with some work in grade twelve), I gradually realized that each grade seemed to involve its own type of challenge that the child would have to meet and get through. Because I taught each grade twice, I did, at a certain point, have an idea of what to prepare for. And I also was privileged to see how two very different children met those same challenges, given their different temperaments and destinies.

Core Challenges for Each Grade
 Kindergarten: structured daily life. Kindergarten at home is a gradual transition from rhythmic family life to time spent specifically with the teacher and other students in a new rhythm to the day. This includes stories (fairy tales and nature stories) and artistic activities (painting, drawing, and modeling). So, the main task for the kindergarten child is to come into a rhythm that is set by the teacher, and which goes beyond the usual daily life rhythms. It can take the whole year to accomplish this joining with rhythm. Engaging in circle movement activities and music, listening to stories, and doing creative art activities all require a certain amount of concentration and exercise of the will. If the adult in these situations does not hold the child very carefully and attentively, the demands can be beyond her level of attention. If that happens, the

teacher has to shift the activity to allow the child to participate. If the teacher cannot do that, the rhythm can literally spin out—and the form of the kindergarten day can fall apart.

In our school, we had structured "in-house" school days only three days a week. The Nature Day on Mondays—free exploration outdoors— prepared the students to attend and concentrate on the next three days. The last day of the week was lessons away from home or time with other children and families. By calling these days "school days" I let the girls know that there would be a certain rhythm to the day and they would be called on to participate. Everyone took this seriously. But four-, five-, and six-year-olds might not want to walk in a circle while singing, or sit still to listen, or take up the paints. But over time and with steady persistence on the part of the teacher, the rhythm of school can be established. Taking Mondays as an exploring day was a great transition for me as a teacher, too, because I didn't have to present material and hold class all day, and instead could take time with them in nature—and prepare mentally for the school days to come. The time outdoors did me good, too. My intention to provide what we all needed helped me to "stick with the program." When Claire was in kindergarten, Sara was just in a pack on my back, or playing nearby as we did school. Yet sometimes Claire, the kindergartner, did not want to take the walk to the arroyo where they would explore and play; sometimes she resisted going out for our exploring day. To this I just chose to say, "No, this is school, and this is what we are doing." She would then get going and would soon be involved in following a stream or making a "house" with her little sister—or perhaps playing in the mud. The challenge was to stay with the rhythm, but it was well worth it. By the time Sara was in kindergarten, Claire was in grade two and I was coordinating two sets of challenges.

At this young age, children are not self-conscious and are only beginning to think. In joining in with a daily rhythm, the child develops the ability to "breathe"—in the larger sense. This is the breathing back and forth of waking and sleeping, of inhaling and exhaling, of concentrating and dreaming, and of being outer-focused and inner-focused. All these ways of breathing are strengthening—for the physical body that is still growing and developing and for the soul that needs rhythmic engagement and disengagement from the world. And all this strength and health is needed for the more intellectual challenges to come.

Grade 1: Initiation into structure. Grade one is the first time that the children are expected to fit into the structured school day and week and season. Children after age seven are generally ready for this experience, but such an integration of the child into the structure of circle, main lesson, movement, handwork, and art lessons is not achieved in a day. Learning to fit with other people and with the school day is a process; it develops over the course of at least the first half of the year in grade one. Different children meet this challenge in different ways, partly depending on their temperaments. But for every child, they are becoming a member of a purposeful group that has a pathway to a certain point in time and to a level of development. The teacher is the guide on this path, but the student must walk it, step by step.

My older daughter, Claire, with her strong tendencies toward the melancholic temperament, took school very seriously. Even on the first day of first grade she knew that she was now a "Grader," and that she would have new responsibilities and that more would be asked of her than had been before. And her choleric side made her unable to resist a challenge. So she was determined to do well, and to be the leader of her younger sister. She was, and is, also a morning person, with her circadian rhythms lending her mental clarity in the morning. She only had to sit still and concentrate for thirty minutes in the morning three days a week, and only after fun and enlivening rhythmic physical activities. Claire was up for this challenge and joined school readily. She had been wanting to read and she took immediately to the letters and numbers. She loved the fairy tales and the handwork, and she was good at eurythmy and music. My challenge as a teacher was to be sure that the rhythm held and that no one was overstimulated or tired. The choleric temperament, combined with very active and open senses, easily leads to tantrums and breakdowns. But our small group at home and plenty of quiet time was a real benefit.

In contrast, Sara—with her sanguine temperament, and after two years in kindergarten—seemed to "float" into first grade. She listened to her older sister on the first day of school when she said, fiercely: "This is serious! This is school now; it's not playing around!" But Sara was very butterfly-like in her attention, with it lighting here and there and not staying any one place for very long. She loved drawing, so the letters and numbers as they emerged out of natural forms and actions kept her attention. And her imagination was so alive that the fairy tales captured her, no matter how many times we told them or acted them out. She also adored her older sister, which provided a kind of gravity that drew her into the school structure and work.

No matter the temperament of the child, when they turn seven, they are at the point of completing an important cycle—the transformation of the most mineral part of the body, that is, the skeleton. This is evidenced by the preponderance of permanent teeth that have pushed their way out in the gums. In a way the child has come into their own in their body, and is now ready to engage the outer world in a new way. The cycles of transformation will continue, and the seven-year cycles will continue, but this point in development means that children are capable of joining in activities that require some thinking, and of coordinating themselves with others a little more consciously than before.

And the new faculty? By fitting into a structured day that includes some beginnings of thinking and written sign-making, children develop the beginnings of self-control—the ability to wait to do something they want, and the ability to do something they don't feel like doing right then. In an accumulation of moments of self-control in order to "stay with" a structured school day, the higher self of the child very gradually begins to manifest. And this self-control will eventually become self-direction. This nascent ability will be critical in facing life on earth.

Grade 2: The best and the worst. Grade two continues a very similar structure and mood to grade one. The routine is similar and the mood of the fifth is held. But there is a major change in the stories of the curriculum, from the fairy tales to the stories of the saints and to Aesop's fables, where animals represent human qualities and human social situations. The stories of the saints are not presented in a religious context, but as stories of human beings who face extreme challenges by strengthening their best qualities and, thereby, giving to others. They are not hero stories, but, rather, stories of transformation from weakness to strength, no matter the particular context. But because the stories are very specific to time and place and to the qualities of the saints and their actions, the tales are very rich imaginatively and figuratively. They capture the children's attention, reverence, and awe. On the other hand, and the contrast is purposeful, the stories of Aesop cast human weakness in terms of animal characters, actions, and moods. The curriculum for grade two specifies stories of these two types; the particular stories are up to the individual teacher's choice.

In our case, for both girls, the grade two play was a narrative from a saint's life, so they dressed and acted out, with others, these scenes. This made the story very real for them! Claire's play was about St. Clare, the companion to St. Francis of Assisi. The story was about how Clare came to devote herself to Christian service. In one scene Clare was given the plain monastic robe, instead of her beautiful clothes, in a small chapel by St. Francis. When I drew this scene on the blackboard so Claire could put it in her main lesson book, she asked, "Wasn't the altar against the wall?" I didn't know how altars were constructed at that time, so I couldn't answer. But when I looked it up, I found that the altars in the early medieval chapels *were* against the wall. The imagination of these events had been very vivid for Claire. When we performed the play for family and friends, there was a hush in the room afterwards, and the audience didn't want to leave the room. In the month or so before we performed the play (which was done at the end of grade two, in May), Claire said two things that are closely related to the two paths shown in this grade. I always ended the school day with a verse that said:

> In every seed that will be a tree
> There lives an image of all it will be.
> When I find the image of all I can be,
> Then I will be free.

After listening to that, Claire said, "What if I am bad?" Good question! And it wasn't a question a younger child would normally think to ask. I just smiled and changed the verse to "The best that I can be," and left it that way for the rest of younger grades. A little later she was talking to a friend about what one sees in the mirror. She said that you can't see yourself, to which he replied that you could. To this she replied, "Not your *real* self."

This consciousness of the physical and nonphysical realms is the beginning of waking up to incarnation on earth—the earth where the animals are, and where we have animal tendencies. So Aesop's fables form a polar opposite to the stories of the saints, and the blocks on these two topics alternate through the year. Aesop's fables are not nature stories; they are morality tales in which the lower tendencies and emotions of human beings are shown by using the appropriate animals as protagonists. "The Fox and the Grapes" is about greed and rationalization, "The Wolf and the Heron" is about helping others only because it benefits you, and so forth. In hearing and writing these stories, children see the consequences of the emotions and actions that are not ideal, or based on ideals. I never explicitly stated a moral with a fable; the feelings, actions, and results were obvious. I made "The Wolf and the Heron" into a verse, thus:

> The Wolf in his greed
> Swallowed a bone, and it stuck!
> He went looking for relief,
> And found a Heron, what luck!
> The Wolf offered the bird a fee
> To remove the bone and
> The Heron put his head in
> Pulled out the bone, and said:
> "I've succeeded! Give me my reward."
> "What?" said the Wolf
> "Your head is free,
> Safe out of the Wolf's mouth
> And you also want a fee?"

Claire's comment after hearing this story was that the Wolf letting the Heron go *was* the fee, and he shouldn't ask for more. Here she was entering into the Wolf's thinking. This alternating immersion first in the saint's lives and then in the "lower," more animalistic urges serves to show the young child two opposite human tendencies, and, in a way, two possible ways of being. When presented to children of around eight years old, these stories function just to illustrate. But this contrast of higher and lower qualities is a preparation for the changes that will happen at ages nine to ten when children become much more aware of earthly life, and of their being on earth. But when children are around age seven, they do not yet have to choose a way of being. Yet in grade two they are shown very concretely, as a kind of preparation, two very divergent paths through life.

By facing the difference between the animalistic and the saintly, children develop some intimations of being able to restrain their own "animalistic" sides and to see how the saintly can be an ideal. Ideals are beyond us, but they lead us in the right direction.

Grade 3: Choose a path, keep choosing the good one. The curriculum for grade three revolves around the Old Testament and the practical activities of farming and gardening—and the math here focuses on measurement, again very practical. The Old Testament stories describe a people constantly seeking and trying to communicate with their God, and repeatedly falling away and being chastised. In Genesis the communication with God is direct: the human being is created and shown the Garden, and given the rules of conduct. But after the separation of the sexes, one of the human beings, Eve, listens to a different divine being and acts in order to expand her awareness—an act that oversteps the rules. She also enlists Adam in the act, and, consequently, both are driven from the Garden to live in pain and toil. This story captures the soul experiences of young children undergoing the "nine-year change"— in which consciousness for the physical, material, earthly world, and for other people in that world, sharpens and awakens. An earlier "at-oneness" consciousness is fading and an awareness of one's self, and therefore, of one's self as separate from the world, is awakening. The stories of people who are gradually leaving paradise and learning to live with each other on earth mirror the child's changing consciousness. This mirroring affirms for the children that the teacher understands what they are experiencing and shows them that she wants to support them. Just telling the stories, remembering them, making drawings of scenes and events from them, and writing in the main lesson book is ongoing support and affirmation.

When I read the story of paradise and the expulsion from the Garden of Eden to Sara in October of her grade three, I got the strong impression that she knew the story was true. Also, both times I taught the story of Noah and the ark, a lightning and thunderstorm was whirling outside, with lashing rain, even though such storms rarely happen in Southern California. I don't know what to make of that, except that the particular context certainly deepened the experience of the story.

For both girls the play for grade three was our adaptation and simplification of the Paradise Play from the Oberufer cycle. This medieval

German play tells in verse form and with songs the story of the second chapter of Genesis, which includes the differentiation of male and female, Adam and Eve's time in the Garden, their eating from the Tree of Knowledge of Good and Evil, and their expulsion from the Garden by the cherubim with a flaming sword who stands guard against their untimely return. This play seems to encapsulate the challenges of grade three, like a forewarning of what is coming with the change of consciousness of ages nine to ten, when children become much more aware of earthly life. In a way, this play captures the essence of grade three.

The first time we did this play, when Claire was in grade three, I was the cherubim and Claire was Eve. We were working with another homeschool family on this play, and a grade five girl played Adam. That girl's mother played the Devil and Claire's father was God. At the point where Eve is driven from the Garden, Claire turned back and looked fiercely at the avenging angel (and I was the receiver of that look) as if to say with determination, "I will return!" This is a certain path through life: fierce determination. When it was Sara's turn to be Eve three years later, we had moved to the East Coast and were working with a different set of families. This time Claire was the cherubim (a continuation of fierceness) and Sara was Eve. (A boy her age was Adam, his mother was the Devil, and Sara's father was again God). I played lyre music for the singing. We began this play with singing and playing a mood-of-the-fifth song, because the play begins in the Garden, in a certain expanded, heavenly consciousness. But it ends with a very different consciousness, with Adam and Eve having been driven from Paradise. Sara did not look back when she left the Garden. Reflecting on this, one could say that Snow White took the expulsion from Paradise very differently than did Rose Red. Sara is twenty-five now, and when I recently asked her what she remembered from that play, she said, "The angel."

So, after being immersed alternately in the animals of the fables and the lives of the saints in grade two, the students in grade three hear about the need for continual effort toward the good—in the context of working the earth out of necessity and responsibility. Building a structure requires hard work and is not done in a day. The same is true of tending a garden, preparing seeds during the winter for spring planting, and taking care of animals. All of these situations present opportunities for selfishness or the opposite—working for others. The strength to try again, and to keep trying, can begin to develop at this time. The teacher who values trying over achieving gives the children the possibility of a valuable, lifelong model.

Grade 4: Face evil. Grade four is the time when most students turn nine and go into the transition that will end with a more adult consciousness, that is, a more earthly awareness. One adult described an experience she had as a nine-year-old that expresses this change quite eloquently. She remembers sitting on a large rock at the edge of the sea, wearing a yellow bathing suit on a sunny day, and enjoying the summer air and light. At a certain moment, she felt a change and she described it as "all the color draining away" from the sky, from her suit, from everything. After that moment, the world was grayer and less alive. Not everyone one has such a momentary and vivid awareness of the change of consciousness around age ten. For most the change is more gradual, but is still a necessary step in the child's changing consciousness as they grow up. Grade four includes in the curriculum the stories and poems of the Norse myths, which were sung and then written down in a clear four-to-one rhythm. For example, the beginning of the *Poetic Edda*, the rune "Voluspa," which is a prophecy by a seeress, goes thus (in an English translation from the Old Icelandic, Hollander, 1962):

> Hear me, all ye hallowed beings,
> Both high and low of Heimdall's children:
> Thou wilt, Valfather, that I well set forth
> The fates of the world which as first I recall.

And the *Kalevala* of Finland begins:

> I am wanting I am thinking
> To arise and go forth singing
> Sing my song and say my sayings
> Hymns ancestral harmonizing.

These rhythms performed in swaying, stepping, speaking, and ball passing, several times over the course of the school year, can help children to establish rhythms of circulation and breathing that allow a more waking and centered consciousness than they have had so far in their childhood. But this consciousness is not just more awake, but more aware of earthly life, which includes forces that counter growth and development—and could even be termed evil. The content of the Norse myths, even when taken at the level appropriate for fourth graders, deals with evil beings that must be faced and countered—for example, the Fenris Wolf in the *Edda*, and the witch of the north in the *Kalevala*. And the Norse myths explicitly end with a type of apocalypse called the Twilight of the Gods. In this Twilight, called *Ragnarök*, many of the gods die and the world is all but destroyed. As images of changes in consciousness, they are quite powerful. And these images are something that the children can very much live in and learn from. The good path isn't always an easy one.

By the time I was teaching grade four for the first time, it started to dawn on me that each grade held a certain challenge for the children, and that, as teacher, I had the role of trying to be conscious about the challenge, and of helping the children meet it. But it is difficult to see an event or a development before it is complete, which only happens toward the end of the year. And children of very different temperaments and destinies meet the challenges in very different ways. So, I was often just working hard to keep up. However, the second time I taught a grade I was a little more prepared—and felt that I was better at practicing the art of teaching. One cannot predict, of course, what will happen in a coming grade, as each child and classroom is unique, and life is an ongoing play of actions and influences, but one can be a little prepared and observant as life in school progresses.

Evil, meanwhile, is a fraught subject—but one that is denied only at one's peril. Personal details are not relevant here, but I did notice, looking back on the two times I taught grade four, that those were the years when we had the most intense social challenges within our group of homeschooling families. Evil often has the face of deception—and children must become able to discern a trick or a lie. Again, this is hard work that extends through one's life, but the stories of Loki, the trickster, and Odin, who poses as a traveling peasant to question and instruct individual farmers, are very educational. There is a difference between a mystery (something hidden for a progressive reason) and a lie (something hidden for nefarious reasons). As children change in their consciousness of the outer surroundings, they begin to encounter lies and mysteries, and true stories about the difference can help them develop discernment. Steiner suggests that the task of our current cultural age is to confront and understand evil (see Steiner, *Inner Impulses of Evolution*).

Grade 5: Face death. The curriculum in grade five covers the ancient cultures through Greece, mostly in terms of legends and myths. It ends with the somewhat historical time of Greek philosophy, embodied by Plato and Socrates. The challenge for grade five turned out to be the facing of death, which, if one thinks about it, only happens on earth. After teaching the Indian and Persian ancient stories and cultural achievements, I next taught the ancient Sumerian *Epic of Gilgamesh*. In this epic, Gilgamesh, who is two-thirds god and one-third human and is the king of the city-state, becomes close friends with an outsider, Enkidu. Enkidu is eventually "humanized" and lives in the city until he is killed after the two friends anger the goddess Tiamat. Up to this point Gilgamesh has not known death; it is a great mystery to him. In the great pain of missing Enkidu, he goes in search of his friend, even if it means going into the underworld. This story of a great figure who is part human resonates with present-day children who have passed the nine-year change. Gilgamesh seeks Utnapishtim for advice in traveling in the underworld; Utnapishtim is ancient and immortal and comes from the time before the flood. Gilgamesh does go into the underworld, meets Enkidu, tries to bring him back, and does not succeed. This is a story that teaches about mortality on earth, which fifth graders are waking up to.

In our case, one of our daughters in grade five gradually stopped eating most foods for six weeks, until she realized that if she were to stay with us she would have to eat. This became almost a destiny choice: understanding life on earth and consumption of food—and everything that this entails. The other daughter got Lyme disease the summer before grade five (I also developed symptoms) and took antibiotics as well as alternative therapies. Lyme disease is an encounter with an extremely "cold" illness, and the antibiotics only enhanced that aspect. In both cases, physical well-being was severely tested.

In each year the birthday verses are given to help the child meet the core challenge of the grade. For the one who began to withdraw from life on earth, I gave the prologue to the John Gospel (based on the version rendered by Jon Madsen) as her birthday verse. So, after mid-November every school day during the circle, she would walk toward me, balancing on a low balance beam, and when she reached me, the teacher, she would recite:

> In the beginning was the Word,
> And the Word was with God,
> And the Word was a divine Being.
> He was in the very beginning with God.
> All things were made by him,
> And without him was not anything made
> That was made.
> In him was life,
> And the life was the light of human beings.
> And the light shines in the darkness;
> And the darkness accepted it not.
> Of his fullness have we all received grace upon grace.

And when it was time for grade five for the other daughter, she also would recite to me after walking on the balance beam. She had a very different, but also supportive, verse (based on a First Nation text):

> In beauty may I walk.
> All day long may I walk.
> Through the returning seasons may I walk.
> Beautifully will I possess again
> Beautifully birds
> Beautifully joyful birds
> On the trail marked with pollen may I walk
> With grasshoppers about my feet may I walk.
> With dew about my feet may I walk.
> With beauty may I walk.
> With beauty before me may I walk.
> With beauty behind me may I walk.
> With beauty above me may I walk.
> With beauty all around me may I walk.
> In old age, wandering on a trail of beauty, lively, may I walk.
> It is finished in beauty.
> It is finished in beauty.

So, in one case, grace, and in the other, beauty, is there to strengthen and support the child in their tenth year. The faculties they develop through experiences such as these relate to facing the reality of life on earth now and still continuing to make the choice to be here—to be incarnated on earth now.

Grade 6: Face beginnings of own destiny. In this grade, children are eleven turning twelve and are on a threshold, a doorway, looking out on their own particular destiny. They are about to take the first steps on their individual path. The curriculum includes the first steps into *history*—from myth and legend. Specifically, they are taught the history of the founding and development of the Roman Empire. The founding of Rome, known only from legend, took place at the beginning of the zodiacal age of Aries, 747 BC, which makes it contemporaneous with the time of Homer in Greece. But Rome has a completely different character and historical trajectory than Greece, so why study Roman history in the year children turn twelve? At the end of history in grade five, the curriculum comes to Socrates, to individuality, and to individual conscience and the expression of individuality in social form, that is, of democracy. What comes next in the child's consciousness is the awareness of social rules and "laws" with which they must reckon in their individuality. In one of our astronomy lessons in grade six with Claire, I illustrated how the stars move across the sky at night—as viewed from the earth. I did this by moving my arms in parallel, as if pointing at two stars and following their movement. When I said, "The stars move together, in parallel lines, they don't go every which way," and I moved my arms at all angles, Claire laughed and said, "That would be a riot! They have to have some rules, like the cars on the roads." In Roman times, the old theocracy that regulated society became separated into two parts: religion and rights. Thinking became more abstract, and the idea of rights and the correlated idea of citizenship became possible (see Steiner, *Rethinking Economics*). The corresponding change for eleven- and twelve-year-olds in our time is the awareness that they have their own path through life, but it must be coordinated with the social forms in which they live.

We did not experience particular crises in grade six, either time, but the mood was more one of preparation for something that would be coming in the future. The image of the twelve-year-old Jesus in the

Temple, a child suddenly imbued with wisdom, was very helpful to me as the teacher of children turning twelve.

The last day of school, the school assembly day for grade six, included a ceremony in which the sixth grader was prepared for the coming year, which would cover the Middle Ages, by being made a "squire," a person to support a knight. The student knelt while the teacher, holding a sword, recited the verse that follows, and then tapped the student on each shoulder with the sword and declared her a Squire.

> Let me behold thine inmost life, o world...
> Let me pierce slowly through the senses' seeming...
> As, in a house, brightness is slow unfurled
> Until the rays of day wing through it streaming –
> And then, as if this house could sacrifice
> Even its roof and walls to heaven's gleaming –
> So that at last, gold-brimming, it might rise
> Wholly transfused, a spirit-building, standing
> Like to a monstrance, radiant spirit-wise.
> So also might my rigid walls, expanding,
> Let thy full life find entry into mine,
> And, unto thy life my full life remanding,
> Let life in life twine purely, mine and thine.
>   (Christian Morgenstern, translation Sophia Walsh)

The ideal for grade six is that the children grow in stature and wisdom because they are becoming more internally integrated. The saintly and the animal become more differentiated and, at the same time, more integrated; also, so do the light and the dark, the waking and sleeping, the focused and the diffuse, and the self-focus and the other-focus. This integration, certainly, is just beginning, as are the other abilities, but the beginning is critical. What is beginning as integration and new abilities of judgment will, according to Steiner, come to a fruition at age fourteen (see his *Education for Adolescents* and *Life of the Human Soul*).

Grade 7: *Becoming more conscious of own destiny on earth*. A progression from the Chemistry block at the beginning of grade seven, the first time I taught it, is representative of a core theme and challenge of the grade. In our observations of materials, we moved from how they participate in fire processes (burning), to water processes (dissolving), to earth processes (solidification, condensation, crystallization). This mirrors the progress of the human soul as it is incarnating on earth. Here is a conversation Claire and I had in the lesson regarding crystallized salt, in our case large blocks of sodium chloride:

> Teacher: Do you remember what the salt looked like?
> Claire: It's a block.
> Teacher: Yes, and transparent.
> Claire: It's hard. Is this earth?
> Teacher: Yes! We've had fire and then water and then earth. What's happening there?
> Claire: It's becoming more material.
> Teacher: Yes, more dense.

In this way the chemistry lessons, which depend on the direct observation of the transformation of materials, mirror something the child is experiencing inwardly about themselves. They are becoming more dense and more focused on the earthly life around them, and beginning to make judgments about that life. An image that might capture this transition or transformation is the difference between the almost aerial, diffuse view in Breugel's scenes of agrarian life, and the point-centered perspective paintings that emerged later in the Renaissance. Young children have a diffuse consciousness that takes in what is all around them, but only rarely focuses for long on one point. Adolescents are beginning to develop that "pointed" consciousness.

The sword became somewhat of a theme for grade seven the first time I taught it. For years as part of the Michaelmas festival we had a small play, in which one of the children would use a wooden sword to fight and subdue the "dragon"—an adult in a large, green mantle—while other children helped. But now, in grade seven, the child who fought the dragon got to use a real sword—one that was metal and large and heavy! It was also very effective against the large and scary dragon! The sword is traditionally an image of intellect and incisive thinking. And Steiner (in *Michaelmas and the Human Soul Forces*) shows that realistic thinking about the beings of the earth and their relation to the cosmos is what is required to be developed, especially as part of a true Michaelmas festival. The dragon is a picture of certain types of beings that the human soul must face and overcome or subdue, and acting out these images can be a powerful support in young students' development. The importance of Michaelmas, which takes place in the autumn, has to do with the shift from nature-consciousness in spring and summer to the possibility of a self-awakening to a spirit consciousness.

Then, in the spring, the sword came in again in the grade seven play on the life of Joan of Arc, the young woman who miraculously led the French to expel the English from the Continent in 1403. Here the sword is a tool of a warrior to show strength. In the Joan of Arc play it was now Claire who held the sword in a kind of mirror image of the archangel who, in grade three, had guarded paradise with a flaming sword. Now four years later, at age thirteen, the student faces the world with the sword, and must develop her intellect and her determination.

The second time we held grade seven, for Sara, the chosen play was adapted from the "Knight's Tale" in Chaucer's *Canterbury Tales*. Here, the sword and battle are not the focus; instead, courtly love is the theme. The story is a medieval adaptation of one from ancient Greece which was then used in a Latin poem—about two brothers vying for the hand of a princess. The story provides adolescent students an ideal of selfless love. This is a time when they might become overwhelmed by the physiological changes in their bodies and succumb to the tendency to be focused only on themselves. The ideal is just that, something to provide a positive influence, but not necessarily an experience of everyday life. Grade seven also includes lessons on human physiology, including all physiological systems, e.g., reproduction. Materials from Waldorf education can be very helpful here, as they go beyond the typical mechanical models of the body (for example, see Walther Buhler's *Living with Your Body*).

As children experience changes in their bodies, and in their consciousness of the world around them, they develop the new faculty of consciousness of their own particular destiny. They sense their own interests and what attracts them, what steps feel "right." And they may begin to develop the determination to continue on their own path.

Grade 8: Trusting one's own senses. As part of developing interest in the surrounding world, students must come to trust their own senses. And one area of school lessons is focused on just this point—the science blocks. The science taught and practiced in the Waldorf curriculum differs from mainstream materialist science specifically in its emphasis on direct experience with nature. This is the phenomenological approach to science in which the student-scientist learns to systematically make observations of natural phenomena, consciously choosing to postpone hypotheses or speculations about causes or histories to the phenomena. (For more see H. Bortoft's *Taking Appearance Seriously*.) Perception can be more and more complete and systematic with careful effort—and this is what has been taught in Waldorf science from the beginning. But in adolescence, when the intellect is "waking up," observation can become more conscious and accurate if students are guided in developing certain abilities. So, the challenge of grade eight is to build up—over time and with patience and interest—an awareness of certain natural phenomena.

    I will describe our Acoustics block in physics as an example of developing nature consciousness through systematic observation and, therefore, at the same time developing an inner consciousness. Autumn is the time that these two types of awareness are in transition and can be in balance. We started with the translated Greek root words for *physics* and *acoustics*, that is, "pertaining to nature" and "pertaining to hearing," respectively. Then our first observations were with the Chladni plates, which are thin metal plates balanced so they are free to vibrate. We scattered a small amount of very fine sand in a thin layer over the plate and then carefully moved an old violin bow vertically, touching the edge of the plate. If you are lucky and everything works, a tone sounds and a geometric pattern forms in the sand! Higher tones were associated with more distinct forms. Also, drawing the forms into a physics lab notebook helps the student become fully involved in the form, and this is similar to what we did at younger ages with form drawing. It is important not to jump to the conclusion or speculation, however, that the tone *causes* the form in the sand. All we know at this point is that they co-occur. The teacher stays open in her thinking and, therefore, keeps alive for the student the possibility of open thinking related to formative force and matter. That is, we do not assume in the beginning that all of existence is material. But we also do not speculate about unperceivable "forces" called on to explain observations. Teaching physics is walking a tightrope in the current day and age!

    The next step was to make observations with tuning forks and stringed musical instruments. I used a set of chromatic tuning forks from middle C to one octave above, plus one tuning fork for lower C (128 hertz). I was careful to say that the sound or tone can be there when the fork vibrates. We held a vibrating fork to the body of a lyre and listened to the body resound. We also noticed which strings sounded slightly (those of the same tone, the same tone in octaves, and the overtones). These studies help the student to coordinate their perceptions of sound with the visual rhythm of waves that are related to pitch and loudness. Then we used the lower C tuning fork against a container of water and on a plate darkened with smoke. The latter two demonstrations make visible the vibrations that we previously had only heard. These observations of tone can be recalled and built on when one comes to the grade eleven History through Music block. Finally, we went on to optics—mirror observations and studies with light through a pinhole or crescent-shaped hole to observe that both the light and shadow forms are cast. The laws of reversal in the mirror and of shadows can be drawn out of these observations and gradually arrived at by the student. Thus, they are thinking actively, but only and especially in the context of directly observing phenomena in nature in a systematically built-up manner. The students gradually become aware that they can observe carefully, and that they will experience new and fascinating phenomena. They often see something that the teacher has missed and so they come to trust their own potential. This provides them a start on the lifelong road of learning to discern actual phenomena from speculations, pronouncements, and assumptions.

I always experienced the teaching of physics as a time of clarity and certainty in dealing with the world—a welcome relief from the complexity and ambiguity of the humanities. But nearing the end of the Physics block I would begin to feel the "dryness" of it, and be ready for the richness and linguistic aspects of the literary blocks. I'm sure the students sensed the same rhythm, to some degree, and drew strength from the alternation between physical solidity and clarity versus human complexity and richness.

This is the year the students turn fourteen, and therefore have completed their second seven-year cycle. They are solidly into adolescence and their perceptions and consciousness are changing. They are moving out of the stage of looking up to authorities and into the stage of needing to, and of being able to, *choose* who will be an authority for them. And, further, they can now begin to make their own judgments and depend on them. Judgment is developing, and judgment is a function of feeling. As odd as it sounds, Steiner describes how we think concepts with our heads, judge with our hearts and arms, and conclude with our feet (Steiner, June 14, 1921). While this system is developing, adolescents are undergoing extreme changes in the relation of the soul with the physical and etheric bodies, especially in relation to the heart (Steiner, May 26, 1922).

Some teachers may also find the image of the twelve-year-old Jesus in the temple very important at this time. (In his lectures on the Gospel of Saint Luke, Steiner describes how what took place at age twelve at the time of the events in the New Testament now takes place more likely at age fourteen). Luke 2:41 describes the twelve-year-old Jesus child as he went with his parents to Jerusalem for Passover (David Hart, translator). His parents "returned to Jerusalem looking for him. And it happened that after three days they found him in the Temple, sitting amid the teachers, both listening to them and posing them questions; And those listening to him were astonished at his intelligence and at his responses. And seeing him they (his parents) were struck with wonder… And he went down with them and came to Nazareth, and was obedient to them. And his mother treasured all these sayings in her heart. And Jesus progressed in wisdom and age and favor before God and men (sic)." The ideal is that young people, who are feeling the first stirrings of adolescence should progress in "wisdom and age and favor." Perhaps the teacher holding this thought and image can support their development. The effects of the developments that take place at this age may not be clear until later, even years later, but there is the potential at this age for the student to begin to be more internally integrated and to wake up to their intelligence and the power of their own choices. The other possibility is that this integration does not have a good beginning at this age, and has to be worked on more at a later time.

To sum up the two seven-year stages from grades one to eight, I would like to quote from a lecture by Steiner (June 19, 1921):

> The effect (of a free relationship between teacher and students) will be the students' healthy growth into the *true* that was given to them by the spiritual world as a kind of inheritance, so that they can merge with, grow together with the *beautiful* in the right way,

so that they can learn the *good* in the world of the senses, the good they are to develop and bring to expression during their lives.

Grade 9: Challenges to physical body, deal with injury. In grade nine the students are fifteen and beginning their third seven-year period of life. The integration of the I and the soul into the living physical body continues. At this age and grade there are often extreme experiences with the physical body, even injuries, that interrupt the wholeness of the individual—and require healing. Wholeness and healing are themes at this age. In some ways this process of injury down to the level of the physical, especially of the bones, allows for the body to become more individualized by and for the I. When Sara, our younger daughter, returned from a week-long camp for homeschooled children in the mountains of Vermont in the fall of her ninth grade, she said: "I like people who have school at home. They're more individual."

That year Sara hurt her wrist and her leg. Healing is a process in time in which the organism regains its wholeness after an insult. But the whole is also changed in some ways, in its own form and organization (see van der Bie's *The Healing Process*). Healing is a four-phase phenomenon—recovering the integrity of the organism, allowing the wound region to interact with the rest of the organism, recovering lost tissue in wound area, and recovering the original form of the organism. These phases are "orchestrated" by the self-regulation of the body and the organ of repair. These are all processes in time, and fit the metaphor of music quite well.

A healed injury can be seen as an opportunity for a child to "individualize" their living physical body, to make it more "their own" and more compatible with soul and spirit. An injury in grade nine is not necessary to the work that year, clearly. And grade nine is not the only time in which there will be injuries. But an injury then, when the young adolescent is becoming more conscious of time, can be of particular importance. One of our early blocks in grade nine with Sara was History through Art, which concentrated on visual art. At the beginning of the block we briefly remembered what we could of history from previous years. I brought out that before history, there was prehistory, that is, artifacts from civilizations from which we have no writing. I then asked: "What is the opposite of history?" This question led to a discussion about time. Sara said: "Time isn't our measurement of it—it is something real.

When you think about it, it is freaky. I don't want to think about it!" I gradually built up to the idea that eternity is the opposite of history, and that very slowly human beings have been "coming out of" eternity and into time. (When Sara was four and a half she said to me: "I know the difference between infinity and eternity." I said: "Oh! Okay, what is the difference?" She replied, moving her hand and arm as though to throw something, almost as if to temporarily join a line that continued behind and in front of her: "This is infinity." And then she said, while lying down to grab her toes with her fingers in order make her body into a circle, "This is eternity." So at that young age she knew that infinity had to do with movement and eternity with stillness!) We then went over the cosmic facts of the position of the rising sun on the spring equinox in relation to the zodiac, and the precession of the equinox, that is, the rising sun's moving "backward" through the zodiac. In the Paleolithic period, that is, from 38,000 to 9,000 years ago, it was rising in Libra, and before that Scorpio, and so forth. The cosmic qualities of the zodiac configuration of stars influences human activities and levels of existence, and this is how I led into the subject of art in prehistory, beginning with the cave art in France from more than 30,000 years ago. We looked at high quality photographs of the cave walls, and Sara did paintings on watercolor paper that had been wadded and then pressed flat and rubbed with sienna chalk to simulate a stone background. She also copied some of the art onto a dark stone slab with hard pastels. When I speculated to Sara that people so long ago might have done paintings in dark caves to somehow join with animal consciousness, or to have power over them, she replied, "Or to partner with them." I found this an interesting thought. Had human beings come to a point at that time when they had, as part of evolution, shed some animal qualities, that, now being separate, could be depicted?

Grade nine is a further step in gradually coming into time, and coming into the current moment of time culturally. Healing at the level of the organism can be a deep support for this process.

Grade 10: Beginning to sense effects on the world of one's being and action. The student in grade ten turns sixteen, a moment that is marked explicitly in various cultural practices. In High German, the adolescent begins to be addressed with the formal, adult pronoun *sie*. In America, many groups have "sweet sixteen" celebrations. Students at this age are continuing to become more aware of the world around them, and of their place in it—physically and socially. In biology they study the anatomy of the human skeleton and in physics they study mechanics. The skeleton is the part of the body that is most mineral, and most directly the function of the mechanics of levers, weight, and acceleration. Galileo is a central figure in the study of mechanics because he was not content to think abstractly, that is, just mathematically, about nature. Instead, he was determined to sense mechanical processes. Before the Renaissance, medieval thinkers saw the world as a kind of curtain that obscured the reality of the spiritual world. With Galileo, the curtain became reality—a reality that could be perceived, measured, and described mathematically. Thus, Galileo's experiments on moving bodies are recreated, measured, and graphed. Trigonometry is taught in the math blocks so that variables of mechanics can be computed. Students at this age are near a time of self-authority, but they are in the process of *choosing* who will be an authority to them. They need to trust their own senses, not just accept authority, but at the same time, and in contradiction, they are moving away from their own rich experiences and into the realm of mechanization and mathematization. Self-assertion without a developed self is a complicated situation, and social exploration and mistakes are inevitable.

Ancient History is another block in grade ten, and here, again, time is a theme. The teacher leads the students to consider a time before there were texts, and to imagine what culture and civilization might have been like then. Here they can study material such as Plato's *Critias* dialogue, where Critias narrates a story about the time of Atlantis—and its destruction. The students can also study the *Epic of Gilgamesh*, which I have shared about previously, and which was written more than three thousand years ago—and which described a much earlier time. The Ancient History block, meanwhile, concludes with Classical Greece, and here I will quote from the end of Sara's main lesson book:

> Euripides (485–406 BC) was the first playwright whose plays showed skepticism about the gods, their motives or even their existence. His views were very radical, they marked the beginning of a new time, where not everything was directly connected to religion, where humans *thought* instead of relying on a higher

power to know what was right, a time when people came into their own. ...Euripides had brought the world one more step forward.

This could very well be a description of the developmental process of the tenth grade student.

Grade 11: Moral choices. As the student's individual conscience begins to awaken, it will be challenged; the individual who is moving out away from the sheltering family will be called upon to make moral decisions and choices. The theme of the blocks for grade eleven is "transformation," and this is exactly what the students are undergoing. The second time I taught grade eleven, the main lesson blocks were Projective Geometry, Chemistry, English Grammar and Composition, Electricity and Magnetism, Bible and Literature, Mechanics, Algebra, and Botany. Our play that year was *The Tempest* by William Shakespeare. The figure of Miranda, who has been raised alone by her father on an uninhabited island, and who is faced with moral complexities when a ship wrecks nearby in a tempest, is a fitting one for grade eleven students. Her response to all the new people and events that are such a mixed blessing is: "O brave new world that has such people in it!"

In comparing Euclidean and descriptive projective geometry, the student moves from assuming finite elements that must be added or synthesized logically to thinking in terms of movement and infinity. In projective geometry, parallel lines eventually do meet, but only at infinity. In chemistry the core phenomena are those of transformation, even though there is quantitative balance. Acids and bases with their opposite properties combine to form salts, which have qualities distinct from either of the components. The whole is other than the parts. In English composition we looked at the qualities of simple, compound, complex, and compound-complex sentences and how these qualities affect a composition. Sara wrote an essay on the knight's horses from *Parzival*, the epic poem by von Eschenbach. With her inveterate interest in everything equine, she explored how the horses embodied the qualities and values of knighthood: nobility, faith, courage, and hard work.

One of the greatest challenges for Sara that year was to accept the responsibilities of being the oldest student in our homeschool group. She was also thrust into the leadership position as art director for the Shakespeare play, in which she also acted two main parts, Miranda and Stephano, the drunken butler. Sara, as the younger sister of a choleric

Sara Read after John William Waterhouse "Miranda"

Figure 14: Sara's drawing of Miranda for the Grade 11 play The Tempest

and capable sibling, was used to following and being ordered about. And her sanguine and loving nature was happy, most days, with that arrangement. Yet Sara had to design and execute costumes and sets, and direct others in doing this, for a very complex play. For example, there was a magical scene where a banquet needed to vanish into thin air. We used no electronics in any of our work, and did not make recordings of anything either, aside from a few still photos of scenes that were reenacted after the production was complete. Sara had to go against her own comforts to contribute to something larger in order to bring about an event that was educational and nourishing for all. It was difficult, but she did it. We had a banquet made of foam that would collapse under a black blanket and be available for use again, and Sara was a main figure in almost every scene, including some almost magical costume changes! Sara also did the drawing for the program (see Figure 14, above), which captures the feeling of the play, torn by the winds of a tempest, and at the same time, captures something of the experience of the grade eleven student as she stands on the threshold of taking on responsibility and choices.

Grade 12: Beginning to look outward: "Where am I? Who are these people?" I did not teach grade twelve, even though I prepared for it in teacher training and taught an optics lesson in a grade twelve Waldorf school class. We had always taken homeschool one year at a time and decided each spring or summer about the next year. It just happened that each year until grade ten or eleven, it was clear that the next year would be school at home. However, both Claire and Sara decided they wanted to do their last year in an institutional school. Claire went to a small liberal preparatory school near our house for grades eleven and twelve, and then went on to college at the University of Vermont. Sara decided to do grade twelve in a Waldorf high school and to live with Claire's godmother's family, who lived near the school. She then took a gap year to work on equine therapy and to work in a painter's studio, and then went on to college at Skidmore in upstate New York. I did not teach grade twelve at home, but we did have a school-leaving ceremony at the end of grade eleven. Claire, therefore, went through the developments of the age of grade twelve without the Waldorf curriculum. Claire found it difficult to adjust to the lack of a steady rhythm, the long hours in school, the homework, and the overwhelming presence of groups of people. In some ways it was a bitter pill. But she did well academically and made a few lasting friends, and she learned to adjust to a variety of teachers—and made her way to a college that was a very good fit for her. She has now graduated from the College of Veterinary Medicine at Cornell University as a Doctor of Veterinary Medicine—a literally lifelong dream of hers. Sara, on the other hand, did have the grade twelve Waldorf curriculum, just in a very different setting than she had had in school up to that point. She fit in well with the class, as she already knew some of the students, and she did very well academically. She graduated with her class and after a gap year went to a selective liberal arts school in upstate New York. She graduated with honors and worked for a year, and is now in graduate school for art therapy, something she had set her sights on in high school.

Meanwhile, by grade twelve, students, who are now from seventeen to eighteen years old, are beginning to wake up to the questions of "Who am I?" and "Who are these people around me?" And those questions herald a new consciousness, a new self-awareness, and the beginnings of a new and personal conscience. In some ways, students in grade twelve come full circle with where they started in grade one, but at a new level. So it is not really a circle, but a spiral of development. One way for the teacher to see this development is to turn to the links between the zodiac constellations and the twelve senses. It is a complex picture, but it helps us understand what is happening for twelfth grade students. They are at the beginning of a time in which they are able to use their freedom rightly, if, that is, they were given goodness to imitate as young children—and natural authority to look up to as adolescents. Twelfth grade prepares students to begin to know on their own, and freely, and in a new way. If we look at the developmental progression of the twelve senses, touch predominates at the younger ages—in helping the child determine her own boundaries. From there, each sense in turn predominates as the child develops, until eventually she can concentrate on sensing another's self or I—and being aware of another's boundaries. At that point, as pointed out by Steiner in *Man as a Being of Sense and Perception*, we can see that the senses make a circle. Also, the senses mirror each other around the circle, just as touch and the aforementioned I-sense mirror each other at the ends. For more on this, see Soesman's book, *Our Twelve Senses*. If we link this with Steiner's description of the zodiac as a living organic process, and with his description of the image of a snake consuming its own tail (from his lecture of September 2, 1921), then we can see the development of the senses from birth to age eighteen as an example of the individual arriving at a new kind of knowing. Steiner describes this process as the snake not just biting its tail, but consuming it, and, therefore, transforming it, spiritualizing it. This process of swallowing or digesting leads to an inversion of the original state. One might say that experience becomes a consciousness of one's own experience. Therefore, in grade twelve the teacher can be aware that students are becoming conscious of themselves and the world at the same time, just as in grade one they felt themselves and the world at the same time. The senses develop over the whole course on one's life, but there are certain moments of transformation. And age eighteen is one of these moments. The teacher of grade twelve strives to be aware of preparing students to be free in their thinking as they transform into adults. Meanwhile, some of them will go on to college.

Although there are presently no Waldorf-inspired colleges in the United States, there are those working to bring Waldorf methods into teaching at that level (see the epilogue).

The Teacher's Challenges

The teacher's challenge is to be aware of the tests the children will meet at each grade, and to support them through the experience. The exact details of the "test," of course, will vary for each child (given their temperament, previous experiences, life intention, and so forth), but the teacher's awareness will allow them to be open to just how each challenge for each child is shaping up as it happens. I was teaching two grades at the same time, so I had two sets of challenges. Also, I never knew what each grade would pose the first time I taught it, but by the second time around I knew better what to stay aware of. So, for each grade I first had something new to discover and later had a more known "quantity" to deal with. For example, when Claire was in grade four, Sara was in grade one. So while I knew I was helping Sara gradually accept and want to be in the structure of school, I was also becoming aware that Claire was "coming down to earth" and learning to face evil. I had to be very positive for the first grader and very resolute for the fourth grader. Two thoughts that we held on to during this time were, first for Sara, "This is a good place to come to," and second, for Claire, "We will get through this." For me the only way I could carry on this work was to have help—from the people and teachers around me, from my husband and other mothers, from my Waldorf teacher training teachers, and also from reading and studying anthroposophy. The important thing is for every teacher to find his or her own sources of strength and support.

Making the curriculum your own

There are as many possibilities for homeschool as there are homes. But if one chooses the Waldorf Curriculum, then there are many ways of working with it. The homeschool teacher is uniquely suited to having an overview and knowledge of all the lessons, and, therefore, she can relate them to each other in ways most teachers in institutional schools would not be able to. The teacher even knows the continuity of the lessons with life outside of school. What a rich treasure trove to draw on in creating lessons and in creating the school day! In this way, teaching the Waldorf Curriculum at home is one renewal of the work that Steiner set out for teachers in the first school. Gather up the courage and go forth!

Epilogue: Waldorf after High School

Our Waldorf homeschool came to an end gradually. Our older daughter, Claire, went through grade eleven at home, and then she went into a small preparatory school near us. We had a year-end assembly with guests that year (in all other years, except grade eight, the year-end assembly was presented to just their father). It was a kind of graduation from our school, which I describe in Appendix 3. She then lived at home with us, went to that school for two years (their grades eleven and twelve), and then moved out to go to college at a relatively small state school in another state. The year Claire started in the prep school was our younger daughter, Sara's, grade nine. We then had three high school years in school at home with just the two of us (of course, always working with different homeschool families and with various specialty teachers). I had taught those grades before, and she was an interested, capable, and hardworking student. It was a joy! I was ill during her grade ten, but we did it anyway. Sara had a beautiful year-end assembly for her father and older sister, and the next fall she entered a Waldorf school to complete grade twelve and graduate. There she lived with a family that were friends of our family, and in the school she jumped right into their curriculum and daily life. It was tiring for her, but she did well there. After graduating, Sara then took a gap year to work in painters' studios, as she had known since she was five years old that she would be an artist. Then she went to college at a small liberal arts school in upstate New York. As one would expect, both daughters had challenges making the transition to institutional environments, but they met the challenges and went on.

Meanwhile, toward the end of teaching Sara at home, I was also preparing to go back to teaching university, which I had left sixteen years earlier. While preparing for this, I realized I couldn't just lecture and give tests as I had before (when I knew hardly anything about teaching) and call that education. Yet I would be teaching classes of around twenty-five students, mostly in their second and third years in college, on the topics of gender and science. I wouldn't be using a block structure, but I would be able to group the topics in three steps that progressed from one to the next. I also knew I would have to present material and assign reading in class, but I wanted to completely change the class time activity and do away with lectures. I also wanted to respect the students' sleep cycles, and use it for their educational benefit, as I had done with my daughters in our homeschool.

How I wished to translate this to the university environment is that I would, or hoped I would, present a lesson one day and engage the students in working with it. Then, in the next class, after they had slept on it, I would work with them to recall what we had done previously. As with my work with my daughters, this recalling would not be just a rote "reeling off" of facts. Instead, the students would work together in a group, with my assistance, to build up a "picture" of what they had done the day before. But could I adapt this for university teaching—in an environment where the classes met only twice a week, and not even on consecutive days?

I decided that every class meeting after the first one would begin with a group class activity of recalling what we had done the session before, without looking at notes. I as the professor participated, too, without preparing ahead of time. Everyone could contribute and anyone could correct statements if they were inaccurate. When this activity was complete, I emphasized points that were important, and brought in any questions they had given me from the previous session (written on cards at the end of each class). In this way I could highlight certain points and also be sure that the particular material was clear. We then went on to new material by discussing the new reading, with my questions guiding their understanding. At the midpoint of the class we took a break, not just to move around and chat idly, but to do some mental "gymnastics." That is, we worked on a particular kind of problem, as a group, depending on which third of the semester we were in. I started with about four weeks of Euclidean geometry constructions, for example, bisecting a line segment and working up to finding the three types of centers of triangles. The method here was to pose the question to the whole class and let them work it out mentally and to "throw out" possible solutions. Anyone could speak at any time, and I only pointed out if the solution would not work. And then we kept trying. Eventually, building on what the others had said, someone would get the answer. It was rarely the same person twice who arrived at the solution. And the solving definitely felt as if it were a group accomplishment. In the next section I used nature riddles for this midpoint class activity, and in the final section I used projective geometry constructions. By that point, the students were used to the method (and participated enthusiastically), and they commented that projective geometry, with its assumptions that were so different from Euclidean geometry, "blew their minds." At the end of each class, they wrote whatever new question they had on a card, and I read these before the next class. This is how I brought Waldorf teaching methods into the classroom. This way of teaching was new and unfamiliar to the students, but they gradually warmed to it and realized the value of this rhythmic way of working, and of working with recall. Some of them even commented on how they took to using these methods in their own studies and observations outside of the classroom. Mission accomplished!

I am still teaching university sporadically, and I find that the above methods also work in a small honors seminar. I am also now on the faculty of a new program of post-high-school study based on anthroposophy and Waldorf methods. This is the M.C. Richards program offered by Free Columbia in Philmont, New York. It is a year-long program of study including science, literature, art, and practical arts. My course is entitled "Attending to Experience through Nature Observation," and I will be concentrating on color experiences in the lab and in nature.

A few days ago, I was outside with Claire and Sara (who, at the moment of this writing, have both been working here, from home, for about six weeks because of the coronavirus pandemic) and it was a breezy, sunny, cool spring day. Sara, the synesthete artist, said: "I see what you mean about the sky now. It's like the light is different." We all looked up at the clear blue arch above us with a few light cirrus clouds in the heights. I said: "Yes, it always changes right around Easter, becomes such a lighter blue, even at the very top." Claire, the clinical scientist, said: "It's like you're seeing it with new eyes." It struck me that the artist concentrated on the light, and that the scientist brought the human being directly into her observations of nature. I hope that the

Waldorf education they had was indeed able to give them living ideas that would change and grow with them. Sara will be using her art to provide care as an art therapist, and she, rightly, questions when human beings are seen as objects. Claire has had a standard mainstream science education since high school, after having had a Goethean science education at home. She studied biology at university, then worked toward a masters in animal science, and then studied veterinary medicine in Scotland and in New York. And yet she includes the human being in the observation—a mark of living thinking. May they both live and grow in wisdom.

Bibliography and Resources

Appenzeller, K. (1976). *Die Genesis im Lichte der menschlichen Embryonalentwicklung / Zeichnungen vom Verf.* Basel: Zbinden.

Armstrong, C. (1998). *Women of the Bible: with Paintings from the Great Art Museums of the World.* New York, NY: Simon & Schuster Books for Young Readers.

Barfield, O. (2011). *Saving the appearances: A Study in Idolatry.* Oxford: Barfield Press.

Bloom, H. (1987). *Ursula K. Le Guin's The Left Hand of Darkness.* New York: Chelsea House Publishers.

Bock, E. (2011). *Genesis: Creation and the Patriarchs.* Edinburgh: Floris Books.

Bortoft, H. (2002). *Taking Appearance Seriously.* Edinburgh: Floris Books.

Brierley, D. (1998). *The Sea of Life Enisled.* Oslo, Norway: Antropos Forlag.

Burton, M. H. (1989). *In the Light of a Child: A Journey through the 52 Weeks of the Year in Both Hemispheres for Children and for the Child in Each Human Being.* Hudson, NY: Anthroposophic Press.

Buhler, W. (2013). *Living with Your Body: Health, Illness and Understanding the Human Being.* Forest Row: Rudolf Steiner Press.

Carlgren, F. (1996). *Education Towards Freedom.* London: Lanthorn Press.

Channer, M. (2020). *Xavier Sings of His Alphabet Friends.* Hudson, NY: Waldorf Publications.

Down, R. (2018). *Color and Gesture: The Inner Life of Color.* Sacramento, CA: Lightly Press.

Durant, W. (1992). *The Life of Greece: Being a History of Greek Civilization from the Beginnings, and of Civilization in the Near East from the Death of Alexander, to the Roman Conquest; with an Introduction on the Prehistoric Culture of Crete.* New York: MJF Books.

Foster, N. (Ed.), (2013). *Mood of the Fifth: A Musical Approach to Early Childhood.* Waldorf Early Childhood Association.

——— (2013). "The Mood of Early Childhood: Music in the Kindergarten." In Foster, N. (Ed.), (2013). *Mood of the Fifth: A Musical Approach to Early Childhood.* Waldorf Early Childhood Association.

Friberg, E. (1988). *The Kalevala.* Helsinki, Finland: Otava Publishing Co.

Goethe, J. W. von. (1989). *Tales for Transformation.* London: Owen.

——— (1995). *Scientific Studies.* Princeton, NJ: Princeton University Press.

Gombrich, E. H. (2013). *A Little History of the World.* New Haven, CT: Yale University Press.

Grimm, J., Grimm, W. (2016). *Grimms' Fairy Tales.* London: Puffin Books.

Holdrege, C. (Ed.) (2002). *The Dynamic Heart and Circulation.* Fair Oaks, CA: Association of Waldorf Schools of North America.

Hyland, D. (2004). *Charles Dickens: Hard times.* London: Longman.

Jacquet Hélène, & Harwood, A. C. (2013). *Christmas Plays from Oberufer.* Forest Row, East Sussex: Sophia Books.

Johns, S. (2013). "Music, Mobility, and the Mood of the Fifth." In Foster, N. (Ed.), (2013). *Mood of the Fifth: A Musical Approach to Early Childhood.* Waldorf Early Childhood Association.

Johns, S. (2013). "The Erosion of Listening." In Foster, N. (Ed.), (2013). *Mood of the Fifth: A Musical Approach to Early Childhood.* Waldorf Early Childhood Association.

Le Guin, U. & Wood, S. (1993). *The language of the Night: Essays on Fantasy and Science Fiction.* New York: HarperPerennial.

Le Guin, U. (2019). *The Left Hand of Darkness.* New York: ACE.

König, K. (2009). *Embyogenesis and World Evolution.* Reprinted by AWSNA.

Kovacs, C. (2002). *Parzival.* Edinburgh: Floris Books.

——— (2004). *Ancient Greece.* Edinburgh: Floris Books.

——— (2005). *Ancient Rome.* Edinburgh: Floris.

Kramer, S. N. (1961). *History Begins at Sumer.* London.

Lockyer, H. (1995). *All the Women of the Bible: The Life and Times of All the Women of the Bible.* Grand Rapids, MI: Zondervan Pub. House.

MacDonald, G. (2019). *At the Back of the North Wind.* DIGIREADS COM Publishing.

McAllen, A. E. (2004). *Sleep: An Unobserved Element in Education.* Fair Oaks, CA: Rudolf Steiner College Press.

Post, L. V. der. (1989). *A Mantis Carol.* Harmondsworth: Penguin.

Ransome, A. (2008). *We Didn't Mean to Go to Sea.* Oxford: Oxford University Press.

Ragan, K. (1998). *Fearless Girls, Wise Women, and Beloved Sisters: Heroines in Folktales from Around the World.* New York: W.W. Norton.

Read, C. (1997). "Family Festivals: Coming Full Circle, Part I." First published in: *The Peridot Journal* 9 (3): 17-18. thegeniusofhome.org

——— (1998). "Family Festivals: Coming Full Circle, Part II." First published in: *The Peridot Journal* 10 (1): 14-15. thegeniusofhome.org

——— (2000). "Transitions in Consciousness." First published in: *The Peridot Journal* 12 (1): 12-13 & 16. thegeniusofhome.org

———(2000). "Finding Ourselves in Community: Class Plays in Family Settings." First published in: *The Peridot Journal* 12 (3): 12-15. thegeniusofhome.org

——— (2001). "Connecting with Nature." First published in: *The Peridot Journal* 13 (1): 13-18. thegeniusofhome.org

——— (2004). "The New Harp: A Grade Four Play Enacting a Kalevala Rune." First published in: *Lyre Association of North America Newsletter.* thegeniusofhome.org

——— (2005). "Goethe's Magic Flute: Working with a Mystery First." *Rudolf Steiner Library Newsletter.* thegeniusofhome.org

——— (2007). "The Class Play as Fever." First published in: SteinerBooks Education Catalog. thegeniusofhome.org

Riccio, M.D. (2002). *An Outline for a Renewal of Waldorf Education: Rudolf Steiner's Method of Heart-thinking and its Central Role in the Waldorf School.* Spring Valley, NY: Mercury Press.

Robbins, R. (2005). "New organs of perception: Goethean science as a cultural therapeutic."*Janus Head, 8*(1), 113-126.

Rohen, J. W. (2016). *Functional Morphology: The Dynamic Wholeness of the Human Organism.* Hillsdale, NY: Adonis Press.

Sachs, J., & Aristotle. (1995). *Aristotle's Physics: A Guided Study.* New Brunswick, NJ: Rutgers University Press.

Saemundar, E., & Hollander, L. M. (1962). *The Poetic Edda. Translated with an Introduction and Explanatory Notes by Lee M. Hollander.* Austin: University of Texas Press.

Sayers, D. L. (2005). *Are Women Human?* Grand Rapids, MI: William B. Eerdmans Pub. Co.

Seidenberg, C. (2002). *I Love to be Me: Songs in the Mood of the Fifth.* Stourbridge, England: Wynstones Press.

Shaw, G. B., & Topolski, F. (1975). *Pygmalion: A Romance in Five Acts; Definitive Text.* Harmondsworth: Penguin Books.

Soesman, A. (1998). *Our Twelve Senses: How Healthy Senses Refresh the Soul.* Stroud: Hawthorn Press.

Steiner, R. (1994). *The Archangel Michael: His Mission and Ours: Selected Lectures and Writings.* Hudson, NY: Anthroposophic Press.

——— (1981). *The Being of Man and His Future Evolution.* London: R. Steiner Press.

——— (2003). *The Calendar of the Soul 1912/1913, Facsimile Edition.* Great Barrington, MA: SteinerBooks.

——— (1996). *The Child's Changing Consciousness: As the Basis of Pedagogical Practice.* Hudson, NY: Anthroposophic Press.

——— (1956). *The Cycle of the Year as Breathing-Process of the Earth. The Four Great Festival-seasons of the Year.* London: Anthroposophical Pub. Co.

——— (1981). *The Education of the Child in the Light of Anthroposophy.* London: Rudolf Steiner Press.

——— (2005). *Eurythmy as Visible Speech.* Weobley: Anastasi.

——— (1998). *Faculty Meetings with Rudolf Steiner, Vol. 2.* Hudson, NY: Anthroposophic Press.

——— (1981). *The Festivals and their Meaning*. London: Rudolf Steiner Press.

——— (1996). *The Foundations of Human Experience*. Hudson, NY: Anthroposophic Press.

——— (1996). *The Four Seasons and the Archangels: Experience of the Course of the Year in Four Cosmic Imaginations*. London: Rudolf Steiner Press.

——— (2007). *"Freemasonry" and Ritual Work*. Great Barrington, MA: SteinerBooks.

——— (2015). *From Symptom to Reality in Modern History*. Forest Row: Rudolf Steiner Press.

——— (2013). *Harmony of the Creative Word: The Human Being and the Elemental, Animal, Plant and Mineral Kingdoms*. Forest Row: Rudolf Steiner Press.

——— (1987). *The Inner Nature of Music and the Experience of Tone*. Hudson, NY: Anthroposophic Press.

——— (1995). *The Kingdom of Childhood*. Hudson, NY: Anthroposophic Press.

——— (1985). *Life between Death and Rebirth*. Spring Valley, NY: Anthroposophic Press.

——— (2001). *The Light Course*. Great Barrington, MA: Anthroposophic Press.

——— (1958). *Man as a Being of Sense and Perception*. Vancouver, Canada: Steiner Books Centre.

——— (1982). *Michaelmas and the Soul-forces of Man*. Spring Valley: Anthroposophic Press.

——— (2005). *An Occult Physiology*. Forest Row, England: Rudolf Steiner Press.

——— (1997). *An Outline of Esoteric Science*. Hudson, NY: Anthroposophic Press.

——— (1999). *A Psychology of Body, Soul, & Spirit: Anthroposophy, Psychosophy, & Pneumatosophy*. Hudson, NY: Anthroposophic Press.

——— (2000). *Practical Advice to Teachers*. Great Barrington, MA: Anthroposophic Press.

——— (2010). *Six Steps in Self-development: The Supplementary Exercises*. Rudolf Steiner Press.

——— (2007). *Speech and Drama*. Hudson, NY: Anthroposophic Press.

——— (2004). *The Spiritual Ground of Education*. Great Barrington, MA: Anthroposophic Press.

——— (2009). *The Stages of Higher Knowledge: Imagination, Inspiration, Intuition*. Great Barrington, MA: SteinerBooks.

——— (1994). *Theosophy*. Hudson, NY: Anthroposophic Press.

——— (1981). *Truth and Knowledge: Introduction to "Philosophy of Spiritual Activity."* Blauvelt, NY: SteinerBooks.

——— (1979). *Truth-wrought Words: with Other Verses and Prose Passages*. Spring Valley: Anthroposophic Press.

——— (2020). *Wonders of the World: Trials of the Soul, Revelations of the Spirit*. Forest Row, England: Rudolf Steiner Press.

——— (2021). *World History in the Light of Anthroposophy*. Forest Row, England: Rudolf Steiner Press.

Stevenson, L. L. (1998). *Women's History*. Princeton, NJ: Markus Wiener Publishers.

Stockmeyer, E. A. K., Everett-Zade, R., & Avison, K. (2015). *Rudolf Steiner's Curriculum for Steiner-Waldorf Schools: An Attempt to Summarise his Indications*. Edinburgh: Floris Books.

Tendler, J. (2017). *The Return of Martin Guerre*. London: Taylor and Francis.

Thomas, H. (1998). *A Journey Through Time in Verse and Rhyme*. Edinburgh: Floris Books.

Uehli, E. (1999). *Norse Mythology and the Modern Human Being*. AWSNA

Van Dam, J. (2013). *The Eightfold Path*. Forest Row, England: Temple Lodge.

Van der Bie, G., Scheffers, T., & Tellingen, C. (2008). *The Healing Process: Organ of Repair*. Driebergen NL: Louis Bolk Institut.

Von Ems, R. (1993). *Gerhard the Good*. West Sussex, UK: Steiner Schools Fellowship Publications.

Weihs, T. (2017). *Embryogenesis in Myth and Science*. Edinburgh, UK: Floris Books.

Appendices

Three previously published articles by Catherine Read on topics related to homeschooling with the Waldorf Curriculum.

Appendix 1:
Anthroposophic Homeschooling:
Fostering the Life of the Soul

(1999)

Sending one's child to a Waldorf school to be educated can, and often does, bring about a transformation of family and soul life. Grace before meals, seasonal activities, and the cycle of festivals often become a part of living at home. When one decides also to school at home, using indications from Rudolf Steiner and practices developed in Waldorf schools, one enters into an encompassing, and sometimes overwhelming, transformation of life in the family. This article describes our family's experiences with kindergarten, first grade, and second grade, the resources we have drawn on, our decision to homeschool, and some of the challenges and satisfactions of schooling at home with anthroposophy as the guiding force. Parenting and teaching the same children is a unique path of inner development and outer work. In all my work I strive to remember that the children are coming from a higher sphere and that they are bringing particular gifts they must learn how to use. As Rudolf Steiner has said, "Reverence will have an immeasurable formative influence on the child; the teacher's feelings are certainly the most important tools of education." (See his *Balance in Teaching*, p. 18). Thus, the soul life of the teacher is all-important for the children; and the soul life of the children is the teacher's primary focus.

The Rhythm of the Day

The girls and I wake to the morning sun shining and the birds singing—my husband, their father, has already gone to work. After talking a little we say our morning prayer and rise for breakfast. Claire, seven, Sara, four, and I, their mother, are embarking on another day of school at home. After breakfast the girls play while I clear up and then we all dress up for school. While they finish, I prepare the schoolroom. I move a play stand to make a "doorway" into the room, I arrange materials for the day, and finally, do my preparatory eurythmy. I do "Halleluiah" in eurythmy, say my prayer about guiding the children, and then do "Amen" in eurythmy. At last I ring a brass bell with a clear high tone to tell Claire and Sara it is time for school. More often than not they call out from the bedroom, "We're not ready!" So, I wait, and ring the bell again, and, finally, they come running down the hall.

I greet them, holding their hands and singing "good morning" and their names, and then step back to admit them into the classroom, and we begin our circle. We have a greeting song, then we stand and say the morning verse while looking up to a sunny window, and finish the circle with seasonal songs, fingerplays, cat's cradles, or riddles, as well as with material related to the main lesson, such as beanbag tossing with rhymes or walking and clapping while counting.

At the end of circle, we have main lesson at the blackboard. The blackboard is a three-panel, free-standing screen that my husband made—each panel is the size of a standard household door. On one panel is my blackboard art, usually a seasonal scene including children, gnomes, and fairies, in the first grade; in second grade a picture of the Archangel Michael with sword raised and pointing upward was on the board all year. On the center panel I draw the form or letter picture or number scene (first grade) or write the fable or draw the saint picture (second grade) depending on the main lesson block. On the left panel Claire does her writing and drawing.

When we have finished at the board, we breathe out by tracing a form with finger and toe, drawing the form in sand and running the form (or equivalent actions with letters or numbers). Then we come back in to do focused work on the blackboard slates and on paper. Sara comes and goes as she chooses—she joins in for the parts of the circle that are at her level and steps out to play with her kitchen or dolls at the other times. She draws on the slate and on paper with crayons—her own free drawings. Then we have a light lunch followed by an activity such as rope jumping, games, gardening, or painting. The end of the main lesson comes when we gather in the Rainbow House for a story—for first grade a fairy tale from Grimm's collection or a nature story, for second grade animal fairy tales, animal fables, nature stories, or legends of the saints. We end with our final verse:

> In every seed that will be a tree,
> there lives an image of what it will be.
> When I find the image of all I can be,
> my heart and soul are then free.

The profound effect of such a verse was brought home to me when, after about six weeks of school in first grade, Claire was quiet for a moment at the end of the verse, and then her eyes lit up and she smiled and exclaimed "*I can be me!*" About three-fourths of the way through second grade (when she was eight and a half years old), Claire said: "'... all I can be...' what if I'm not good?" I thought, "The first intimations of the nine-year change!" I changed the verse to "when I find the image of the best I can be." This verse turns out to be very revealing of Claire's soul life!

After the main lesson, we have snack and do handwork, knitting or stitching, often while I read to them. At transitions in the day they have a break to play outside, and sometimes I go with them to do jump rope and other games. At the end of the day, we are rosy-cheeked and content—smiling when my husband comes home. I feel that this alone is quite an achievement in modern-day middle-class life! Soon after the school day is finished, the girls' father comes home and plays with them, and then after dinner takes them to bed while I prepare for the next school day. This is one of the primary transformations in our family life; the girls have more time with their father.

The Rhythm of the Week

The rhythm of the week consists of three and a half days of school and one and a half days in groups with other children and teachers. We sometimes had "exploring days" or Nature Days on Mondays when we went on hikes in the hills or to the beach. Sometimes we went with another family. On these days we walked at a slow pace, determined by the children, to see what we would see. I did not talk with them unless they brought something to me or showed me something. The adults did not talk to each other, except to share in something with the children. We had these days to immerse ourselves in nature. We often made our way to the same place, a bird sanctuary in the hills, and no one was ever bored. How wonderful to experience the changes of season in one place over the course of the year!

Tuesdays, Wednesdays, and Thursday mornings were always school days at home, unless someone was ill. Thursday afternoons we attended a parent-child eurythmy class. On Fridays Claire, the seven-year-old, spent the mornings with a German-speaking family to begin learning German, and had pentatonic flute lessons on Friday afternoons. Thus, I am not my daughter's only teacher—I have the support of many others in educating her. All her teachers receive gifts we have made in handwork and are a much loved and appreciated part of my daughter's life.

Toward the end of first grade we joined with another family homeschooling out of anthroposophy and worked on a play—Snow White told in song and verse (written by Elizabeth Moore-Haas). We had three days over a period of several weeks in which we had school together, and the main lesson consisted of play rehearsal. At the end of the year we put on the play for several mothers with their young children—and for one grandmother. My husband drew the castle and forest scene on the blackboard as backdrop and worked as prompter and backstage manager. The play was wonderful and we all felt so accomplished afterwards, especially the children. A friend of mine who saw Claire from a distance a few days after the play mistook her for a third grader, she was standing so tall. In the second grade our play was performed by just our family—it was a play about St. Clare and St. Francis. I wrote the play, the girls and I acted in the play, including singing and playing instruments, and my husband was the narrator as well as drawing the backdrop on the blackboard. This play was a powerful experience for us all, especially the second grader, who is getting ready to enter the consciousness of being incarnated here on earth, and of the choices for human beings—to go the way of the animals or to lift themselves to a higher level.

At the end of each of these plays I felt the kind of joy and peace I always do after a festival. Which leads into the rhythm of the year.

The Rhythm of the Year

I just finished my third year of homeschooling our two daughters—this year we finished second grade and kindergarten. For three years our family has been part of a group of families who celebrate festivals in an effort to renew the festivals, based on indications from Rudolf Steiner, the founder of Waldorf education. As I continue with anthroposophic homeschooling and with celebrating the transformed festivals, I begin to awaken to the ways in which teaching out of the Waldorf curriculum is itself festival work. I begin to realize that the festivals are not just a handful of days during the year on which we perform outer celebrations, but that every day belongs to a festival time. And I realize that the festival time directs me to the stories, lessons, activities, materials, colors, and even foods that form our school days at home.

The Cycle of the Year

To provide a clearer picture, I will briefly describe the cycle of season-related festivals that we celebrate.

Michaelmas, September 29. Michaelmas celebrates the Archangel Michael overcoming the dragon of unspiritualized desires, thoughts, and deeds. This is a festival of courage to face the dying of nature and certain qualities of our own souls. This festival of the autumn and early winter prepares the way for Advent, the deepening of winter.

Martinmas, November 11. This Saint's day celebrates St. Martin as a person who gave of his own to the poor, a person who kindled the light of kindness and caring in his open heart. The festival is celebrated by making paper lanterns and carrying their light through the dark evening.

Advent, Fourth Sunday before Christmas. Advent is the time of waiting for a momentous event—the birth of Jesus as watched over by higher spiritual beings. This is the time of shorter days and longer nights, a time in which we begin to turn inward. We celebrate with a spiral walk, carrying a candle to light at the center of the spiral.

Christmas, December 25. The culmination of Advent is the celebration of the birth of Jesus, which we celebrate by caroling in one of our neighborhoods. In the depth of winter, we try to light our consciousness and warm our hearts, as well as those of our neighbors.

Easter, first Sunday after the first full moon after the spring equinox. This is the first in the year with a movable date—it is determined by both the sun and the moon. This is a three-day festival celebrating the death and resurrection of the Christ which took place in spring, when earth life begins to grow. We have a festival in a park, with a meal, a story about rebirth, and outdoor games for the children.

St. John's Tide, June 24. This festival celebrates the birth of St. John the Baptist and occurs at the height of summer. In such intense summer sun, we are aware of the sky and the atmosphere and we must try to take in the goodness of the golden light to use later in the year. Our festival consists of a meal at the beach, jumping over a bonfire, and singing songs around the fire.

Festivals and the Waldorf Curriculum at Home

The festivals can guide work for all grades from kindergarten through high school. I will give examples from K-2, as that is what I know best. Stories, songs, and handwork all through kindergarten can come directly from the festival of the time. For example, during St. John's, the children can be swung over a "fire" made of red, orange, and yellow silks by an adult on either side of the child, singing a song about summer and the sun.

In the first grade I used a continuing story as the context for the form drawing. The story was about a wise old woman whom a prince was seeking for help in finding his princess. In the fall he had to face the dragon in its cave and in winter walk a spiral and come back out. As the Michaelmas festival approached, I told a story of Michael, and before the end of school for Christmas, I included songs about Mary preparing for the birth of her Child. The qualities of numbers and the arithmetic processes are more difficult for me to connect to the festivals. I am exploring the connection between the tones for the vowels of the Archangel's names and the musical intervals and rhythms that can be used in songs to teach intervals in arithmetic. Although the connection between mathematics and the festivals is less obvious to me, even these topics are always related to the human being in our unique relation to heaven and earth, which all the festivals celebrate and strengthen.

In the second grade the first Form Drawing block can be based on Michael legends. This work strengthens the life body and gives renewed vitality to perform difficult tasks. All the festivals have associated saints, and this can help guide the choice of saints' legends. The animal fables show the opposite of the distinct qualities celebrated in each festival. The qualities of the festivals are mirrored in the foibles of the animals—weakness and fear versus courage, greed and egotism versus love, self-serving versus self-sacrificing.

Why Celebrate the Festivals?

Festivals help us wake up to our humanity, our connection with others, and our work here on earth. For those of us who are our children's teachers as well as their parents, the festivals are a continuous source of strength in family life as well as a beacon of guidance in our work as teachers. Each festival builds gradually, peaks, wanes, and then gradually becomes the next festival through each cycle, as well as the cycle of years. We and our children gain inestimable strength and essential treasures from participating in the festivals that grow out of connecting the spiritual world with life on earth. We are truly strengthened by weaving the festivals into our daily lives and thereby teaching out of celebrating. A group celebrating the festivals also provides, for homeschooled children, experience with adults other than their parents as authorities and time in large groups of children playing games, listening to stories, sharing meals, and importantly, engaging in free play.

In first grade last year, Ascension, the day forty days after Easter on which we celebrate Christ's rebirth and transformation into the nonphysical realm, fell on a school day in which we did watercolor painting. Although I did not plan it consciously, the color exercise we painted, red ovals on a gold ground, with orange inside the ovals, looked like a butterfly. When my daughter asked what the picture was, I said maybe it is a butterfly. She then added a body and antennae to hers, and made a beautiful painting. I did not realize until that night, when I did the review of the day, that it had been Ascension. Even though I was unconscious about it, when we painted the perfect picture of transformation, I was being guided by the festival! All the more can we enliven our work when we consciously connect with the ongoing festival time.

How Did We Get Here?

When it was time for Claire to start five-day kindergarten, the nearest Waldorf school was a forty-five-minute drive away. In our family all of us have much better days when we wake on our own and when we return for the day when we are ready. It would have been impossible for Claire (who took afternoon naps until she was over six years old), as well as for me and her younger sister if we sent her to school. Although it was frightening, we made the commitment to school at home. I began taking Waldorf teacher training courses in the middle of the kindergarten year and continued the courses through the first-grade year. In

Appendix 1: Anthroposophic Homeschooling: Fostering the Life of the Soul

addition, I took summer workshops specifically on teaching grades 1, 2, 3, and 4, and kindergarten. I have found the training immeasurably enriching and helpful in my teaching. Finally, I consult with Ms. Barbara Dewey, editor of the Waldorf Without Walls Newsletter, as well as with practicing Waldorf teachers on questions of material, organization and, artistic work.

Some of the problems and challenges we face as a homeschooling family include a lack of understanding of what we are doing, and why, as our work is unusual—both among traditional homeschoolers and among traditional Waldorf school communities. We also face challenges in fitting schooling into our family life in such a way that each enhances and strengthens, rather than causes conflict with, the other. Marking school time, and working on transitions into school, are challenges that require conscious effort and continual refinement. For me, however, and I believe also for my daughters and husband, the rewards and satisfactions far outweigh the challenges and problems. I find the inner work that is part of teaching to be a significant aid to my development. Facing the challenge of learning and singing songs, playing musical instruments, doing artwork, and memorizing and writing stories and verses, all in the context of organizing main lesson blocks, has greatly helped my self-confidence and increased my joy in my work. My meditative work on connecting with my daughters and taking the schoolwork into sleep has brought clearer focus to my thoughts and feelings, and increased my calm during the day immeasurably. My daughter is thriving, the younger one is happily joining in, and our family life is much more peaceful than it used to be.

Waldorf education requires that the teacher work out of anthroposophy (Dancy, 1998), and homeschooling as well as any other kind of schooling will only succeed when the teacher is developing personally and is committed to self-knowledge (Williams, 1998). Homeschooling is increasing in this country, and those working out of anthroposophy sometimes decide to take on the demanding task of teaching their own children. Just as the role of teacher has come to include some aspects of parenting in independent Waldorf schools (Elkind, 1987), parents sometimes take on the additional role of teacher. In both settings, institution and home, teachers work now to help the children meet their destiny in a "life in common with people of all the world" (Bock, 1955,

p. 271) and to emerge from confinement within one's own folk group and nation.

I am grateful for the work Rudolf Steiner did to initiate anthroposophic education and for all that those in the Waldorf movement have done and are yet now doing to bring this work to fruition. I sincerely believe I would not be able to give my daughters what they need in their daily lives and in their education without the inspiration of anthroposophy. Homeschooling is one of the most demanding tasks a person can undertake, and homeschooling out of anthroposophy is one path that transforms the soul life of everyone in the family by awakening us to the joy and beauty of the world and to the truth of our work in this world.

Bibliography and References

Spring, Summer, Autumn, Winter (1983). Gloucester, UK: Wynstones Press.

Almon, J. (Ed.). *An Overview of the Waldorf Kindergarten.* Silver Spring, MD: The Waldorf Kindergarten Association.

Anderson, A. (1993) *Living a Spiritual Year.* Hudson, NY: Anthroposophic Press.

Barz, C. (1991). *Festivals with Children.* Edinburgh: Floris Books.

Bock, E. (1955). *The Three Years.* London: Christian Community Press.

Burton, M. (1989). *The Light of the Child.* Ghent, NY: Adonis Press

Carey, D. & Large, J. (1982). *Families, Festivals, and Food.* Gloucestershire, UK: Hawthorn Press.

Dancy, A. (1998). "What is Essential in Waldorf Education?" Presentation at Conference on Waldorf Methods and Homeschooling, Sacramento, CA, September 19-20.

Elkind, D. (1997). "Waldorf Education in the Postmodern World." *Renewal,* Vol. 6, #1.

Querido, R. (1995). *The Esoteric Background of Waldorf Education.* Fair Oaks, CA: Rudolf Steiner College Press.

Read, C. (1997). "Family Festivals: Coming Full Circle (part 1)". *Peridot,* Vol. 9, #3.

——— (1998a). "Family Festivals: Coming Full Circle (part 2)." *Peridot*, Vol. 10, #1.

——— (1998b). "Family Festivals: Fruits of Esoteric Christianity in Family Life." *Perspectives*, October, forthcoming.

Schmidt-Brabant, M. (1996). *The Spiritual Tasks of the Homemaker*. London: Temple Lodge.

Steiner, R. (1965). *The Education of the Child*. London: Rudolf Steiner Press.

——— (1982). *Balance in Teaching*. Spring Valley, NY: Mercury Press.

——— (1988). *Practical Advice to Teachers*. New York: Anthroposophic Press.

——— (1994). *Theosophy*. Hudson, NY: Anthroposophic Press

——— (1996). *The Festivals and their Meaning*. London: Rudolf Steiner Press

——— (1996). *The Foundations of Human Experience*. Hudson, NY: Anthroposophic Press.

——— (1997). *Discussions with Teachers*. Hudson, NY: Anthroposophic Press.

Williams, L. (1998). "What is Essential in Homeschooling?" Presentation at Conference on Waldorf Methods and Homeschooling, Sacramento, CA, September 19-20.

APPENDIX 2:
COLORED SHADOWS AND AFTERIMAGES

RESEARCH FOR THE PHYSICS CURRICULUM
GRADE 12 OPTICS BLOCK

(2009)

The physics curriculum in Waldorf schools calls for a block on optics in Grade 12. In this block the activity of light is experienced, and the methods and ideas of Goethe and Newton are contrasted. Newton's work was in line with current methods of mainstream science which involve testing hypotheses. The method of hypothesis testing is useful, but only if the hypotheses are warranted, that is, they are about objects or events that are potentially perceivable (Steiner, 1996, Lecture 1). Notice that atoms and molecules are not potentially perceivable. Goethe's method, in contrast, involves direct experience of as many instances of a phenomenon as possible until experience of the underlying archetype or fundamental primal form arises. Steiner, in his lectures to Waldorf science teachers on physics, says that Goetheanism should "continue its education" (Steiner, 2001). He points out a misstep in Goethe's thinking about afterimages,[1] and describes one method to experience the true situation. He also describes a different general method of scientific endeavor, one of "gathering" experiences from the periphery and eventually coming to a central point. This contrasts with Goethe's method which begins with an experience in nature and then analyzes it into simpler component experiences.

The research I report here delves into one of Goethe's investigations of color and brings this study up to date based on

---

[1] An image, usually visual, that persists after the external source is removed; it is the opposite of the original image in brightness and color

Steiner's critique of Goethe's explanation of colored shadows.[2] *I report on a method for distinguishing colored shadows and afterimages that is available to any observer. I also explicate Steiner's description of the relation of colored shadows and afterimages as equally objective phenomena that exist at different levels of reality. The results and method of this study could easily be part of the Grade 12 Optics block, and the thinking behind this work might prove valuable to the physics teacher.*

Colored Shadows and Afterimages

"Thinking consideration must encompass what is perceptible...and must seek the interrelationships within this area."
    Goethe, "Against Atomism," *Scientific Studies*

Abstract

In lecture 5 of *The Light Course*,[3] Steiner states: "Goethe died in 1832, and we don't confess to an 1832 Goetheanism, but rather to one of the year 1919—in other words, to a Goetheanism that has continued its education" (p. 94). Steiner goes on to take Goethe's work a step further by showing that light and dark work in the human eye the way they do in nature. We use the eyes as instruments to see color of various types. He specifically points out that afterimage color is no less objective than colored shadows, and that the two are related. Colored shadows are objective, and not contrastive (that is, not due to afterimage effects), and, also, afterimage colors are objective. Although this idea contradicts the usual understanding of afterimages, I will endeavor to trace out the consequences of the idea that afterimages are objective.

---

2 Shadows are usually thought to be black, or the relative absence of light; close observation reveals that most are, to some degree, colored.

3 "First Course of Natural Science" was the name Steiner originally gave to this series of ten lectures for teachers of the first Waldorf School in Stuttgart from December 23, 1919 to January 3, 1920. Over the following years it became known as "The Light Course." (*The Light Course*, Anthroposophic Press, 2001, CW310). This course and the two subsequent courses on the natural sciences given in 1920 (*The Warmth Course*, Mercury Press, 1988, CW321) and 1921 (*Interdisciplinary Astronomy*, CW323) were intended by Steiner as a basic schooling in the Goethean approach to science and as an introduction to his impulse to anchor natural science in a science of the spirit.

Prior to demonstrating the relation of colored shadows and afterimages, I worked with prismatic color observations in order to "tune" the instrument of the eye and to begin to educate my attention to pure color phenomena. I then observed colored shadows in several ways, as described by Goethe in *Farbenlehre*, and as explained by Steiner in lecture 7 of *The Light Course* (Dec. 30, 1919) where he details how phenomenological work based on spiritual science goes beyond that of Goethe. Steiner shows that Goethe's conclusion that "colored" shadows are afterimage colors is incorrect and that the theory of color must be changed. Steiner's direction for making a critical observation has not yielded clear-cut results, at least as reported in published literature. Others have taken steps to photograph colored shadows, and to observe them through prisms and to photograph the result. My method takes a different tack: I work on systematic observations of the qualities of colored shadows and of afterimages. Out of this work comes the idea: One cannot make afterimages of afterimages—therefore, if one can make afterimages of colored shadows, the latter cannot be afterimages. I describe the results of this investigation, which are clear-cut, consistent, and available to anyone without involving physical image-making in the form of photographs. The end of this report consists of ideas for future work based on Steiner's statements about the primacy of velocity (e.g., lecture 2, *The Light Course*), and the relation of this idea to afterimages that come about from moving through the world. Specifically, I ask: Is visual flow analogous to velocity in being the real quality from which we divide out and thereby create such concepts as image or layout-of-surfaces and time-to-contact? These are questions for future research based on the method of making a reasoned series of observations.

Introduction

In 1919–1920 Rudolf Steiner gave a series of lectures to science teachers of the Waldorf School in which he endeavored to give them some basic ideas in the study of nature (Steiner, 2001). He said (on page of 95 of *The Light Course*): "It's really a matter of precisely following through to their conclusion what is present in the natural phenomena. And light gives us the most clues for pursuing that course." Does light give these clues because it exists at the border of the material and the immaterial, and thus can bring our attention to the spiritual beyond the physical? We do not see light, but we see the world by means of the light. Is color a relationship between light and the world, so that our sense of sight can be especially educated by experiences with color? The method of following clues does not necessarily lead one in a straight line in one's thinking and observations. Indeed, Steiner described his course thus:

> I would like to guide you to a certain insight into the natural sciences, so please regard everything I present before that as a kind of preparation, which isn't done by progressing in a straight line, as is otherwise the custom, but by gathering the phenomena we need and creating a circle, so to speak, then pressing forward to the central point (p. 111).

In describing my observations of light, and demonstrations of prism and colored shadow phenomena, I will try to follow Steiner's method of "gathering the phenomena." In the final section of the paper I will contrast this approach to Goethe's method of experiencing as many instances of a phenomenon as possible until the "archetype" emerges. (See Goethe, *The Metamorphosis of Plants*, 1988.) Where Goethe moves to explaining, Steiner stays with perceiving, including, for him, perceiving the living aspect of the world, which he terms the "etheric" world. This term resonates with the ancient Greek word "*aether*" which designated a world surrounding the physical world, and existing above or beyond that world.

Steiner studies the phenomenon of color resulting from the interaction of light and darkness in many ways, one of these being to demonstrate and explain colored shadows. Goethe laid out in great detail in his *Farbenlehre* that colors result from the interworking of light and darkness. Steiner works through this interaction in several careful steps in lecture 7 of *The Light Course*. He shows that one should observe as many real phenomena as possible before coming to conclusions about the causes of the interaction of light and darkness. One phenomenon that can help us to understand color is that of colored shadows. He then demonstrates a setup that Goethe had described originally in the *Farbenlehre* (p. 31); two candles are placed in front of a white screen with a vertical rod between them and the screen. Two shadows are cast, that is, certain dark spaces are created. Then if red glass is placed in front of one of the candles, the light from that candle is dimmed, and because it is dimmed red, its shadow becomes green. Goethe explained this phenomenon as due to the "required" color or afterimage; Steiner concludes that this explanation is incorrect. My project reports on Goethe's observation and explanation of colored shadows, Steiner's further observations and descriptions, others based on Steiner's ideas, and finally my own, new, systematic observations of colored shadows and afterimages. Through all these steps, one might see a pressing toward a central point, that is, the true nature of colored shadows.

Tuning the instrument: Preliminary experiences with prismatic color

To begin the study of color that is independent of solid objects, that is, not pigment-based, I did a series of observations with prisms. This work was intended to tune and educate my eye and attention with regard to color phenomena that form at the boundaries of light and dark. Proskauer, in his book *The Rediscovery of Color*, gives directions and black-and-white figures to guide one in recreating in a certain sequence some of the prism observations that Goethe reported in *Farbenlehre*. I used glass prisms of two angles and Proskauer's Plates 1–6. I worked with Plates 1–4 in January 2007 and Plates 3–6 in May 2007, recording my experiences and checking that I experienced what Proskauer described. These plates move intentionally from complex to simple following Goethe's method based on mathematics: to "analyze complex problems until one arrives at the simplest, indivisible, self-evident facts" (Goethe, *Maxims and Reflections*). I did experience what Proskauer noted, with the exception of red pressing into the darkness, and blue spreading out from the darkness. I could not see these movement qualities.

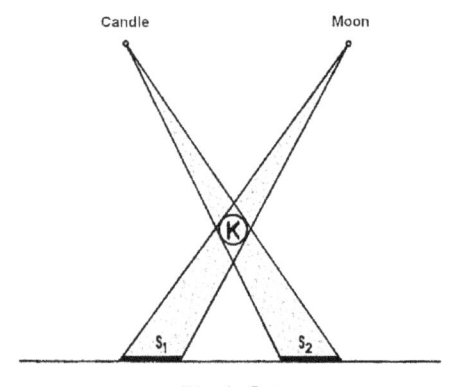

Fig. 1: Setup

Appendix 2: Colored Shadows and Afterimages

Fig. 2: Shadow in moonlight

Fig. 3: In moonlight and candle

In conjunction with these prismatic color observations, I studied prismatic colors in nature, that is, rainbows, sundogs, and color fringes.[4] I watched, for example, a sundog in March in the afternoon with some small, elongated clouds in the sky. The sundog was to the lower right side of the sun in front of a cloud, which looked darker on the sun side of the sundog, and lighter on the outer side. As I watched, the cloud moved, but the sundog didn't, so that the cloud continuously moved through or behind the sundog—the cloud emerging on the outer side of the sundog becoming lighter than it was on the inside. I also saw color fringes at the edge of the moon, which is a classic light-dark boundary. In late May around 9:00 PM at around latitude 42 degrees, I looked at

---

4   Sundogs are small arcs of rainbow that appear to be near the sun and stay in a fixed distance from it. Color fringes are red-to-yellow or violet-to-blue sequences of prismatic color that occur at the boundary of light and dark.

the moon, which was nearly full in a sky almost completely dark, but with a slight tinge of intense dark turquoise still in the sky. Contemplating the moon, I noticed a red to yellow fringe on the upper left, and an indigo to light blue fringe on the opposite side. The next night when the sky was hazy, no color fringes were present.

Goethe's Work on Colored Shadows

Goethe begins his section of the *Farbenlehre* titled "Colored Shadows" with a detailed description of colored shadows in nature. This passage lays the groundwork for the phenomena that are the focus of the present study.

> 75. Once, on a winter's journey in the Harz Mountains, I made my descent from the Broken as evening fell. The broad slope above and below me was snow-covered, the meadow lay beneath a blanket of snow, every isolated tree and jutting crag, every wooded grove and rocky prominence was rimed with frost, and the sun was just setting beyond the Oder ponds.
>
> Because of the snow's yellowish cast, pale violet shadows had accompanied us all day, but now, as an intensified yellow reflected from the areas in the light, we were obliged to describe the shadows as deep blue.
>
> At last the sun began to disappear and its rays, subdued by the strong haze, spread the most beautiful purple hue over my surroundings. At that point the color of the shadows was transformed into a green comparable in clarity to a sea green and in beauty to an emerald green. The effect grew ever more vivid; it was as if we found ourselves in a fairy world for everything had clothed itself in these two lively colors so beautifully harmonious with one another. When the sun had set, the magnificent display finally faded into gray twilight and then into a clear moonlit night filled with stars.
>
> 76. One of the most beautiful examples of colored shadows may be observed when the moon is full. It is possible to find a perfect balance between the light of a candle and that of the moon; both shadows are formed with equal strength and clarity so that the two colors are in complete equilibrium. The surface should be placed in

Appendix 2: Colored Shadows and Afterimages

the light of the full moon with a candle at an appropriate distance a little to one side; an opaque object should then be held in front of the surface. A double shadow will result; the one cast by the moon and lit by the candle will seem an intense red-yellow, while the one cast by the candle and lit by the moon will appear in the most beautiful blue. The area where the two shadows meet and merge will be black. There is no more striking demonstration of the yellow shadow. The close proximity of the blue shadow and intervening black shadow make the phenomenon all the more attractive. When we look at the surface for a long time, the blue required as a complement by yellow will impose its own demand on the yellow which produced it; it will intensify the yellow and force it into the yellow-red. This in turn will bring forth its opposite, a shade of sea green.

77. Here it should be noted that it takes some time to produce the complementary color. Before the complementary color will appear vividly the retina must be affected fully by the color that calls it forth.

Note that Goethe moves from *describing* colored shadows, and the phenomenon of complementary colors observed there, to, in paragraph 77, *explaining* the complementary colors as "required" colors or afterimages formed by the eye.

Observations of Colored Shadows under Specified Conditions: Observations in Moonlight

The configuration diagrammed in Figure 1 shows the arrangement Goethe described (quoted above) for observing the yellow shadow cast by a candle in moonlight. I observed the shadows he describes on three occasions in February and March of 2007. In all cases the moon was nearly full and about halfway between the horizon and its zenith. I first used a flashlight and then, twice, a candle. The candle cast a more yellow shadow, but in both cases the shadow cast by the moon and lighted by the candlelight became golden, and its shadow was slightly bluish. On the last occasion, in March near Easter, we photographed the shadows with a digital camera and immediately afterward looked at the pictures on a computer screen. I had a clear memory of the colored shadows I had just seen, and the colors in the photographs were not exactly the same, but were close. The shadow cast by the moon alone is shown in Figure 2, and the shadows when the candle was added are shown in Figure 3.

Observations with Light through Colored Film

The arrangement of objects used to display colored shadows as described by Goethe and Steiner is portrayed in Figure 4. An opaque object stands before a screen, between the screen and two light sources. These two lights cast two shadows, one lighter and more indistinct than the other. When red film or glass is placed in front of the latter light, its shadow immediately becomes a light sea green with a light red background. The other shadow stays dark and mostly black, depending on how wide the red film is. The darker shadow can also become somewhat reddened. These steps are shown in Figures 5 through 9. Again, the photographs were produced digitally, and though they show the colored shadow (even reflecting off the white ceramic candleholder that is the opaque object in Figure 7), but not in the same hue that I saw. These observations were made several times in April before they were photographed in May.

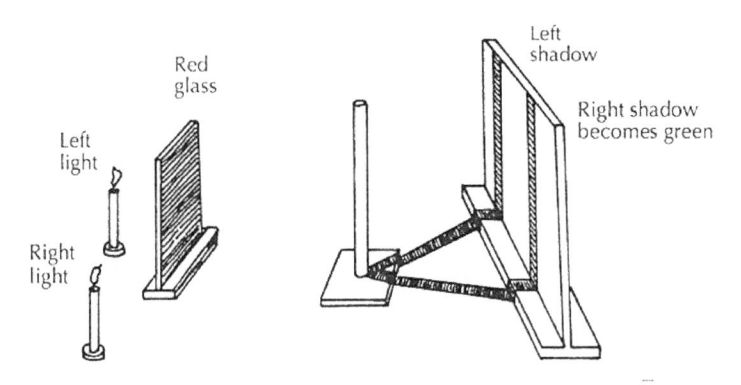

Fig. 4: Setup for colored shadows

Appendix 2: Colored Shadows and Afterimages

Fig. 5: Shadow in "white" light

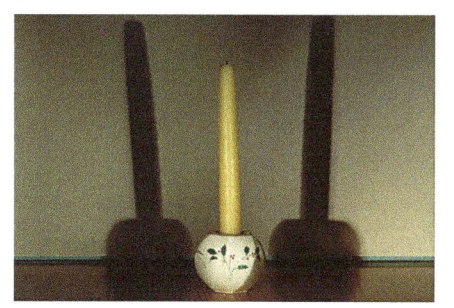

Fig. 6: In two "white" lights

Fig. 7: In "white" and red lights

Fig. 8: Red and green in "white" light

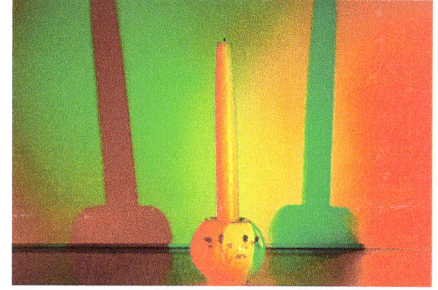

Fig. 9: Red and green, no "white" light

Are Colored Shadows Afterimages?

Steiner diverges from Goethe in his characterization of colored shadows. In fact, Steiner says that Goethe's explanation is incorrect, and that the *Farbenlehre* should be modified to take this into account (Steiner, 2001, p. 113). Goetheanism, because it is living, evolves, or as Steiner says, "continues its education" (Ibid. p. 94).

Steiner stated: "The differentiation between subjective and objective, between color that is temporarily fixed here (on the screen) and color 'required' by the eye as an afterimage has no justification on the basis of objective facts." To elaborate this point he goes on to say: "When I am seeing the red here with my eyes, I am dealing simply with all the pieces of physical equipment I have described to you—the vitreous body, the lens, the fluid between the lens and the cornea (of the eye). I am dealing with a highly differentiated physical apparatus. The relationship of this physical equipment, which mixes light and dark with each other in the most varied ways, to the objectively extant ether is no different than that of the pieces of equipment I have set up here—the screen, the rod, etc."

Thus, the process is not different when one sees it in a "subjective" way with the eyes, or when one fixes one's gaze on it on the screen. Steiner then describes: "You float in the ether. Whether you become one with it by means of your eyes or this equipment, it is just a different series of events." And he goes on to conclude: "There is no real essential difference between the green image that has been produced in space by darkening with red and the green afterimage that only occurs temporarily. Looked at objectively there isn't a tangible difference—in one instance the process takes place in space, in the other instance it takes place in time" (lecture 7, p. 115). Clearly, there is a difference between processes in space and time, but Steiner's description draws our attention to the eye as an instrument with certain qualities that form color over a span of time and then dissolve it. Perhaps color in the world is at the physical level; color in the eye is at the level of the etheric.

The radical idea that afterimages are objective colors, and that colored shadows are not afterimages, requires that we think clearly about the two phenomena, that we make careful observations, and that we develop methods for distinguishing the two-color experiences. Steiner, in lecture 7 of *The Light Course*, says that if one looks at the colored shadow through a small tube so as to see only its color, and not the complementary color of the background, one will still see the single color of the shadow.

The controversy regarding methods of observation

A footnote to lecture 7 of the *The Light Course* describes that a physicist tried the experiment of looking at the colored shadow with a

Appendix 2: Colored Shadows and Afterimages

small tube, with negative results.[5] Subsequently he met with other scientists to try to make the observation that Steiner described; this group had mixed reports of the results. They then turned to the method of photographing colored shadows, presumably with the thought that if photographs showed color, it could not be just within the eye. The first results were not reliable, but with advances in film technology, Hans-Georg Hetzel did produce color photographs that showed the colored shadow and he included a grayscale in the photo to show that not all gray had become the color of the shadow. There is agreement that even the most careful color photographs do not show the colors seen in person.

Hetzel later published an article which took these observations one step further (Hetzel, 1987). In reference to the setup shown in Figure 4, Hetzel states that the question arises again and again whether the color of the shadow is produced by the eye. He notes three points: 1) the color of the shadow is the complementary color to the surrounding color, 2) the color appears strong and intense, even if the surround is only faintly colored, and 3) the colored shadow is photographable. He goes a further step to observe the colored shadow through the prism and finds that it gives rise to the same kind of colored fringes as black shadows, and shadows colored with one light source (that is, with no complementary color involved). He compared the colored fringes from a green shadow from a single green light source to those formed from a green shadow as the complement to the red light surrounding it. Hetzel describes the prismatic colors from the two types of green shadow as the same. He photographed these three cases and presented these photographs in the article. There are clear color separations in all three cases; from his photographs the colors for the two green shadows do not look the same to me. The ones for the plain green shadow look

---

[5] See the footnote to Lecture 7, p. 190, *The Light Course* for details on attempts to view the colored shadow through a small tube, and various attempts to photograph the shadows. V.C. Bennie, a physicist at Kings College, University of London, could not see the color through the tube. Subsequent experiments by a group at Dornach, which included Steiner, resulted in different reports by different participants. My own attempts to view the shadows through a small tube with a group of observers yielded similar results. A further thought was to photograph the shadows; this Hans-Georg Hetzel worked on in detail. The main claim is that the photographs show that the process developed for ordinary colored surfaces also reacts to colored shadows.

yellow and blue; the ones for the complementary green shadow look orange and purple/blue. The article ends with the question: Does not this photographic documentation show that the color of colored shadows exists independent of our eye?

To replicate these prism observations with colored shadows, I used my setup, as shown in Figures 5, 6, and 7, and observed all the steps with an equiangular glass prism. I did see color fringes on the edges of dark objects and the dark shadows, but I saw absolutely no color fringe or color separation in relation to the colored shadows. Photographs of my setup through the prism are shown in Figures 10, 11, 12, and 13. Again, these photographs show the colors, but not exactly as I remember seeing them. The surprising result is that the colored shadows *are* differentiated from the gray shadows in that the prism does not at all change how they look. I did not try the case of the colored shadow with the same color background. The question of the differences in results is not resolved. Hetzel may have used a very large prism, and I would have to try my observations again with such a prism to see if his results were replicated. The fact that the complementary colored shadow behaved so differently from all other surfaces around it when viewed through the prism is also a puzzle. Perhaps the complementary colors balance each other so perfectly that a light-dark boundary does not develop, consequently the conditions for a color fringe are lacking.

Fig. 10: Shadow from one white light seen through a prism

Fig. 11: Shadow from one "white" and one red light seen through a prism

Appendix 2: Colored Shadows and Afterimages

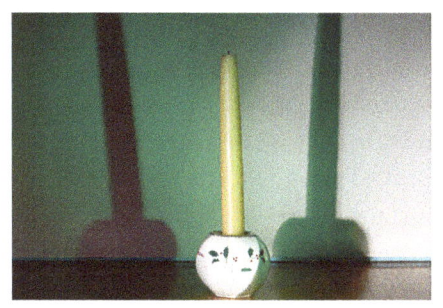

Fig. 12: Shadow from one "white" and one green light seen through a prism

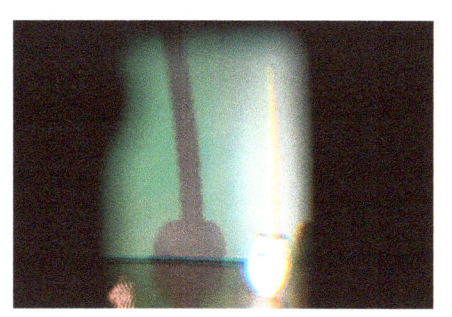

Fig. 13

So far, I have not dealt with the question of photographs as evidence of the independence of the colored shadow from the afterimage processes of the eye. Goethe placed his topic "colored shadows" in the section of the *Farbenlehre* titled "Physiological Colors." As we saw from the quote above, he assumes that the color of the shadows is due to the colored background light calling forth a "required" light from the eye. Is it sound thinking to propose that a photograph that shows a colored shadow proves that the color is independent of the eye? What is a photograph? The photograph is a mechanically produced image on paper based on chemical reactions on film or digital correspondences to measured light-dark areas that the camera is exposed to. The image on paper is an object that we perceive as we do any object in the world, except that it is two-dimensional and formed based on linear perspective. Because it is produced using a mechanical instrument, we think that it is objective. But perception of the image involves the eye, just as perception of the scene that was photographed involves the eye. If we are forming afterimages in the scene, we could be forming afterimages in perceiving the photograph. Photographic evidence does not lead us closer to distinguishing colored shadows from afterimages.

A New Method for Distinguishing Colored Shadows from Afterimages

If we return to Steiner's statement that colored shadows exist in space and afterimages in time, we have a clue for beginning to differentiate the two phenomena. Anyone can see that in the experimental setup, the colored shadow appears instantly, that is, coincidentally with the background color formed by the light shining through colored film. This observation fits with Steiner's statement, but counters Goethe's characterization that the color called forth from the eye takes time to develop. My experience of afterimages, in addition, is that they are fluctuating—changing in color and form—and that they, therefore, exist in a pulsing, breathing movement. This quality is the opposite of the colored shadows that jump instantly into existence and "stay put" as long as the conditions for their existence hold. Light in nature, especially at sunset and dawn, is always changing. Colored shadows formed in this setting would have a more dynamic quality than those in the experiment, but the changes in the complementary colors remain exactly coincident in time, and are thus, of a spatial quality. Further, colored shadows can be explored visually just as any surface in the world can be explored. That is, we can focus on any part of the colored shadow at any time, move our gaze, look away and look back, without changing the shape or quality of the color of the shadow.

What are the Corresponding Qualities of Afterimages?

To form afterimages for one's own observation, one must focus on a point on a colored surface for at least thirty seconds, and look away from the colored surface to a white or light gray, smooth, indirectly lit surface—or close one's eyes. The complementary color will form in an image with the basic form of the object one focused on. The afterimage, however, stays in the periphery—one cannot focus on it, and therefore one cannot explore it visually. It gradually fades away, sometimes changing color and disappearing and reappearing before it fades. If one forms an afterimage looking first at a colored surface and then at a white surface, and then places a colored surface in the same space as the image, the color of the afterimage remains the same, if somewhat darkened by the colored surface added. If one makes an afterimage, and then tries to concentrate on it for several seconds, even though one cannot focus on it, and then looks to a different white area, the same color as the original afterimage is seen. Given these conditions and qualities, I maintain that it is not possible to make an afterimage of an afterimage. Therefore, if one can make afterimages of colored shadows, the colored shadows cannot, themselves, be afterimages.

Afterimages of Colored Shadows

I worked with all the colored shadows formed in the experimental demonstrations described in this paper to test whether I could make afterimages of them, and whether the color of the afterimage was the complementary color to the colored shadow. In every case I stared at a point in the colored shadow near the center of the shadow for about thirty seconds and then looked away to a non-colored surface. The yellow shadow of the moon produced a pale blue; the blue shadow a pale yellow. The green colored shadow was the condition for a red afterimage, and vice versa. Interestingly, the quality of the color as ephemeral and translucent without radiating brightness was the same in both the colored shadows and afterimages. I formed afterimages of moon shadows in electric light and in candlelight, of the colored film shadows in electric light and in candlelight in both daylight and at night. In all cases the afterimages were readily formed from the colored shadows. The afterimage method has one final advantage: one is not required to somehow isolate the eye from the background color; both the colored shadow and its complementary background color form their own opposite afterimage color. Anyone with normal color vision can observe this set of phenomena.

Conclusions

I maintain that colored shadows are at one level of phenomena and afterimages at another level. Colored shadows exist outside the eye; afterimages through the eye—but both are *objective*. These levels should not be mixed in understanding and explaining the phenomenon of colored shadows, as Goethe does. It is misleading to step from one level to the other in explanation. Colors are vital and they work or tend toward balance or completion at each level, not across the levels. Steiner describes color phenomena thus: "We are thoroughly in things with our being and are in things all the more as we ascend from certain physical phenomena to other physical phenomena. We are not in color phenomena with our ordinary bodily nature but with our etheric and, therefore, our astral nature" (Lecture 7, p. 116). Perhaps colored light and shadow, as "free" color—that is, not bound to the surface of a physical substance—is a higher physical phenomenon in which we float with our etheric and astral natures. For this reason, these phenomena would be important to experience in a systematic manner in order to raise our senses to the level of perception required by these delicate phenomena.

I conclude that colored shadows are not afterimages—they are shadows that are colored.

By proceeding from simplified observations in nature (moon shadows) to more controlled demonstrations with colored light, and forming afterimages in parallel with observing colored shadows, the method gathers experiences that place color itself, rather than colored objects, at the center of inquiry and thinking. Rather than working to allow an archetype or primal underlying form to arise, one begins to develop sensitivity to different levels of the phenomena in relation to one's own senses and activities. The *Farbenlehre* would have to take into account at least a threefold human being in order correctly to describe the workings of color in the world, in our eye, and in our perception. Thus, Goetheanism continues its education, and we ours.

Future Investigations

In lecture 2 of *The Light Course* Steiner says that velocity (as a vector, that is, movement in a direction) is primary and that distance and time derive from it. I will work on the idea that color coincides with the movement of light into darkness or darkness into light, and the question of whether these movements could be characterized as vectors. Vector analysis arose in mathematics and usually involves calculation. Is it fruitful to think of color as deriving from the movement of light or darkness? Certainly, light is directional in relation to objects, as is shown by the shadows that are cast. Goethe's famous statement that colors are the deeds and sufferings of light might be explicated by such an analysis as I suggest here.

I will also continue my investigations of developments in Goetheanism by studying visual flow as one moves through the world and consequent afterimages of movement in relation to Steiner's statement that velocity is primary and that distance and time derive from it. If visual flow is primary, then such concepts as the visual image and its transformation would be derivative, rather than formative as is thought in mainstream physiological and perceptual studies of perception. (See Gibson, 1979, for a critique of this view.)

I take seriously the statement of Steiner that the psychologists have failed to support the physicists in their study of light. He states, in lecture 7, p. 122:

> Our psychology, you see, is actually in even a worse state than our physiology and physics, and we can't really blame the physicists very much for expressing themselves so unrealistically about what is in the outer world, because they are not supported at all by the psychologists. The psychologists have been conditioned by the churches, which have staked a claim to all knowledge about the soul and spirit. Therefore, this conditioning, which the psychologists have accepted, has led them to regard the human being as only the outer apparatus and to see soul and spirit only in the sound of words, in phrases. Our psychology is actually only a collection of words, for there's nothing there about what people should understand by "soul" and "spirit." And that's why it appears to the physicists that it is an inner, subjective experience when light at work out there affects the eye and the eye counteracts it or receives the impression, as the case may be. A whole tangle of ambiguities begins right there, and the physicists repeat this in quite the same way for the other sense organs.

Perhaps we can work toward untangling these ambiguities by clarifying our thinking about perception through a careful experience of central phenomena—by gathering the phenomena until they point to a center.

References

Goethe, J. W., (1998). *Maxims and Reflections*. New York: Penguin.
—— (1988). *Farbenlehre* (Theory of Color), tr. Douglas Miller. Princeton, NJ: Princeton University Press.
—— (1988). "The Metamorphosis of Plants." In D. Miller (ed. & tr.), *Goethe's Scientific Studies*. Princeton, NJ: Princeton University Press.
Gibson, J. J. (1979). *The Ecological Approach to Visual Perception*. New York: Houghton Mifflin.
Hetzel, H-G. (1987). Der "Fargibe Schatten." "*Optometrie*," Ausgabe 4, Median-Verlag.

Proskauer, H. (1986). *The Rediscovery of Color: Goethe vs. Newton Today*. Spring Valley, NY: Anthroposophic Press.

Steiner, R. (2001). *The Light Course*. Great Barrington, MA: Anthroposophic Press.

——— (1996). *Physiology and Therapeutics*. Spring Valley, NY: Mercury Press.

Related Works

Steiner, R. (2005). *Goethean Science*. Chestnut Ridge, NY: Mercury Press.

——— (1988). *Warmth Course*. Spring Valley, NY: Mercury Press.

——— (1983). *The Boundaries of Natural Science*. Spring Valley, NY: Anthroposophic Press.

——— (1968). *A Theory of Knowledge Based on Goethe's World Conception*. New York: Anthroposophic Press.

Von Zabern, B. (1999). *Organic Physics*. Spring Valley, NY: Mercury Press.

Appendix 3: Seeing the Twelve Grades through the Lens of the Twelve Senses

Or, The School-Leaving Speech I Didn't Give

(2009)

This would be the last year of homeschooling for Claire. Our eleventh-grade daughter, homeschooled since kindergarten, had decided to enter a college preparatory school near us for the following year. The end of our last year marked a life change from school at home to school in an institution, and I wanted to celebrate the transition with a kind of graduation from our school. At the end of each school year prior to this we held an assembly in which my two daughters and I presented a program of music, movement, and speech taken from the circle activities that had begun each school day.

I thought that as the teacher in this last assembly for Claire I would present a speech that would encompass the twelve years we had been together. As I thought about how to look back over the twelve years of school, and about what could be a unifying theme, a lens through which to see each year, I remembered Rudolf Steiner's description of the twelve senses. (See the bibliography below for references.) The senses all function together at all ages of life, but they differentiate, develop, and shift in balance as one moves through the different stages of life. (See Albert Soesman, *Our Twelve Senses*, Hawthorn Press, 1990.)

The first four senses are the so-called "lower" senses, and they relate to sensing one's own physical body—they are touch, life, self-movement, and balance. With the sense of touch, we feel the boundary of our own body. With the life sense, we are aware of the wholeness or health of the body as a living whole. With the sense of self-movement, we are aware of the movements of the body in relation to other parts of the body (also sometimes called proprioception). With the sense of balance, we are constantly assessing the orientation of the body in relation to gravity (the vestibular sense). These lower senses develop early as the infant is touched and held, moves, and eventually begins to gain uprightness.

The "middle" four senses, sometimes characterized as soul senses, have to do with the relation of the person to the world. The senses in this group are all recognized in mainstream psychology and physiology—they are smell, taste, sight, and warmth (inaccurately, called temperature). The sense of smell is the first to relate to physical material from outside one's own body, but it also relates to morality and a sense of good and bad. Recall the line from *Hamlet* (Act I, Scene 4): "Something is rotten in the state of Denmark." Taste takes physical matter and dissolves it, making it fluid and able to enter a flowing, living system. Taste involves a process of meeting the world; we say people have taste when their clothes and homes are harmonious and beautiful. The sense of sight or vision takes us farther out into the world, at a farther distance from our own body. Sight gives awareness of color and of the lightness and darkness of the surfaces in the world around us. Light links us to the surfaces of the world through vision. The sense of warmth is the next step in moving out into the world. Warmth or coolness fills the air and water in currents, but also fills the solids in our world. When we feel the warmth of a sun-warmed stone, we sense deeper into the stone than just its surface. At another level, warmth is interest that one can pour into one's attention for something in the world, or for another person.

The "higher" four senses take us even farther out of our body and into the world and other people—they are hearing, word, concept, and I. Hearing leads to sensing the inner qualities of things—when we hear a bell ring, we hear into the material and the shape, in a way we hear through them into something beyond them, into the immaterial. Word, concept, and I are not to be found in mainstream science as senses. We understand language using our sense of word; we must be able to sense the meaning of what is said, and hearing sound is not sufficient for this perception. Then, we use the sense of thought or concept to reach the idea behind the word. Finally, the most complex sense is that which allows us to perceive the I or self of another human being. We sense the presence of another human being at the level of self.

Appendix 3: Seeing the Twelve Grades through the Lens of the Twelve Senses

The senses as a lens to view the grades

Though I use the progression through the senses as described above to work through the progression of the school years from kindergarten through Grade 11, I do not mean that there is one correct correspondence between qualities of the senses and the content of the curriculum grade by grade. But I wanted to see whether coherent themes would emerge from a sequential view of the grades using the senses as a focus. Therefore, starting with kindergarten, I thought back over the school year in the light of, or through the lens of, the qualities and tasks of the sense of touch. What came to mind about Claire's kindergarten year when I thought about touch, the boundaries of the body, and boundaries in general? Contemplating the qualities of touch and thinking about the kindergarten year, I found that certain scenes came to the fore. I saw that they had to do with boundaries and so I took heart in the method—and continued on through the senses and the grades.

THE SCHOOL-LEAVING SPEECH

Below is an abridged version of the speech I wrote for the celebration of my daughter's leaving of our school at home.

Touch

The first day of kindergarten at home was an exploring day. We walked out our back door across our bare California soil to a dusty path through parched yellow grass to the arroyo—then down the bank into the creek bed sheltered by scrub willow. There we found some mud, good for smearing and packing and covering skin and anything else! The next day we were fresh for school—the bell and handshake, the circle in verse, songs, movement and then snack, painting, drawing or modeling, and the final gathering into the Rainbow House for a fairy tale. Two more days of circle and story would finish each fairy tale. And the last day of the week we were ready to go *out* to a play day in the park with other children. I especially remember one painting day, when Claire and Sara, her little sister, sat next to each other at the table. They each had their wetted, white paper ready before them and their nice big brushes and two beautiful colors of paint. I painted first, saying a little about the colors, then they started. Claire was irritated that Sara sat so close. I just quietly proceeded, with Claire getting more and more vocal, when suddenly Sara calmly raised her brush full of red paint and with a quick flick of the wrist flung paint everywhere—just happy to see the paint fly. The red splatters were not only all over the table and me and Claire, they were on Claire's *painting*! Outrage! I quickly separated them, repaired Claire's painting, and we went on with the day. What an art—judging space and closeness.

Life

First grade was a step across a threshold, and Claire knew it. When I rang the bell, she and Sara appeared at the doorway of the classroom, having dressed themselves in their fancy Easter dresses. So beautiful! This was really school. The structure and rhythm of the days and of the week stayed the same, and our old friends the fairy tales were there. But now a main lesson was added—serious work. The straight line and the curve, the letters and numbers, work in painting, modeling, and something new, a musical instrument—the pentatonic flute. All this work, but everything had a life. The straight line and curve went on a journey through the whole year, related to the festivals. The lessons came out of nature and scenes from fairy tales, the numbers related to gnomes, the colors and tones had a life of their own. Our play, enacting Snow White with scenes and songs, was about life and death. Claire was Snow White, who had to "die," but who was also awakened. The seriousness, the life or death, of school was an undercurrent the whole year—even with all the laughing and fun that went on day by day.

Self-movement

In second grade, two paths gradually came into view: the one leading to the saints, the other to the animals. We went a ways down each path with our stories of the saints, and in contrast, with the fables. We saw how far they diverged. Claire loved the humor of the animal fables, and their exaggerated gestures and schemes—and the path of the saints was also very real to her. In preparing for a scene in her play of St. Clare and St. Francis, she insisted that the altar in their little church be against the wall. I later found out this was true of old churches in the Middle Ages. There was no space behind the altar where people could stand—the altar met directly with the other world.

Appendix 3: Seeing the Twelve Grades through the Lens of the Twelve Senses

Now the rhythm of the days of the week was familiar, and the festivals were well-known enough to begin to sense the movement from one to the next. At the beginning of school was Michaelmas, which quickened into Advent, which then deepened into Christmas. Then gradually with Candlemas and then Easter, we came out of winter into warmth in nature, ending the school year with the beginning of summer.

Balance

Third grade brought farming, house building, and stories from the Old Testament, as well as measurement. We grew different grains in the backyard, built a teepee covered with palm leaves, worked on a straw bale house, and learned gardening and baking. All this practical activity was countered by the other pole: the hard work of thinking, questioning, and knowing. We studied all kinds of measurement: length, volume, and weight, using our beautiful brass scale with weights to balance and measure. We studied the people of the Old Testament. We saw how they lived in Paradise but didn't know it, and how they were tempted and ate of the Tree of Knowledge and then had to labor in the fields and the house—the long, long road back to Paradise. Claire loved to climb on top of the swing sets, stand and walk along the single beam at the top, high above the shocked adults standing below. She built her own "fort" out of huge straw bales and clambered all over it. She was upset that Jahve accepted Abel's sacrifice but not Cain's, and that Isaac was tricked into choosing Jacob as his successor and not Esau, the firstborn. She looked for the justice, the balance of deed and consequence.

Smell

Fourth grade brought big steps into the world—Claire had a new friend with whom to play and work, and also with whom to take trips and with whom to perform in the class play, a story from the *Kalevala*. She had lessons on the animals in relation to the human being and saw cougars, eagles, deer, and others in the mountain zoo. And she saw dolphins frisking by the boat on our trip to Catalina Island for her birthday. We studied fractions and even dividing fractions. She heard the Norse myths and the *Kalevala* and the *Poetic Edda*, and read stories about Vainamoinen and Odin who both had a good nose for evil—they couldn't be tricked or deceived. Claire discovered that she has a good nose—she can tell a place by its smell.

Taste

Grade 5 found us in a completely new place—our new home in Pennsylvania. New beginnings! We studied botany and did many drawings of plants, spending our exploring days at a wildflower preserve nearby. We drew beautiful geometric forms.

We also had lessons on ancient cultures, and then Greek stories that moved into Greek history. The play for the year was about Pandora, the metamorphosis from the dead to the living—and then the choice to defy the gods. At least hope was left at the end. Claire was taking the world in more deeply, getting a taste for it, deciding whether she liked it or not.

Sight

Grade 6 brought geology, business math, and Roman history. In geology, she learned about the layers of the earth and types of rocks, as well as about mining and uses of minerals. She learned about interest and the uses of money. She had lessons on the Romans and the critical event that happened at that time—the birth and life of Christ Jesus. The year's play on St. Paul showed the experience of being blinded to this world by the sight of another world—and then to a new, changed life and vision in this world. She finished sixth grade having found her stride in the work and could see her way forward.

Warmth

In the seventh grade, we worked through life in the Middle Ages, ending with Joan of Arc. We studied the beginnings of algebra, and also astronomy and chemistry. In chemistry the focus was on fire—fire as a force of transformation, as warmth, as activity. In the class play Claire fit the part of Joan to a "T," with her own inherently fiery nature and her urge to lead. She took up the banner (which she made herself) with joy and determination.

Hearing

Eighth Grade was the end of lower school. We had American history through the civil war, poetry, algebra and geometry, and physics, where we concentrated on sound and tone and hearing. Claire played the lyre with me at the Waldorf school Advent garden celebration. She braved weather and judges to show her special lamb, Hero, at a county fair. In the spring Hero was shorn and Claire spun her fleece into yarn and then wove it into a beautiful herringbone-pattern scarf. The class play was a huge work, with Claire taking two leading parts—both men—in Goethe's *Magic Flute: A Comic Opera Fragment*. We also played the lyre and violin for the play.

Word

The Ninth Grade was serious work. We had geology again, but this time we studied the geology of the whole earth, and the evidence of changes in the earth. We looked for fossils and strata and types of rocks in a streambed, and we learned about the theory of plate tectonics. We studied the Industrial Revolution and modern times in history; then history through drama, and combinatorics in math. Claire worked on an organic dairy farm in the fall and the spring for her farm practicum—and wrote a report on this work. The year's play was *Pygmalion* by G.B. Shaw—so Claire had to learn Cockney and Received Pronunciation, and also learn about the social power of the word. This play was again about transformation—this time through language. It was a triumph!

Thought

Grade 10 became even more intense. We studied mechanics in physics, which required a lot of math—vectors and trigonometry. Claire got to try some of Galileo's experiments on moving objects and then work on the math related to the movements.

We studied ancient history and saw how all she had learned from fifth and sixth grades laid the foundation for understanding those ancient cultures in their geography and their time. We studied Euclidean geometry and mensuration. Claire again worked on the dairy farm during the year. The thread running through this year was the effort to grasp the thinking of people at different times in history—from the ancients in the Middle East to the Western Europeans in the Renaissance—and to see the transformations in their thinking.

I of the Other

In Eleventh Grade, I added more blocks of study and changed my presentations to a lecture format. Claire took notes and had homework assignments. We both had to work toward sensing the other as an individual in order to even begin the schoolwork. We studied the chemistry of salts, acids, and bases, and then moved on to the history of atomic theory, the periodic table, and experiments with the elements. The fiery acids, soapy bases, and their combination into salts began the year, and our fine observation of substances and the work to single out and characterize the elements ended the year. In between, we studied the Bible and literature, *Parzival*, projective geometry, algebra, botany, music theory, and electricity and magnetism. Claire also worked in the weavery at a nearby Camphill community, continued horseback riding, and took up viola and basketball. The grand finale was a major production of Shakespeare—*Much Ado About Nothing* (which we combined with Sara's Grade 8).

Claire applied to prep schools in the winter, interviewed, and was accepted, and that's where she's off to. To meet and see people she doesn't know, and who don't know her. Starting fresh. May she be blessed.

What Actually Happened

I had written my speech and prepared for the celebration. The morning of the assembly I woke with the realization that the old form of our celebrations was all wrong. Speeches just would not fit the occasion. I tried to envision the celebration, and I thought of a Quaker meeting process in which each person listens until they have something to say. So when we gathered, we moved the desks and put a vase of flowers on a stool in the center of four chairs. My husband and I and the two girls sat with each other. I said we would have a Quaker meeting—everyone could say what came to them. My husband spoke first—"I am impressed with how self-possessed you girls are." Sara—"I'm glad you're getting to do what you want and I'm sure you'll be happy in the school." Catherine—"We've done a lot of good work together and now we're going into a new phase." Claire—"I want to go to the school, but I'll miss having school at home." I asked Claire to read a favorite poem of hers.

Appendix 3: Seeing the Twelve Grades through the Lens of the Twelve Senses

THE MOMENT
by Kathleen Raine

> To write down all that I contain at this moment
> I would pour the desert through an hourglass
> The sea through a water clock
> Grain by grain and drop by drop
> Let in the trackless, measureless, immutable sea and sands
> For the earth's days and nights are breaking over me
> The tides and sands are running through me
> And I have only two hands and a heart
> To hold the desert and the sea
> What can I contain of it?
> It escapes and eludes me.
> The tides wash me away
> The desert shifts under my feet.

Then we stood, and I gave her flowers and shook her hand and congratulated her for completing twelve years in our school—"Blessings on you as you go on." Then Sara hugged her, crying, and we hugged all around, and I comforted Sara with how we would go on to *her* high school. Then we all went swimming in a quarry pool to celebrate—having traversed the moment.

Postscript

The transition to school in an institution was not without stress, but Claire ended the year with grades at the high honors level and a letter of commendation from the faculty that included such phrases as: "The teachers raved about your work ethic and outstanding attitude in class," "Your transition from homeschooling was seamless," "Your contributions to the basketball team were outstanding," and "Your positive attitude is infectious." Hurray for the Waldorf curriculum!

Bibliography: Rudolf Steiner on the Senses

"The Real Basis of Intentional Relation" in *The Case for Anthroposophy,* Rudolf Steiner Press, 1970, GA 21.

Anthroposophy: A Fragment, Anthroposophic Press, 1996, GA 45.

A Psychology of Body, Soul, and Spirit, Anthroposophic Press, 1999, GA 115.

Lectures of June 20 and July 18, 1916, in *Toward Imagination,* Anthroposophic Press, 1990, GA 169.

Lectures of August 12 and September 2, 1916, in *The Riddle of Humanity,* Rudolf Steiner Press, 1990, GA 170.

Lecture of August 25, 1918, in *Human Evolution: A Spiritual-Scientific Quest,* Rudolf Steiner Press, 2015, GA 183.

Lecture of July 22, 1921, contained in *Man as a Being of Sense and Perception,* Steiner Book Centre, Vancouver, 1981, GA 206.

Lecture of August 8, 1920, in *Spiritual Science as a Foundation for Social Forms,* Anthroposophic Press, 1986, GA 199.

Lecture of August 29, 1919, in *The Foundations of Human Experience,* Anthroposophic Press, 1996, GA 293.

Beitrage zur Rudolf Steiner Gesamtausgabe, Nr. 34, Dornach, Sommer 1971, *Aufzeichnungen Rudolf Steiners zur Sinneslehre.*

About the Author

Catherine Read holds a PhD in developmental psychology from UCLA and is a Visiting Scientist at Rutgers University and an Associate at Ithaca College. She is the editor, with P. Zukow-Goldring of *Evolving Explanations of Development* (Washington, D.C.: American Psychological Association Press, 1997). She homeschooled her two daughters from kindergarten through the eleventh grade using the Waldorf curriculum. Catherine studied Waldorf Teaching in the Lower School at the Waldorf Institute of Teacher Training in Los Angeles and in Orange County, California, where she also taught craft work. She took summer courses for Waldorf Teachers at Gradalis, Sunbridge College, and Rudolf Steiner College. She has conducted workshops on a variety of topics, including music in the mood of the fifth, festivals, dyeing with plant dyes, nature meditations, and on homeschooling grades one through eight. She took Waldorf Teacher Training for the High School through the Center for Anthroposophy in Wilton, New Hampshire, where she majored in Physics and minored in English. Catherine has served on the Board of the Lyre Association of North America, and taught in the Resonare Music Foundation Course and the Dorion School of Music Therapy. She is now on the faculty of a new one-year program for students post High School, the M. C. Richards program, offered by Free Columbia in Philmont, New York.